From Surrealism to Less-Exquisite Cadavers

Léo Malet and the Evolution of the French *Roman Noir*

FAUX TITRE

288

Etudes de langue et littérature françaises
publiées sous la direction de

Keith Busby, M.J. Freeman,
Sjef Houppermans et Paul Pelckmans

From Surrealism to Less-Exquisite Cadavers

Léo Malet and the Evolution of the French *Roman Noir*

Michelle Emanuel

With a foreword by Peter Schulman

AMSTERDAM · NEW YORK, NY 2006

Cover illustration: © Marc Gantier/TCS.

Cover design: Pier Post

The paper on which this book is printed meets the requirements of
'ISO 9706: 1994, Information and documentation - Paper for documents -
Requirements for permanence'.

Le papier sur lequel le présent ouvrage est imprimé remplit les prescriptions
de 'ISO 9706: 1994, Information et documentation - Papier pour documents
- Prescriptions pour la permanence'.

ISBN-10: 90-420-2080-6
ISBN-13: 978-90-420-2080-1
© Editions Rodopi B.V., Amsterdam - New York, NY 2006
Printed in The Netherlands

Table of Contents

Acknowledgements

The realization of this manuscript would not have been possible without the support of my family, friends and various colleagues. A complete list would be longer than the manuscript itself, but I would be remiss without acknowledging a few people:

Dr. Peter Schulman, who encouraged me to revise my dissertation for publication, even before it had been defended. I have been grateful for his guidance and editorial advice, and I look forward to working with him on future projects.

Alain Regnault at the Bibliothèque des Littératures Policières (BiLiPo) in Paris, who pointed me in the right direction when my research was leading me astray.

The Fulbright Commission, which facilitated my research in Paris by sending me to France as an *assistante d'anglais* in the *région parisienne* (1997-98), and the University of Mississippi Office of Research and Sponsored Programs, which provided funding for conducting additional research at the BiLiPo in 2004.

Dr. Deborah Hamilton, who led me to discover Léo Malet after reading his obituary online.

Drs. Lauren Doyle-McCombs and Claudia Nadine, who read many early versions of the manuscript, and my professors at the University of Alabama.

Christa Stevens, the editorial board at *Faux Titre*, and others at Rodopi, for their assistance during the preparation of the manuscript for publication.

My colleagues at the University of Mississippi Libraries, whose patience and indulgence during the completion of this project have been appreciated.

My mother, for always listening, and for giving the advice I need to hear.

Michelle Emanuel, University of Mississippi
Oxford, Mississippi, 2005

Foreword

Léo Malet's Post-War Paris

"There are many ways to take a walk through Paris," Georges Perec wrote in *Perec/rinations*, his whimsical *visite guidée* of Paris in twenty-one crossword puzzles, "one can have fixed goals for oneself or go off on ones'own; one can want to systematically explore each neighborhood, with a guide in hand, or get on the first bus that passes by and take it to the end of its line."[1] Although Léo Malet never got to the "end of the line" of his epic series of novels, *Les Nouveaux mystères de Paris*, in which he set out to write one mystery for each of the twenty-one *arrondissements* of Paris, he did quite well for himself, managing to get through an astonishing fifteen of them.[2] One can only imagine what atmospheric delights would have been in store for readers had Nestor Burma, his tough gumshoe alter-ego, been able to also explore the rest of the *arrondissements* such as the seventh, the eighteenth, or the twentieth . . . perhaps he left that job for another generation of writers such as Daniel Pennac, who so lovingly sets his mysteries in the Belleville section of Paris, or Alain Demouzon who infuses the Parisian *banlieues* with the existential weight of his detective hero, Melchior.[3] As François Rivière recounts, the idea of making a new type of *Mystères de Paris*, by updating Eugène Sue to

---

[1] Georges Perec, *Perec/rinations* (Paris: Zulma, 1997) 8 (my translation).
[2] Because of the many printings of his novels by different publishers, all references to Léo Malet's text in this book will come from the five-volume *Oeuvres complètes*, edited by Francis Lacassin, (Paris: Laffont, 1985-89). Volumes 1 and 2, *Les enquêtes de Nestor Burma et les nouveaux mystères de Paris*, are heavily cited in the format: (*Enquêtes*, volume: pages).
[3] Malet, in fact, wrote the preface to one of Alain Demouzon's earlier novels, *Château-des-rentiers* (Paris: Flammarion, 1982).

suit modern Paris and 1950's sensibilities[4] came to Malet in a perfectly surrealist moment, by chance, and fittingly, during a walk with his ten-year old son near the Bir-Hakeim bridge with its elevated metro stop: "Il se perd dans la contemplation du métro aérien et se dit qu'il y a vraiment quelque chose à faire avec un si prestigieux décor, si négligé depuis les auteurs de *Fantômas* et Louis Feuillade.' L'idée lui vint spontanément . . ."[5]

Indeed, if the *Nouveaux mystères* are so captivating, and go far beyond the regular *roman policier* genre in their scope, it is because Malet was successful not only in capturing a slice of the Parisian quotidian of his era, but also appreciating its poetic value. In this way, Michelle Emanuel's groundbreaking study, *From Surrealism to Less-Exquisite Cadavers*, is particularly insightful in its treatment of Malet as a pioneer within the French *roman noir* literary genre, of course, while making sure to focus on his surrealist roots as well. If Malet has been able to fascinate the French public for so long, it is because, as Emanuel rightfully points out, his work "reveals multiple literary and cultural influences as [he] forges a link among popular culture and concurrent genres in twentieth-century French literature." Through his unflappable protagonist Nestor Burma, Malet was, above all, a modern *flâneur*, as he not only sought out exciting crime stories, but also, snippets of the quotidian that are usually within the jurisdiction of poets and urban studies specialists rather than crime fiction novelists. As such, when Burma takes a spontaneous break from pursuing a suspect he has been following, he pauses to admire the (still to this date) beautiful outdoor Passy metro station – a station that many every day users of the metro might not even appreciate for its beauty and elegance (especially if they happen to be late for work!). In truth, Malet's tastes are refreshingly simple, and his appreciation of every day Paris, not very dissimilar from his surrealist predecessors such as André Breton or even, in his early poetry, Raymond Queneau:

> Une des plus agréables du réseau – à mon goût, mais j'ai des goûts simples
> moi – presque champêtre, avec ses portillons qui semblent donner de

---

[5]François Rivière, "Léo Malet: Un noir jeu de l'oie," *Magazine Littéraire* 332 (1995): 61-63.

l'intérieur des wagons. C'est à cet endroit que la ligne Etoile-Nation, direction Nation, sort de terre pour devenir aérienne jusqu'à Pasteur dans le quinzième. La station Passy est séparée de la verdure que l'on aperçoit en passant, de la largeur d'un escalier, aussi bien à droite qu'à gauche. Ces escaliers sont bordés de terrain en pente, boisés, couverts de buissons. (*Enquêtes*, 2: 126)

Yet, it is somehow fitting that Malet's project remain unfinished, as the Paris evoked by Malet, and then so atmospherically interpreted by Tardi in his *bande dessinée* adaptations of Nestor Burma's adventures, has changed radically since the fifties. Writing at the dawn of France's remarkable thirty years of prosperity known as *les trente glorieuses*, Malet sensed and almost melancholically depicted a Paris at the crossroads of intense modernization *cum* gentrification on the one hand, and a city desperately trying to hang on to its old neighborhoods, folkloric streets, and traditional values on the other. Although Malet was not quite as graphic in his wistfulness *vis-à-vis* the vanishing parts of Paris (often "embodied" by a disappearing cadaver in Burma's cases) as Jacques Tati who in his 1957 film *Mon Oncle* so humorously described a hyper-modernized flip-side to the quaint *vieux Paris* so adored by Monsieur Hulot, Burma's Parisian peregrinations are nonetheless historical testaments to a Paris that no longer exists. In his most famous novel, for example, *Brouillard au Pont de Tolbiac,* the thirteenth *arrondissement* which, today, is so distinctive because of its dynamic Chinatown, was rather bourgeois and traditional in Malet's time. Similarly the *Marais* so colorfully if not controversially described in terms of its Jewishness in *Du Rebecca, rue des Rosiers* or *Fièvre au Marais* has now yielded to fashionable shops and trendy restaurants or cafés.

Perhaps Malet's sudden flashes into a fleeting Paris are what ultimately distinguish him from some of his distinguished colleagues in French crime fiction such as Georges Simenon or Maurice Leblanc. As Emanuel points out so clearly, while Malet "subverts the rules of the canon as well as those of detective fiction itself, allowing literary variation within the existing genre," and his *détective de choc* hero is hard-boiled inside and out, it is his appreciation and interaction with a changing Paris that adds a rather bittersweet quality to the Burma narratives. As Burma laments when noticing a construction site within the once "pristine" 16th *arrondissement*:

> Bientôt dans ce secteur jadis renommé pour ses coquettes residences privées, il ne se dressera que des gratte-ciel, et les espaces verts dont s'est longtemps enorgueilli cet arrondissement, il faudra les chercher dans les académies de billard. Même les terrains vagues seront boulottés. (*Enquêtes*, 2:121)

"Old Paris" will soon give way to a "New Paris," a Paris where even *la pègre* does not abide by the codes it once followed in earlier, more respectful times. Although Malet did not quite imagine a Paris taken over by The Gap and Starbucks, he was prescient in putting his finger on that aspect of urban life that cannot help disappearing if a city wants to remain vibrant and "up to date." As Akbar Abbas has written regarding the constantly disappearing sections of Hong Kong which never ceases to reinvent itself through a process he labels the phenomenon of the "déjà disparu," Malet's Burma inadvertently stumbles on a "visual that is both ineluctable and elusive at the same time."[6] This is why Burma is ultimately and, in opposition to his more *mondain* detective predecessors, a type of Everyman, a man of the people, a man who can understand the thrill of the urban crowds, a quick *coup de rouge* at his favorite café or the majestic beauty of an empty Parisian street at dawn. This is Burma's Paris that Tardi so dreamily portrays in his drawings. As Burma lovingly muses through the caption of one of Tardi's images in *120 rue de la Gare* when standing in front of a *vitrine* (the Passage de l'Argue in Lyons) that resembles the old Parisian "arcades" (*passages*) Walter Benjamin immortalized in his classic essays on the *flâneur* in Paris: "Eh ben dis donc!...le voilà, mon petit rade. Ça n'a pas bougé d'un poil...ils n'ont même pas repeint la façade!"[7] Paris may well have had to adapt itself to the contemporary, globalized world at times, *Burma*'s Paris never changes as he is able, in capturing certain ephemeral pleasures of the quotidian, to keep those images alive for future readers of all classes and walks of life.

Lastly, if Malet can follow in the footsteps of such colleagues as Philippe Marlowe, Sam Spade and Hercule Poirot, as many critics have pointed out, it is not only for his incredible investigative skills and toughness in tackling criminals and unsavory cases. He is indeed

---

[6] Akbar Abbas, *Hong Kong: Culture and the Politics of Disappearance* (Minneapolis: University of Minnesota Press, 1997) 42.

[7] Léo Malet and Jacques Tardi, *120 rue de la gare* (Paris: Casterman, 1996) 36.

the "détective de choc" but also a *détective célibataire*. Long and lonely are his adventures, when he is not having an attractive woman fall into his arms or his bed. There is no room in Malet's life for deep attachments to bourgeois institutions such as marriage or enough sentimentality to be vulnerable to what Philippe Marlowe, referring to romantic sadness, describes as a sensation of "cold as the ashes of love" in *Farewell, My Lovely*.[8] In this way, he is reminiscent of the typical hero of a Jean-Pierre Melville film. Although Melville's heroes are often on the other side of the law, that is almost an irrelevant bit of information as what binds the ideal Melvillean detective or the Melvillean gangster is not the official law of the Palais de Justice, but rather an honor code of the streets which, like the old neighborhoods Burma explores, is also a relic of a more genteel time. As Bob le Flambeur says to his friend the Police Commissioner in the 1956 film *Bob le flambeur*, *la pègre* itself can no longer be considered "civilized" in its breaking of the law as the unwritten codes of behavior that both criminal and detective once followed have given way to pure "chacun pour soi" expediency: "Le milieu n'est plus ce qu'il était. C'est Pourriture et Companie maintenant."[9] Yet, despite the changing times, Burma, like Bob le Flambeur, enjoys the freedom of time and space that comes with being a bachelor. Although Paris during the *trente glorieuses* was in full economic expansion, there was an excitement in the air and a certain speed with which France was recovering from the war (such as the extraordinary amount of governments that came and went during the Fourth Republic alone. From 1944-1958, there were 25 Heads of Governments, the shortest one lasting only 4 days). It is an excitement that Burma seems to encapsulate in his carefree structuring of his days. If Melville's Bob "est un homme libre. Il a choisi de vivre à Montmartre parce que pour lui Montmartre est encore le seul endroit où l'on puisse vivre. C'est le dernier refuge. Il y vit pendant la nuit jusqu'à l'aube, entre loup et chien, puisque le soir, c'est entre chien et loup,"[10] Burma, too, makes the city his playground at all hours of the day and night. As is the case

---

[8] Raymond Chandler, *Farewell, My Lovely* (New York: Vintage Crime/Random House, 2001) 255.

[9] *Bob le Flambeur*, dir. Jean-Pierre Melville, Organisation Générale Cinématographique/La Cyme/Play Art, 1956.

[10] Rui Nogueira, *Le cinéma selon Jean-Pierre Melville* (Paris: Editions de l'Etoile/Cahiers du Cinéma, 1996) 72.

of many fictional detectives, Burma's bachelorhood contributes to his "hunter"-like aura that allows him to keep questing from one adventure to another without ever needing to be satiated to the point of settling down in domestic bliss. As Jean Borie has written regarding the restlessness inherent in the bachelor condition, "le célibataire qui peut donner si facilement l'impression d'être quelqu'un de fini, reste un être de quête,"[11] It is therefore particularly *à propos* that Malet and Burma never finish the ultimate mission of completing the *Nouveaux Mystères* as finishing them all may have endowed Burma with a false note of satisfaction which his perpetual search for urban adventure would somehow never permit anyway.

In similar fashion, Michelle Emanuel does not content herself with simply placing a *point final* to her study of Léo Malet as she might well have been entitled to as one of the only critics to devote a full-length study to Malet's life and work. Indeed she is to be commended for providing such a complex and deep study of the controversial Malet as she is not afraid to tackle his nationalism or the bitterness that characterized the later part of his life. As critics of the much more controversial Céline have encountered, the many facets of Malet – the man and the novelist – can be as maddening as they are rewarding. By providing an in-depth analysis of Malet's surrealist roots, Emanuel perspicaciously puts her finger on what makes him a truly serious writer who, surprisingly until now, has been all too often neglected by "mainstream" literary criticism. Indeed, by contextualizing Malet's work within the framework of his surrealist and anarchist past, she engagingly underlines the originality and unique position Burma plays within the detective fiction genre in France. Since he is playfully *à cheval* between the hard-boiled American model and the rather intellectual esthete that dominates the French model, he is equally fascinating for where he fits in terms of his predecessors such as the brilliant memoirs of the19[th]-century Vidocq (the master criminal turned police chief upon whom Balzac's Vautrin is based), Alexandre Dumas's *Les Mohicans de Paris,* and of course Eugène Sue's *Les Mystères de Paris* as he is for the ways in which he diverges from them. Part Eugène Sue, part Raymond Chandler, Malet concocted, in Burma, a particularly intriguing

---

[11] Jean Borie, *Le célibataire français* (Paris: Livre de Poche, 2002) 37.

fictional hero. Along parallel lines, Emanuel's last chapter, by keeping the book open to potential heirs to Burma such as Jean Amila, Jean-Patrick Manchette and Didier Daeninckx confirms Burma's role as an avant-garde literary hero as well.

"Au final," writes Christophe Evans of the *Service Etudes et Recherche* of the *BPI* (the Centre Pompidou's Bibliothèque Publique d'Information*),*

> curieux miroir, on s'apercevra que les lecteurs de polars [...] ne sont pas si éloignés du sociologue qui cherche à mieux les connaître et les comprendre: même sensibilité à l'importance des enquêtes, même goût pour les efforts d'objectivation et la collecte minutieuse de témoignages. En un mot, même goût pour le réel, aussi difficile soit-il à saisir et à décrire.[12]

It is to Emanuel's credit that the reader of *From Surrealism to Less-Exquisite Cadavers* will be able to experience not only the "réel" within the *roman policier* genre, but especially the *sur*-réel for as Evans confirms, "Lire des romans policiers: un jeu décidément très sérieux."

Peter Schulman, Old Dominion University
Norfolk, Virginia, 2005.

---

[12] Christophe Evans, "Pourquoi lit-on des romans policiers? Une enquête sur les lecteurs," *Bulletin BPI,* 12 (2005): 6.

Introduction

The guilty pleasure of reading detective fiction appeals to a wide cross-section of the reading public as it transcends intellectual backgrounds. Even Jean-Paul Sartre admitted in *Les Mots* to reading "plus volontiers les «Séries Noire» que Wittgenstein."[13] Vanoncini regards the detective novel as "l'expression littéraire la plus poignante de ce qu'on a appelé la modernité, comparable en un sens au jazz et au cinéma," for its fusion of elements to create "un produit populaire par son origine et par son mode de diffusion et, comme [le cinéma et le jazz], il sait concilier l'emploi du stéréotype avec la creativité innovatrice."[14] This book will consider Léo Malet, an innovator in the French detective genre who was able to "concilier" the formulaic genre of detective fiction in France with the legacy of the surrealist movement, yet remains virtually unknown in American academic circles. Due to the great volume of unexplored material contained within the Malet corpus, the primary focus of this book is Malet's fifteen-novel series, *Les Nouveaux Mystères de Paris*, and its "détective de choc," Nestor Burma.

Expanding the boundaries of the detective novel in his use of slang and surrealist imagery, Malet creates a new postwar French icon in the character of Burma: a man of his appetites, culturally adept, and proud of his Frenchness even after the demoralizing occupation of World War II. Malet "introduit dans le genre français un esprit canaille qui préside également à la naissance de son 'détective de choc'."[15] Malet's icon is an emblem of what a Frenchman – detective or not – can be: smart yet streetwise, brash yet cultured, as well as

---

[13] Jean-Paul Sartre, *Les Mots* (Paris: Gallimard, 2003) 65.

[14] André Vanoncini, *Le roman policier* (Paris: PUF, 1993) 5.

[15] François Rivière, "Léo Malet: l'envahissant cadavre," *Libération* 08 Mar. 1996: 28-29.

proud of his cultural heritage in the face of postwar upheaval which further uprooted those who had been displaced by the occupation. Malet's text, which alludes to contemporary postwar concerns alongside avant-garde imagery, complements Kristin Ross's critical analysis in *Fast Cars, Clean Bodies: Decolonization and the Reordering of French Culture* which looks at the period from the late 1950s and early 1960s which she terms as "the years after electricity but before electronics."[16] In Malet's series, Burma rebuilds his detective agency to its prewar status, buys his first car, falls in love with a movie star, a gypsy, and many women in between, chases collaborators, and is held hostage by Algerian FLN rebels. Malet's series is rich with cultural significance, in both language and imagery, which I will analyze and categorize throughout this book from both a literary and cultural perspective.

Evolution of a popular genre

The *roman policier* in France is a hybrid of both canonical and popular literatures. The influence of naturalist writers such as Balzac and Hugo, and Baudelaire's popular translation of Edgar Allen Poe,[17] combined with the development of mass-produced newspapers brought a new awareness of the seedy, crime-ridden underbelly of urban life to the general public. Increased literacy rates during this period fueled the demand for popular genre fiction. The first French detective novel, Émile Gaboriau's *L'affaire Lerouge* (1863), "owes as much to French melodrama and adventure as it does to Poe's model of the cerebral detective,"[18] with the characters Père Tabaret and Inspecteur Lecoq serving as the first French detective figures. The next wave of iconic French detective characters comes during the *Belle Époque* (1900-1914). Maurice Leblanc's Arsène Lupin, the *gentleman-cambrioleur* borrows from the tradition of adventure novels to include "trésors cachés, passages secrets, messages à

---

[16] Kristin Ross, *Fast Cars, Clean Bodies: Decolonization and the Reordering of French Culture*. 3rd ed. (Cambridge: MIT Press, 1988) 2.

[17] In particular, Poe's stories "Murders in the Rue Morgue," "The Mystery of Mary Rogêt," and "The Purloined Letter" were influential to the genre for having "set out an investigative procedure and created an authoritative agent of detection, both of which had been largely missing from earlier literature dealing with crime" In Claire Gorrara, *The Roman Noir in French Popular Culture: Dark Fictions* (Oxford: Oxford University Press, 2003) 11.

[18] Gorrara 12.

déchiffrer"[19] within the detective narrative. Lupin, "aux tendences anarchisantes qui pille les riches arrogants ou les institutions peu appréciées comme les banques ou le Trésor public, puis assistant de la police et agent secret au service de la France,"[20] is both thief and detective, an ambiguous character blurring the line between good and evil. Meanwhile, in novels such as *Le mystère de la chambre jaune* (1907), Gaston Leroux's young journalist/amateur detective Joseph Rouletabille "laid down many of the conventions that would be exploited in the whodunit: murder in a locked room, super-intelligent investigators and their battle against master criminals."[21] The figure of the journalist and the detective remain closely linked throughout the genre, as it is frequently from reading *faits divers* in newspapers that detectives will learn of crimes.[22] Another iconic figure from la Belle Époque, *Fantômas*, "le maître de tout, de l'heure et du temps" in the wildly popular *feuilleton* co-written by Marcel Allain and Pierre Souvestre, "n'existe que dans la conscience du policier Juve et du journaliste Fandor et à travers la designation par les autres personnages qui l'évoquent en tramblant.[23] The cultivation of "l'esthétique de la cruauté" would influence Apollinaire and surrealists such as Soupault, Cendrars, Cocteau, Artaud and Desnos,[24] and, by association, Léo Malet. The fast-paced schedule of writing *feuilletons*

> relève de l'écriture semi-automatique chère aux surréalistes. D'autre part, à une époque rationaliste et légaliste du roman policier, Fantômas représente l'intrusion de l'irrationnel dans la réalité comme il consacre la revanche du rêve et de l'imaginaire sur la logique desséchante.[25]

[19] Franck Evrard, *Lire le roman policier* (Paris: Dunod, 1996) 42.
[20] Evrard 41.
[21] Gorrara 12.
[22] In *Le roman policier: introduction à la théorie et à l'histoire* (Liège: Éditions du Céfal, 1999), Marc Lits points out that in the 19th century, *faits divers* and *feuilletons* "apparus quasi simultanément dans les mêmes journaux, et sous la plume des mêmes auteurs ... Edgar Poe, Emile Gaboriau, Gaston Laroux sont d'abord des journalistes qui sont payés pour transformer le quotidien en sensationnel, pour produire de l'information qui soit aussi du spectacle" (138).
[23] Evrard 45.
[24] Evrard 46.
[25] Evrard 46.

With its supernatural imagery, Fantômas precludes normalcy, thus subverting the *roman à énigme* on which most detective fiction is based. However, the basic structure of the novel does not stray far from the norm.

The interwar period represents the "Golden Age" of detective fiction.[26] While Agatha Christie and Ellery Queen dominated the genre in Britain and the United States, in France, the collection "Le Masque," created in 1927, presented French translations of works in English, as well as a few Francophone authors such as Jacques Decrest and S.A. Steeman. Limited primarily to the *roman-problème* or the *roman-jeu*, the genre embraced codification, outlined by S.S. Van Dine's *Twenty Rules for Writing Detective Fiction*, which "obéit à un protocole fixe qui comprend un meurtre initial, un groupe restraint de suspects, un détective menant l'enquête et la revelation finale du coupable."[27] Compared to its Anglophonic equivalents, the French *roman à énigme* looked to "renouveler le contenu du roman policier en introduisant le réalisme psychologique ou en enrichissant la trame romanesque de themes inédits,"[28] with a "greater emphasis on social context and an openness to mainstream literary influences."[29]

With Inspector Maigret, a "petit bourgeois pantouflard,"[30] Georges Simenon bridges the gap between what was the codified *roman à énigme* of the early 1930s and the splintering of the genre beginning with Léo Malet and the French *roman noir* in the early 1940s.

> Les «Maigret» relèvent à la fois du roman à énigme (la remontée retrospective vers le criminel et les motifs) et du roman noir en ce sens que l'enquête du commissaire le conduit dans des milieux sociaux et des décors différents. L'identité du criminel importe moins que les motivations secrètes qui sont à l'origine du délit, les mobiles qui ont partie liée le plus souvent

---

[26] In her dissertation, Deborah Hamilton writes: "Golden Age refers to the period between the two world wars which was marked by a significant increase in the production of detective novels as well as the proliferation of rules and codes to define the genre." *The French Detective Fiction Novel 1920s to 1990s: Gendering a Genre* (*DAI* 55 (1994): 1576A. Pennsylvania State University) 7.

[27] Evrard 47.

[28] Evrard 50.

[29] Gorrara 12.

[30] Pierre Verdaguer, *La séduction policière: Signes de croissance d'un genre réputé mineur: Pierre Magnan, Daniel Pennac et quelques autres* (Birmingham: Summa, 1999) 9.

avec l'humiliation et les frustrations du personnage. Les coupables ne sont pas des génies du mal mais des êtres médiocres ... La vocation de Maigret est de reconstituer l'individu grâce à des indices existentiels.[31]

In his eighteen Maigret novels, Simenon brings an appreciation of psychological insight, giving the inspector an intuitive, hermeneutic approach to solving crime.

C'est donc une fois terminée la série d'investigations aussi sociologiques que policières qu'est émise une appreciation d'ordre philosophico-moral, sorte de jugement dernier de l'enquêteur qui, chez Maigret du moins, suscite la nausée.[32]

In the classic *roman policier*, the detective is above the crime he is investigating. In the hardboiled novel, which comes to France in the 1930s, mostly in translation at first, the detective is often just as depraved as the criminal he is chasing. Simenon unlocks the door for the genre of French detective fiction to evolve from the *roman à énigme*, but it is the *roman noir*, given a French perspective by Léo Malet, that actually opens it, by bringing a French perspective to the new American style of crime fiction.

The *roman noir* follows the tradition of the American hardboiled detective story, created in the United States in the 1920s and '30s.[33] It differs from the *roman policier* in a variety of ways:

In a roman policier, the crime (usually single) has been committed before the narrative (or at its beginning) by a criminal whom it is the detective's job to identify, in a single narrative; the detective works on his own and is impelled by the desire to defend the moral order. In the roman noir, multiple crimes are committed as an ongoing feature of multiple narratives, by criminals whose identity is known and whom it is the hero's job to destroy (rather than apprehend); heroes are usually part of an organization and are paid to defend a political order.[34]

---

[31] Evrard 62.

[32] Verdaguer 8.

[33] As defined by *Webster's 3rd New International Dictionary*, "hardboiled" is "of or relating to a literary form or production characterized by impersonal matter-of-fact presentation of naturalistic or violent themes or incidents, by a generally unemotional or stoic tone, and often by a total absence of explicit or implied moral judgements."

[34] Peter France, ed., *The New Oxford Companion to Literature in French* (Oxford: Oxford University Press, 1995) 713.

The *roman noir* promises a more complex mystery, with several related murders within the same narrative, all of which are both solved and vindicated. The American style takes "la banalisation du roman à énigme à l'anglaise en misant sur des ingrédients feuilletonesques (péripétie, fait brut, violence)."[35] French readers, hungry for an escape from their war-torn, occupied reality, read this type of American story faster than translations could be printed. It was this hunger from which Malet's friend Louis Chevance, as well as other editors, were trying to profit, though most of the chosen writers had never left the European continent. Looking for something different, Malet chose to place his new mysteries in a familiar setting where he felt comfortable, and subsequently became "le père du roman noir français."

Malet, the man

Malet's biographical information is relevant, as his experience closely parallels that of his readership, many of whom were also displaced in the decades of war and renovation. Malet transcended his relatively underprivileged childhood to become a pivotal figure in the literary production of the postwar era.

Léo (Léon) Malet was born March 7, 1909 in Montpellier to Gaston and Louise (Refreger) Malet. When he was four years old, both of Malet's parents, as well as his younger brother, succumbed to tuberculosis, a fate he himself escaped by being too big to still sleep in their bed. Orphaned Léo was taken in by his grandfather, a *tonnelier*, described by an older Malet as "le prolétaire complet,"[36] who instilled in his young grandson a love for reading, especially the novels of Dumas and Zevaco. Léo attended the Ecole communale Auguste-Comte, and the Ecole primaire supérieure Michelet, but had no other formal education. He passed time by writing poems and songs, hanging out with local anarchists, and working odd jobs: assistant to fabric merchant, bank employee, and "crieur professionel," selling Parisian anarchist newspapers (*Le Libertaire* and *L'Insurgé*) on Sundays.

In 1925, at the age of sixteen, he moved to Paris, where within two months he became a cabaret singer at "La vache enragée" in Montmartre. He frequented anarchist circles and contributed to their

---

[35] Jacques Dubois, *Le roman policier ou la modernité* (Paris: Nathan, 1992) 74.

[36] Michel Abescat, "Léo Malet a quitté pour toujours Nestor Burma," *Le Monde* 9 Mar. 1996: 22.

various publications, but was shipped back to Montpellier after being stopped for vagrancy one too many times. There he held more odd jobs: office worker, ghost writer, cinema extra, manager of a fashion magazine, and newspaper seller, before returning to Paris in 1929. With the bit of money he had saved, he founded the "Cabaret du poète pendu" with Paulette Doucet, whom he would later marry. After an impulse purchase of "La révolution surréaliste," and sending a few poems to André Breton, Malet was invited to meetings of the surrealist group. Though he could not attend the meetings every day due to his full-time job, he belonged to the group from 1931 to 1940 and was a close friend of Breton, René Magritte, Salvador Dalí, and Yves Tanguy. During that period, he produced collections of poetry, including *Ne pas voir plus loin que le bout de son sexe* (1936), *J'arbre comme un cadavre* (1937), and *Hurle à la vie* (1940), and enjoyed the surrealist practice of automatic writing. When World War II broke out, he and Paulette stayed in Paris rather than follow the group into exile.

   With Jacques Prévert as their witness, Paulette Doucet and Malet were married in April 1940[37]. The following month, Malet was arrested for having signed a number of surrealist documents that were perceived by the French government as subversive[38]. He went to jail outside Paris for a few days, but was released when the Germans invaded. As he walked back to Paris to save his train fare, the Germans captured him, thinking him a military deserter, and sent him to a P.O.W. camp between Bremen and Hamburg. While imprisoned, he had an idea for a story about a murder in the *stalag*. When he was freed for "health reasons" after making friends with the *stalag* doctor, Malet returned to Paris and his friends at the Café de Flore, where Louis Chevance, the script-writer for Henri-Georges Clouzot's film *Le Corbeau*, encouraged him to write a *roman policier* for "Minuit," his collection of American-style detective fiction by French authors under pseudonym.

   Since foreign books could not come into occupied France, Chevance reasoned, a lot of money could be made by producing mystery fiction "made in France." Here began Malet's career in detective fiction, with a character named Johnny Metal (an anagram of

---

[37] Their only child, Jacques-Lionel, was born in 1942.
[38] "Il est arrêté pour «atteinte à la sûreté intérieure et extérieure de l'État»," writes Alfu in *Léo Malet: Parcours un œuvre* (Amiens: Encrage, 1998) 157.

Malet), under the pseudonym Frank Harding. Among his other pseudonyms were Jean de Selneuves, Lionel Doucet, Omar Refreger, and Léo Latimer before he began to use his patronym. Like other writers in the series, Malet would set these mysteries in the United States, writing in the style of authors like Dashiell Hammett, though he knew the American locale only from films and popular literature. Encouraged by the success of Johnny Metal among his friends, including Henri Filipachi of Livres de Poche, Malet decided to continue writing detective novels and set them in France among familiar elements. He was not the first French author ever to pen a *roman noir*, but he was the first to make his character French and to have him solve a mystery in France. In 1943, he created the detective "Dynamite" Nestor Burma of the Fiat Lux detective agency, and the story idea from his internment, "L'homme qui mourut au stalag" evolved into the first Burma mystery, *120, rue de la Gare*.

From 1943 to 1949, Malet wrote seven Nestor Burma mysteries before giving the detective (and himself) a vacation. Burma returned in 1954 when Malet had the idea of a series where each mystery is set in a different *arrondissement* of Paris. His editor, Robert Laffont, named the series *Les Nouveaux Mystères de Paris*, inspired by Eugène Sue's nineteenth-century *feuilleton, Les Mystères de Paris*. After writing fifteen novels in four years, Malet suspended the series in 1959, but never completed it, leaving five *arrondissements* untreated, neglecting, among others, the seventh *arrondissement*, which contains the Tour Eiffel. Ten years later in 1969, the Editions Losfeld released in one volume the *Trilogies Noires*, a collection of three novels including the 1948 *La vie est degueulasse*.

Malet's oeuvre was rediscovered, reedited, and reevaluated in the 1970s at a time when he himself was writing less and less. In his 1988 autobiography, *La vache enragée*, Malet speculates that as May 1968 activists were throwing *pavés* in the Latin Quarter, they found used editions of his work at the *bouquinistes* along the Seine. Claiming to friends that he no longer read, Malet went into a depressive seclusion with his ailing wife in their HLM in the suburb Châtillon-sous-Bagneux[39]. When approached, he would give

---

[39] Frustrated by her illness, she committed suicide in 1981 by throwing herself out of a window.

interviews, most notably an inflammatory interview in 1985 at the age of 76 to *Libération* where he proclaimed that "les arabes me font chier."[40] In spite of his racist leanings, his writing was still embraced by both the right and the left.

Malet's innovations were praised with a number of awards during his lifetime. A "Chevalier des Arts et des Lettres," he won the first awarded "Grand prix de littérature policière" in 1948. *Les nouveaux mystères de Paris* took the 1958 "Grand prix de l'humour noir" and the 1979 "bouchon de cristal" at the Festival du Roman Policier in Reims. In 1984 Malet won the "Prix Paul Féval de littérature populaire de la société des gens de lettres." When Malet died on March 3, 1996, shortly before his 87th birthday, media reaction was best expressed on Gallimard's website for the *Série Noire*: "Le père du roman noir français meurt . . . dans son lit!"[41] appreciating the irony that Malet would die of natural causes, and not as a result of one of the various crimes he had written about.

In this study

In chapter one, I will show how Malet expands the boundaries of the detective fiction genre. Malet "écrivit ses premiers 'noirs' pendant la guerre et est donc le premier français dans ce domaine."[42] His work falls between Roger Caillois's 1941 study of the *roman policier*,[43] and Tzvetan Todorov's 1966 study of the genre which, by that time, had splintered into subgenres. Whereas Caillois analyzes how the genre has followed the rules of the mainstream canon, while at the same time becoming increasingly detached from traditional narrative forms, Todorov focuses on the continued marginalization of detective fiction with respect to canonical literature. Influenced by concurrent literary movements in theatre and poetry, Malet subverts the rules of the canon as well as those of detective fiction itself,

---

[40] Léo Malet, interviewed by Phil Casoar, "Le faucon Malet," *Libération* 11 June 1985: 30-31.

[41] <http://www.gallimard-mtl.com/eseriesn.html> 14 Mar. 1996.

[42] Fereydoun Hoveyda, *Histoire du roman policier* (Paris: Éditions de Pavillon, 1965) 167.

[43] Verdaguer theorizes that this study is "peu connu. Peut-être parce qu'il ne fit l'objet d'une publication distincte qu'à l'étranger (Buenos Aires), et pendant les hostilités de surcroît (1941). On le retrouve par la suite inséré dans Puissances du roman (1942) et Approches de l'imaginaire (1974), mais il passe de ce fait beaucoup plus inaperçu" (2).

allowing literary variation within the existing genre. The *roman noir* can remain true to its constants (violence, sordid crime, and the amorality of its principal characters, sometimes including its detective) and still venture in new directions, looking for its own rules. Falling between the two studies, *Les Nouveaux Mystères de Paris* has elements of both trends: tradition and innovation.

Malet's use of slang conveys nationalist sentiment and boosts postwar morale.[44] No longer limited to a pejorative means of description, slang becomes part of the detective's vocabulary. He is streetwise and not an esthete like his literary colleagues. Throughout Malet's series, the author leaves key ambiguities with regard to the character's background and description, opening to possibility that the character is based on the author himself. As such "slippage" is not present in Malet's detective fiction contemporaries, such as in the work of Simenon, this characteristic further contributes to his innovative style. In this book, I use Simenon's Maigret series as a litmus against which Malet's Burma series can be compared, arguing that Simenon represents the Golden Age of French detective fiction which Malet transcends with the *roman noir*.

In chapter two, I will demonstrate how residual traces of Malet's involvement with the surrealist group blend with gritty *noir* undertones to create a new type of detective novel. Imagery in the form of dream sequences, altered states of consciousness, and the appreciation of both *faits-divers* and the *merveilleux* infuse Malet's content, most vividly in Burma's frequent episodes of unconsciousness. Of this infusion, Durozoi writes:

> . . . les allusions au surréalisme vont se multiplier dans les textes tout en devenant éventuellement plus subtiles ou discrètes: leur décompte, si l'on prétendait relever non seulement les noms propres, les références à des œuvres, à des lieux privilégiés, mais également celles à des objets, des faits politiques et culturels, connus pour avoir suscité de la part des membres du Groupe intérêt ou passion, serait impressionnant.[45]

---

[44] Slang citations will include bracketed translations from Colin and Mével's *Dictionnaire de l'argot* (Paris: Larousse, 1994). Refer to the appendix of "Frequently Used Slang" for a more complete listing.

[45] Gérard Durozoi, "Ésquisse pour un portrait anthume de Léo Malet en auteur de romans policiers," *Revue des sciences humaines* 64.193 (1984): 177.

Malet alludes to avant-garde elements such as "œuvres," "lieux," and "objets" in his detective fiction. Surrealism is not just a poetic movement, but rather a new way of looking at the same familiar objects. A detective novel tends to be a series of familiar if not formulaic items: a detective, a dead body, a weapon, a search for the guilty. Burma not only reacts to these familiar items (which he always seems to find before the police) with the detached sarcasm expected in a *roman noir*, but also with the relish of an avant-garde artist.

In chapter three, I argue that the multifaceted character of Nestor Burma reflects the postwar order. A former anarchist, Burma works to maintain his own sense of social order while resisting the authority of the Parisian police, personified by Inspector (promoted later in the series to Commissioner) Florimond Faroux. Burma is not a civil servant like Simenon's Maigret but, rather, an entrepreneur looking to serve his own needs before those of the State. In the *roman noir*,

> Le détective cessera aussi d'être un fonctionnaire de police ou un amateur éclairé de la noblesse ou de la bourgeoisie, la place sera prise par les détectives privés, plus ou moins honnêtes, plus ou moins violents, à l'image d'un monde où le Bien et le Mal ne sont plus très distincts et où les valeurs morales ont tendance à perdre de leur importance.[46]

Plagued by insensitive and xenophobic observations, Burma reflects the resistance of the working classes who see their socio-economic status threatened by the changing face of post-colonial Paris. At the same time, Burma is a champion of French culture, with an emphasis on literary appreciation, who encourages the reader to expand his intellectual horizons by referring in the same series to Baudelaire, Mallarmé, Apollinaire, and La Rochefoucauld, as well as several prominent figures of the postwar artistic scene.

In chapter four, I show that the members of Burma's entourage – the Commissioner Faroux, Burma's faithful secretary Hélène Chatelain, and Marc Covet, the star crime reporter of *Le Crépuscule* – further define Burma himself. His friends function as a surrogate family, supporting the detective physically, emotionally, and sometimes financially when he is between cases. Their relationship creates an informative symbiosis as they help each other to complete

---

[46] Lits 56.

successfully the tasks they are assigned which include the gathering of information useful to Burma's investigation. Their interactions with Burma balance the graphic narrative with both comedic and flirtatious exchanges. Hélène is Burma's ideal woman, yet Malet keeps them apart; in order for Hélène to survive for the next installment, she must remain unattainable. Faroux represents the authority that Burma subverts, yet is sometimes the detective's best friend. Covet is Burma's link to the outside world, keeping Burma's name in the papers, renewing his glory at the end of every solved mystery.

In chapter five, I will demonstrate how the constant presence in Malet's series of the city of Paris functions as a quasi-character. Malet's Paris is a Paris of Nazi occupation, then of postwar recovery. By portraying each *arrondissement* individually with its own character and details, the series stands as historical document to a Paris that no longer exists. Burma reflects the uneasiness of Parisians in the face of renovation, and many of the locations he cites, including the Pont de Tolbiac, have been bulldozed since the publication of his series. Burma serves as the reader's tour guide and presents local curiosities as vital information. He is as fascinated by the city's small details as by the significant historical events for which there are commemorative plaques. Malet's "City of Light" is dark, at times even shoddy and run-down. The story itself is fiction, but the urban topography is both real and surreal. For Durozoi

> . . . il est incontestable que le Paris où évolue Nestor Burma est un Paris d'un surréaliste': certains lieux y apparaissent immédiatement attirants et chargés de mystère, ils suscitent des intuitions du détective ou sont propices à des promenades au cours desquelles ses idées se mettent en place.[47]

Malet writes of Paris with a surrealist eye and a popular sensibility. Like Baudelaire and his *flâneurs*, Malet's Burma encounters people from all walks of life. Malet finds the same inspiration in the streets of Paris as both his surrealist contemporaries and writers like Walter Benjamin. Reading a Nestor Burma mystery is like taking a tour through the underside of Paris clouded by fog, reeking of stale cigarette smoke, and populated by deviants looking out for themselves. Burma himself resembles the very people he is trying to bring to justice, with his bull-shaped pipe constantly lit. Quotidian

---

[47] Durozoi 174.

Parisian life is evoked in these novels in both Burma's life and the lives of his clients.

In chapter six, I examine the evolution of the French *roman noir* from 1960 through 1985 in the novels of Jean Amila, Jean-Patrick Manchette, and Didier Daeninckx, positioning Malet's work in relation to developments in techniques and formulas. Each experiments with the narrative structure of a formulaic genre, removing the detective to focus on the victims and perpetrators of crime. By adding a political message, Manchette and Daeninckx reach out to readers who might not be familiar with their activist agenda, in the same way that Malet reached out to those unfamiliar with the avant garde. With their use of literary techniques borrowed from *la série blanche*[48], the writers both embrace and reject Malet's legacy, but in its consistent evolution, the *roman noir* remains a viable and relevant genre of popular fiction.

> Avec le roman policier, on se trouve en presence d'un texte tout surchargé, tout encombré de references sociales, allant de la bourgeoisie à demi aristocratique de Gaston Leroux jusqu'au milieux banlieusards et populaires du néo polar.[49]

The novels of Amila, Manchette, and Daeninckx take the *roman noir* to the provinces, further expanding the boundaries of French detective fiction by depicting violent crimes outside the *périphérique*.

This study of the work of Léo Malet reveals multiple literary and cultural influences as Malet forges a link among popular culture and concurrent genres in twentieth-century French literature.

> Entre la nouvelle énigmatique de Poe et les romans noirs de Raymond Chandler, entre l'élégance surannée d'Arsène Lupin et la violence déseperée de Manchette, l'écart est grand, mais il reste suffisamment de convergences pour rassembler ces œuvres dans une catégorie identique, surtout si on prend la peine de les situer dans un cheminement historique du genre qui a évolué sous deux pressions: celle de l'évolution littéraire générale, et celle, très forte, de l'univers social dont le genre policier, aujourd'hui, se veut le témoin.[50]

---

[48] This term refers to Gallimard's traditionally literary line, with white covers, contrasting with the Série Noire, with black covers.
[49] Dubois 75.
[50] Lits 157.

This progression "sous deux pressions" would have been much different in France without the work of Léo Malet. His series *Les nouveaux mystères de Paris* witnesses the cultural shift in France in the immediate post-war era as Parisians adjust to both decolonization and electrical appliances. At the same time, Malet mixes an appreciation of France's proud literary heritage with contemporary slang and references to popular culture. His experimentation with a formulaic genre brings the avant-garde to a new audience and clears the way for further experimentation by French writers. Between the Lupin's elegant gentleman-cambrioleur and Daeninckx's suicidal Inspecteur Cadin is Malet's Nestor Burma, "détective de choc."

Chapter One

Expanding Boundaries

Taking his cue from the American style of Dashiell Hammett and Raymond Chandler, Léo Malet launched the French *roman noir* with Nestor Burma, who, for the first time, narrated a hardboiled crime story set in France. The world that he portrayed was not to be found in a Michelin Green Guide;[51] it did, however, exist for those who read local news coverage and crime reports and for those who lived on the fringes of postwar society. Whether imported from England or the United States, or produced in France under pseudonym, hardboiled crime fiction appealed to those readers, both streetwise and intellectual, touched by crime in their everyday lives.

For some, this everyday crime was the occupation of their country by brutish Nazis, for others it was the behavior of fellow French citizens. Nestor Burma's Paris was one of moral mediocrity where petty criminals stole personal possessions to be sold on the black market. Ordinary citizens had dealings with suspicious characters in or out of circles of authority. An individual could be a scoundrel or hero by degrees. The appeal of the hardboiled novel was that in its fictive world, the criminal is brought to justice and the detective is smarter than either the police or the perpetrators. American hardboiled detective fiction was particularly popular as well as influential for the French *noir* style because it

---

[51] In *Pulp Surrealism* (Berkeley: University of California Press, 2000), Robin Walz makes a comparison between Aragon's *Le paysan de Paris* and turn of the century guidebooks. Aragon's guide-like description of the Passage de l'Opéra "served as a technique to force his readers' imaginations out of a common reality and into surreality" (11).

portrays society as inherently corrupt, crime as ubiquitous, and logic and reason as inadequate opponents for brutality, perversion, and greed. Hence, crime is no longer an individual, isolated act of a brilliant, or as in Simenon's work, of a diseased mind, but a symptom of a diseased out-of-joint world, where the laws of the jungle govern the battle for power and material goods.[52]

The Paris of both the occupation and postwar periods was the "diseased out-of-joint world" that Blaha describes; further, its denizens related to the urbanized tone of the *noir* style. Malet's novels appealed to the French reader who yearned to return to a time in which French culture spoke for itself but who lived in a time of moral compromise when culturally vested comforts could be obtained often only through marginally criminal behaviors. The end of Malet's novels produced familiar tension: Burma solved the crime, but his world was still a mess and loose ends remained. Bourgeois order was not restored as it was in a Maigret novel.

In the midst of the French "Golden Age of detective fiction" during which Georges Simenon prolifically succeeded "à maîtriser l'écriture policière,"[53] Léo Malet became the first writer to use the American hardboiled style in a French setting, for which he has been called "le père du roman noir français."[54] Malet's *roman noir* differs from Simenon's *roman policier* in several ways, most notably in that Burma is a private detective with his own agenda, whereas Inspector Maigret is a respected and decorated servant of the State. As his own boss, Burma is accountable only to himself and thereby free to bend rules as he deems necessary. Carl Shutoff writes that Simenon's Maigret novels "follow the traditional crime-investigation-arrest-capitulation pattern," and end with a "statement on the moral problem about which the plot has revolved."[55] Malet's *roman noir* deviates from this formula in that 1) the murder, usually the first among several, is not always in the first chapter, 2) the chapters that follow do not exclusively investigate the first murder, and 3) the novel rarely ends with a statement on moral problems. Burma's last line is likely to

---

[52] Franz G. Blaha, "Detective/Mystery/Spy Fiction," *Handbook of French Popular Culture*, ed. Pierre L. Horn (Westport: Greenwood, 1991) 44.

[53] Vanoncini 89.

[54] Jean-Paul Schweighauser, *Le roman noir français* (Paris: PUF, 1984), 31.

[55] Carl Shutoff, *Simenon's Maigret Novels* (*DAI* 41A no. 1 (1980), 277. Indiana University), 28.

reflect on his own shortcomings or speculate on what will come next for him. There is little or no concern for society at large and its moral dilemmas nor hope of restoration of bourgeois order.

Malet's American-style first-person narration is another departure from Simenon's French model. If Malet has a formula, it is the complacent daily routine of his Fiat Lux agency interrupted by a new client whose seemingly mundane request for service somehow connects to a murder in the same *arrondissement*. As Schweighaeuser summarizes:

> Burma enquête sur une affaire, il tombe sur un cadavre, rencontre des personnes étrangères à son enquête, est imbrigué dans une seconde affaire, reçoit un coup de matraque providentiel et, à son réveil, découvre la solution grâce aux liens mystérieux qui lient ensemble tous les éléments qui paraissaient épars au point de départ.[56]

This is the basic plot of every Nestor Burma mystery: when he finds himself outside his second *arrondissement* office to meet a client in his or her milieu, Burma stumbles onto something he did not mean to see. Burma's investigation to connect the murder to the client's request is a process usually criticized by Commissioner Florimond Faroux until it works in favor of the official police investigation, though Burma almost always stumbles onto more "cadavres" along the way and receives at least one if not multiple blows to the head. Burma is not a hearse-chaser, scouring the daily papers for a new case, and does not look exclusively for murder cases, but he is not disappointed when a blackmailing case leads to something more newsworthy. There may be updates on Burma's theories during the story, in a seeming effort to soothe a confused reader by confirming that he follows the same twist or turn as the detective and is not fooled by a false lead, but there is rarely a capitulation at the end of the novel. Once Burma has committed to an investigation, the narrative does not leave the *arrondissement* of the crime, save for brief scenes at the office here and there. With few exceptions, the novel will end in the highlighted *arrondissement*, at the moment of arrest.

This chapter will look at the role of Léo Malet's *œuvre* in the evolution of detective fiction in France from 1941 to 1966, dates defined by two pivotal genre studies by Roger Caillois and Tzvetan

---

[56] Schweighaeuser 32

Todorov. In framing the *Nouveaux Mystères* series by these two studies, I will argue that Malet's decision to set his writing in Paris proved to be a catalyst for this popular genre's French line to splinter into subgenres which would evolve in the second half of the twentieth century. Malet precipitated change by using the familiar location of Paris, introducing an antiheroic French detective, and mixing slang with literary form, thus expanding the boundaries of the French detective novel. Malet also blurs the line between author and subject, using Burma as a literary alter ego to both critique and praise the postwar era.

Shaking up the Status Quo

In his study of the *roman policier*, Roger Caillois documents the state of detective fiction in France during the occupation, at the time when Malet began to write.[57] It is from this state that Malet deviates in creating the French version of the hardboiled novel. For Caillois, detective fiction offers a formulaic exception to experimental literature with a "tendance générale à l'anarchie."[58] Classic detective fiction writers who adhered strictly to classical-style limits and codes, and *policiers* with clever usage of Aristotle's unities or S.S. Van Dine's rules, as if they were poetry or theatre, were particularly well received by Caillois. The criteria cited by Caillois illustrate the status quo of a popular genre that was on the verge of splitting into subgenres.

Caillois examines the genre of detective fiction and its "évolution" from reading for pleasure to a literature worthy of scholarly attention. Unlike the adventure novel, which often resembles the *policier* in other respects, the *roman policier* "semble un film projété à l'envers [et] prend le temps à rebours et renverse la chronologie [suivant] l'ordre de la découverte."[59] The death of a central character, which would be the end of a novel in another genre, becomes the beginning in a detective novel, with the rest of the

---

[57] Caillois was one of many French intellectuals who sought refuge in the Americas during the war: he in Argentina, Breton and the surrealists in New York and Mexico. Malet, however, remained in the occupied zone, and his experience both colors his prose and links him to his readership through a shared traumatic experience.

[58] Roger Caillois, *Le roman policier* (Buenos Aires: Éditions des lettres françaises, 1941) 10.

[59] Caillois 11.

narrative serving to reconstruct the murder. Caillois claims that the *policier* is not a story but a scientific deduction,[60] satisfying the intelligence of a reader rather than the passions. Most readers of detective fiction would differ with Caillois, however, and argue that they turn to popular fiction, including detective fiction, in order to escape the scientific deduction that surrounds them in everyday life and to indulge their imagination. The dominance of scientific deduction in the mysteries featuring Holmes, Poirot, and Maigret is a trend of detective fiction in Caillois's era which Malet's Burma will break. Malet falls somewhere in between two styles of mysteries: the mystery of pure deduction which the reader only observes, and the *roman problème* or *roman jeu* where the reader plays the game of solving crime along with the detective. The streetwise Nestor Burma is far from the "esthète" detectives that precede him who often solve a crime by pure deduction, without even soiling their hands in an investigation. Authors in the style of Sir Arthur Conan Doyle resort to hiding essential knowledge from readers, in order to provide a surprise, albeit contrived ending, while those in the style of Agatha Christie take care to expose all possible details to the reader, who is "en condition de découvrir la solution . . . à l'égal du detective."[61]

When Burma formulates theories as to why a suspect was where on a given night, it shows the reader a possible direction in which Malet might have taken his story. Burma's theories reveal his creativity, as well as Malet's, and allow us to understand why the eventual solution was the right one. This proto-hypertext is part of the author's game with his reader: while one of Burma's theories in a middle chapter may seem plausible, the four remaining chapters will unveil surprises. Action rather than theory will generate the final accounting. Malet's variation on this game played with the reader is to combine the arrogance of Holmes, who "se présente comme le maître incontestable d'un savoir et d'une technique spécifiques,"[62] with the intimacy of first-person narration which confides in the reader as the investigation plays out. As the reader cannot be allowed to solve the mystery before the detective does, the narrative must include false

---

[60] Caillois 12.
[61] Caillois 20.
[62] Vanoncini 26.

leads, which the detective will claim not to have noticed.[63] The means are often more interesting than the ends, to the extent that Malet's story generally ends when the culprit is identified. There is no follow-up to see if justice is actually served. The guilty usually die on the penultimate page, either from a self-inflicted wound or from a fatal dénouement, but in novels such as *Boulevard . . . Ossements*, the police arrive on the final page. It is not revealed whether the murderer resists while being led away, or even whether Burma is congratulated for a job well done. For Malet, the game is over when the truth is revealed. The game is also over for the reader, who, according to Caillois, reads a mystery novel not only to read the story of a murder but also for the pleasure of solving the mystery, "d'assister à un tour de prestidigitation dont l'illusionniste dévoile aussitôt le secret."[64] Burma investigates the crime in order to uncover the identity of the criminal, but finding the motive behind the crime is no longer as important as in Caillois's study.

For Caillois in 1941, the French *polar* "occupe une place spéciale dans la littérature romanesque, mais il s'en écarte, depuis qu'il est né par un étrange renversement de perspective."[65] Whereas most of a *policier* novel reconstructs the events that led to the murder in the first chapter, forming a narrative circle, in a *noir* novel the search for the motive of one murder usually leads to other murders, which may or may not have been committed by the same criminal. The first murder serves merely as a springboard for the rest of the novel. The self-imposed restrictions of detective fiction limited its capacity for innovation enjoyed by other genres at the time. Caillois maintains that, in detective fiction, there is no place for psychological methodology nor for passions and emotions. The genre is

> toute abstraction et toute démonstration. Il ne cherche pas à toucher, à émouvoir, à exalter, à flatter l'âme par l'image de ses troubles, de ses souffrances, et de ses aspirations. Il est froid et stérile, parfaitement cérébral. Il ne suscite aucun sentiment et ne fait pas rêver. Il s'applique

---

[63] Jerry Palmer says of the nature of crime narrative: "the puzzle-like quality gives the reader the illusion that (s)he has as much chance as the detective of solving the mystery, although in reality . . . the author weights all the chances in the detective's favour". In *Potboilers: Methods, Concepts, and Case Studies in Popular Fiction* (London; New York: Routledge, 1991) 131.

[64] Caillois 35.

[65] Caillois 47.

> seulement à ne rien laisser en suspens ou dans le vague. Tout ce qu'il
> apporta disparate ou mystérieux, il le laisse cohérent et clair.[66]

The state of French detective fiction before the arrival of Nestor
Burma is, then, according to Caillois, "froid et stérile, parfaitement
cérébral." Malet brings the irreverent hardboiled style to a French
setting, creating a series that is far from cold and sterile. His witty
characters are faced with the fallout of the occupation and must find
the compassion to help out those who are on the societal fringe. One
such character is Esther Lévyberg in *Des kilomètres de linceuls* who
wears her hair like Veronika Lake to cover her disfigured face and
changes her name from Alice to Esther out of solidarity for her fellow
Jews exterminated by the Nazis. Where the classic *polar* "ne fait pas
rêver," Malet's novels are colored by their own dream imagery which
encourages readers to reflect on their own dream activity no matter
how insignificant the dreams may seem. The end for Malet is not
always "cohérent et clair," but what is most important is that the
detective survive for the next installment.

Also important for Caillois is that both investigator and
perpetrator be portrayed as evenly balanced as possible, in order to
make the game more interesting. The detective must have distracting
weaknesses so that the element of danger is always present, but the
criminal should also be clever so as not to be found out too quickly.
For Caillois, a story such as Poe's *Murders in the Rue Morgue* is
unsatisfying because the murderer, an animal, neither uses nor rejects
reason when committing a crime. In a detective novel, the perpetrator
must be human. Neither is insanity a *policier*-worthy generator of
criminal activity. In detective fiction, the motives must be clear and
the acts without remorse. The only regret should be getting caught.
The reading of a detective novel for Caillois is an intellectual exercise
where both the reader and the detective work to discover the identity
of and motive behind the murderer and his crime. In this exercise, "le
rôle du hasard diminue, celui de la logique augmente."[67] While the
identity of the murderer is most important to uncover in Malet's
roman noir, Burma is not so concerned with the logic of the crime.
Rather, the concern is how the plan to commit murder and avoid
punishment was flawless enough to puzzle the police but not flawless

---

[66] Caillois 47.
[67] Caillois 17.

enough to stop the snooping detective. Burma's detective is looking for what is hidden by lies and deceit. Sometimes he opens the right door, sometimes not; it is the search that is gratifying, often more so than the answer he eventually finds. The literary focus is the game between the detective and the murderer, as well as between the detective and the reader, often leaving aside the victim who had to die to allow the game to begin.

Caillois reminds us of a fact often overlooked by fans of the genre: characters are murdered to keep the reading public entertained. When Burma tells us in chapter one that he has not worked in many months, or that his name has not recently appeared in the newspapers, the reader sympathizes with him. If, by chapter four, there is no murder (as in *M'as-tu vu en cadavre*), we start to grow as impatient as Burma himself, disappointed that the person he assumed dead was just out of town. We can read about his other *enquêtes* and *filiatures*, such as the pursuit of philandering husbands and vengeful blackmailers, but these subplots, while most are eventually woven in with the murder, are not as interesting as those involving murder, where Burma is truly in his element. For Caillois, "Il exige un meurtrier, un coupable qui ait tué et qui risque la peine capitale," a rather standard feature of detective fiction, as well as "un drame véritable, un duel sans merci entre des adversaires disposés et obligés à recourir aux moyens extremes."[68] It is easy to choose a side in a merciless battle of well-defined extremes, but such a choice does not always make for satisfying reading. When a villain is completely evil, there is no reason to learn why he committed the crime, and when the hero is completely good, there is no interest in watching him. When the detective is flawed, he not only becomes approachable to the reader but also gives the reader a fascinating if inscrutable hero to follow. Even with his "dynamite" reputation, Nestor Burma is still flawed.

Caillois sees celebrating the "maudit" as a dangerous direction glamorizing the murderer instead of the hero solving the mystery. Malet, however, sees the "maudit" as filled with narrative possibility. His novels are colored by images of the seedy underbelly of urban life, and it is this new sensibility that helps to make his *œuvre* so innovative. In the final pages of his essay, Caillois refers to the "détective mondain" as

---

[68] Caillois 54.

> esthète, détaché, ne désirant ni argent ni gloire, qui ne s'indigne ni ne s'apitoie et qui, au dénouement, se lave les mains comme Pilate des conséquences que peuvent avoir les découvertes de sa perspicacité dans le bas monde des sensations, des émotions, et des douleurs.[69]

Caillois's detective is an esthete, solving crimes as an intellectual exercise and not as a way to make a living. While it is unlikely that Malet had read Caillois's essay before creating Burma,[70] it almost seems as if he used Callois's essay as a parallel blueprint for creating a detective that would be nothing like anyone expected from a French writer. Malet's Burma is well read, but is hardly an esthete, and does what he does to keep himself alive. While he desires money, fame is even more appealing, and he fears no consequences if he knows his name will be in the newspaper.

Whereas Caillois's study documents the state of the genre that Malet would penetrate, Tzvetan Todorov's 1966 study (published in 1971) considers the critical progress of detective fiction in the era following Malet's most productive and influential years. Though the detective fiction genre had existed for almost 200 years, it was only then in the mid-1960s beginning to be taken seriously by critics who, until that time, had chosen to undervalue the novels in question for not following the rules of the canon regarding fiction. The romantic rebellion of the nineteenth century, which opened the door for more varied subject matter, Todorov explains, was shortly followed by the rise of newspaper culture, featuring *feuilleton* fiction that appealed to newly literate masses. One of the more popular *feuilletons* at the end of that century was Eugène Sue's *Les Mystères de Paris*, which inspired the title of Malet's series in 1954.[71] By 1966, the classic *roman policier* had splintered into the subgenres of *énigme* (what was formerly the classic *policier*), *noir*, *aventures*, and *espionnage*.

---

[69] Caillois 72.

[70] As Caillois was in Argentina, his and other imported books were not allowed in France during the occupation.

[71] The title of the series was chosen by Malet's editor, Robert Laffont, and not by the author himself. Claude De Grève compares the depiction of Paris in Sue's *feuilleton* to Malet's series in "Des Mystères de Paris d'Eugène Sue aux Nouveaux Mystères de Paris de Léo Malet", *Cahiers de l'association internationale des études francaises* 40 (1988): 156. Paris "crée dans les romans de Malet comme dans les romans de Sue une atmosphère à la fois aimée et haïe, mais il est d'abord participant, rôle actantiel si l'on veut, dans le récit où il sert de cadre."

Todorov writes of the norms of genres established by every new, significant work: the dominant genre that the new work transgresses, and the genre which the new work creates. As an example, he cites Stendhal's *La Chartreuse de Parme.*

> Le genre de *la Chartreuse de Parme*, c'est-à-dire la norme à laquelle ce roman se réfère, n'est pas le roman français du début du XIXe; c'est le genre "roman stendhalien" qui est créé par cette œuvre précisément, et par quelques autres. On pourrait dire que tout grand livre établit l'existence de deux genres, la réalité de deux normes: celle du genre qu'il trangresse, qui dominait la littérature précédente; et celle du genre qu'il crée.[72]

The trangressing genre is hailed as the next great movement and is allowed to exist alongside the dominant genre. In this paradigm, Malet's *roman noir* transgresses Simenon's classic *policier*, and creates a new genre for itself. Todorov, however, argues that this comparison does not apply to popular literature, such as the *roman policier*. He writes,

> Le roman policier a ses normes; faire "mieux" qu'elles ne le demandent, c'est en même temps faire moins bien: qui veut "embellir" le roman policier, fait de la "littérature," non du roman policier. Le roman policier par excellence n'est pas celui qui transgresse les règles du genre, mais celui qui s'y conforme.[73]

To improve upon the formula of a popular genre is to do something "literary" and therefore no longer represents the popular genre. Todorov cites Agatha Christie as an example; she is revered for remaining true to the genre's course without deviation. Different critical standards remain between "le grand art" of literature and popular art. Todorov does not mention Malet by name in his essay, perhaps because Malet's introduction of surrealist imagery into the detective genre constituted a literary experiment and was no longer popular literature by Todorov's definition. His essay does, however, indicate the legacy of Malet's boundary crossing.

In detective fiction, according to Todorov, there are two concurrent stories: the story of the crime and the story of the "enquête." Todorov compares this method to the *fable-sujet* of the

---

[72] Todorov 56.
[73] Todorov 56.

Russian formalists. The *fable* corresponds to "la réalité évoquée . . . des événements semblables à ceux qui se déroulent dans notre vie," while the *sujet* "[correspond] au livre lui-même, au récit, aux procédés littéraires dont se sert l'auteur."[74] With the *sujet*, "l'auteur peut nous présenter les résultats avant les causes, la fin avant le début,"[75] whereas the *fable* is the action of the story in its natural order, without inversion. That the two stories of "crime" and "enquête" can coexist in a detective novel is paradoxical for Todorov, which he dismisses by labeling the story of the crime as a story of absence.[76] Meanwhile, the story of the investigation is "insignifiante," as it serves "seulement de médiateur entre le lecteur et l'histoire du crime."[77] He explains, "Il s'agit donc, dans le roman à enigme, de deux histoires dont l'une est absente mais réelle, l'autre présente mais insignifiante."[78] "Paradoxical" characterization does not hold for a *roman noir*, whose second story, the story of the investigation, is more important than the story of the initial crime. The *noir* story, with its first-person narration, reads as if we are tagging along with the detective, "le récit coïncide à l'action,"[79] as opposed to the flashback *récit* of the *énigme*. In the way Malet writes a typical *noir* story, the novel ends when the criminal's identity is discovered. There is no flashback at the end of the novel to reconstruct the murder as it happened. It is only revealed who committed the crime, and sometimes a motive, though that motive does not change the fact that the detective has successfully solved yet another case.

In the *roman à énigme*, the detective is implicitly immune; he never gets hurt and there is no danger of his succumbing to those he investigates. In the *roman noir*, such immunity no longer holds true. Therefore, the story of the investigation becomes more interesting; the same dangerous element that Burma investigates hopes to bring harm to the detective. The detective is struck on the head in a "coup de

---

[74] Todorov 58.

[75] Todorov 58.

[76] Lits writes of "cette structure particulière du récit policier constitué de deux histoires, celle du crime et celle de l'enquête, la deuxième fonctionnant à rebours pour revenir aux sources du délit. La séparation est claire: le récit du crime est entièrement pris en charge par la recension des faits divers, l'enquête étant réservée au détective qui porte d'ailleurs un regard assez méprisant sur ces articles" (141).

[77] Todorov 59.

[78] Todorov 59.

[79] Todorov 60.

crâne" or "coup de matraque," if not shot at or pushed down a flight of stairs, at least once in every novel. Not only does he "met le mystère K.O.," but he also triumphs over death. Unlike the case in a *roman à énigme*, mystery is less prevalent than "curiosité" and "suspens" because "tout est possible, et le détective risque sa santé, sinon la vie."[80]

For Todorov, the *roman noir* is constructed "autour du milieu représenté, autour de personnages et de mœurs particuliers"[81] rather than following a formula. This is true subsequent to Malet's *Nouveaux Mystères* series. His *roman noir* does not follow the formula of the *policier* leftover from Caillois's era but is set around a fixed location, such as the *arrondissement*. In a *roman noir* the characters and their fringe-culture values are more important than a story with tidy endings. Malet's cast of characters always includes Hélène Chatelain, Burma's faithful secretary; Burma's investigators, Roger Zavatter and Louis Reboul, the latter having returned from the war with only one arm; Marc Covet, the "journaliste éponge" who keeps Burma's name in the newspaper; and Florimond Faroux, a police inspector in *120, rue de la gare*, promoted to commissioner in the *Nouveaux Mystères*. These characters provide constants in a genre where the murderer is not always who we expect him or (sometimes) her to be. Narrative turns are interspersed throughout the narrative and are not reserved for the dénouement.

Todorov discusses eight of the "Twenty Rules for Writing Detective Stories" written in 1928 by S.S. Van Dine[82] in more detail than did Caillois, showing how far the genre had come since Caillois's essay. While these rules were already being violated in Caillois's era, they had become all but completely irrelevant by Todorov's essay, in light of the emergence of various subgenres. Van Dine states that the detective novel should have more than a detective and a guilty party, and at least one dead body; Malet's *roman noir* presents a cast of familiar characters, and several "cadavres" per episode. For Van Dine, there is no room for love or romance in a detective novel; Burma has several romantic entanglements throughout the series, all of which end with the woman's death. Van Dine forbids the use of irrational explanations, fantastic imagery, psychological analysis and

---

[80] Todorov 60.
[81] Todorov 60.
[82] Todorov 62.

descriptions, or banalities; Malet violates all of these rules, deploying surreal imagery in place of the fantastic. Todorov criticizes the *roman noir*, saying that its descriptions "sont faits sans emphase, froidement, même si l'on décrit des faits effrayants; on peut dire 'avec cynisme'."[83] Malet, again, stands apart from other French writers, even in his own subgenre, as his language is always colorful, if sometimes cynical, and never cold. His style approaches that of a *roman à suspens*, noted for its vivid descriptions, but as the *suspens* is a subgenre noteworthy for not always needing a detective, as when a falsely accused person sets out to find the "real" killer, Malet's series definitely remains a true *noir*. Malet expanded the boundaries of detective fiction, to the extent that there are elements of several subgenres in his series.

Though the rules of Caillois's era are no longer relevant, Todorov predicts at the end of his study that a "nouveau code" of rules will help different genres of literature, both popular and avant-garde, coexist peacefully, remaining distinct according to their characteristics. Each genre needs the other to exist, "à partir d'un complexe de propriétés différents."[84] The *roman noir* can thus venture in new directions and still remain true to its constants, cited by Todorov as violence, sordid crime, and the amorality of the principal characters, sometimes including the detective.[85] The elements of "le danger, la poursuite, [et] le combat"[86] found in the *roman noir* also turn up in the *roman d'aventures*, which leans toward the exotic, with its descriptive travel logs. Malet flirts with the *roman d'aventures* in his descriptions of Paris, but his narrative remains fundamentally *noir*.

With the innovation of bringing the *noir* style to a French setting, Malet redefined the detective genre for a new generation of writers. Malet dared to push the boundaries of a codified genre. French writers had followed the status quo by setting their American-style mysteries in the United States. As the majority of these writers had never crossed the Atlantic, they had to rely on other mystery novels and popular films for source material. Malet's first editor, Louis Chevance, commissioned popular writers, including Malet, to write novels which followed a particular formula. There was no room

---

[83] Todorov 63.
[84] Todorov 65.
[85] Todorov 61.
[86] Todorov 61.

for an aspiring artist to deviate. Malet was both stubborn and courageous to write novels in a setting and style with which he was familiar, but having come from an avant-garde milieu, did not see his change of setting as particularly earth-shattering. Under the pseudonym Frank Harding, Malet wrote of an American journalist, Johnny Metal. His ideas were limited, however, as he was familiar with Paris and had never been to the United States, and he did not want to read other hardboiled novels to get details for his own work when he could write about what he knew.[87] His first step toward change led to other changes in terms of language and imagery. He used colorful slang and surrealist imagery to bring a new sensibility to a popular genre. The situating of Malet's Nestor Burma series between both Caillois's and Todorov's studies illustrates the impact his writing had on other *noir* authors who followed his lead and changed the face of detective fiction. If this were not true, Malet would be remembered as a peculiarity in a popular genre, if at all.

Slang: un micmac pour le ciboulot

A detective novel set in France is not in itself something new; neither is the use of slang in narrative new, with Céline's *Voyage au bout de la nuit* as the primary example. Malet's innovation, rather, is in his introduction of slang into the deeply rooted popular genre of detective fiction. Slang is both subversive and suggestive, an instrument of acculturation to a new space where double entendre is a way of life. By having Burma speak the same slang as the street dwellers he encounters, Malet subverts the purity of the language expected from the detective genre. At the same time, this rich language evokes the urban space of Burma's investigations more vividly than a mere traditional lexicon. Malet's favorite use of slang is as *jeu de mots*, and the first place in the novel to find it is in the title. As each novel focuses on a different *arrondissement*, the title's wordplay pinpoints a specific trait of the *arrondissement*, whether a particular site or an indirect reference to activities associated with that

---

[87] Malet maintained: "Le décor de [Paris] n'avait à mon goût jamais été assez exploité; d'où l'idée d'un livre par arrondissement, avec son propre décor, sa propre atmosphère. Mais faire des descriptions est un art difficile. On trouve que Simenon nous met vraiment dans le bain. Il ne fait jamais que donner quelques indications, au lecteur d'apporter le reste" (Jean-Paul Morel, "Le retour de Nestor Burma, *Le Matin* 14-15 July 1979: 21).

sector of Paris. With the ironic title *Micmac moche au Boul' Mich* composed uniquely of slang, Malet pokes fun at the scholarly Quartier Latin, the location of the Sorbonne in the fifth *arrondissement*. In another example, *Corrida aux Champs-Elysées* revolves around the film industry centered in the eighth *arrondissement*. The literal meaning of "corrida" is "course de taureaux," evoking the stubborn tourists that crowd the most famous avenue in Paris, but the slang variation is a "scène plus ou moins violente, en gestes et en paroles, entre plusieurs personnes." Both variations circulate for Malet, who found much frustration in the film industry's inability to adapt his novels successfully to the big screen.[88] Malet further criticizes actors and the film industry in *M'as-tu vu en cadavre?*, a study of washed up actors and teen idols, but the novel is a rare example of a title that is neither *arrondissement* specific nor a *jeu de mots*.

In most cases, Malet's slang-filled verbosity colors the novels' titles, provoking the reader's curiosity and reflecting the narrative's location. Sometimes a place is evoked, other times a plot device or mood. The first novel of the series, *Le Soleil naît derrière le Louvre*, has a poetic title, one that could be expected from any *polar* author, even Simenon. But the slang variation of "soleil" as "un million de francs (anciens)" connects to the story where the murders revolve around the theft of a painting. The verb of the title, "naît," also evokes the homonym "n'est," suggesting that perhaps the "sun" is not behind the Louvre after all but is rather somewhere else. The sun, like the painting, is not where it is supposed to be, thereby disrupting a usually tranquil scene. That the title is the same as the last line of the novel sets *Soleil* apart from the rest of the series. Another title that lures the reader with poetic pretense is *Brouillard au pont de Tolbiac*. The title evokes fog on the Seine in November when the novel takes place, but an alternate reading of "brouillard" gives "dans un état d'ivresse," possibly a reference to Burma's hazy flashbacks to his arrival in Paris twenty years earlier, under the protective wing of an anarchist commune. In the novel, retired police inspector Ballin

---

[88] Looking at the three film adaptations of Malet's works, Claude Gauteur writes, "Or cet ancien figurant, ce cinéphile averti, ce poète surréaliste, a toujours rêvé de voir ses livres, qui regorgent de qualités visuelles et verbales, adaptés à l'écran: il y a là un *rendez-vous manqué*, à propos duquel il vaut peut-être que l'on s'arrête." In "Léo Malet et le cinéma: un rendez-vous manqué," *La revue du cinéma image et son* Apr. 1979: 51.

haunts the *quai* under the bridge looking for the fish that got away, "la clef de l'énigme" (*Enquêtes*, 2:264), the urban character Burma could have become, the case he was unable to close. His presence is like that of a ghost, a hovering human fog. As could be expected, his situation is connected to Burma's case and, because Ballin has the same trenchcoat as Burma, he is stabbed in the back by a disgruntled gypsy seeking revenge against the *détective de choc*. Confused by the suggestion of the trenchcoat, the gypsy kills the wrong detective.

Of the six possible slang terms for a "protestation, opposition violente," the most appropriate for the title of the *mystère* set in the Jewish district, known as the Marais, is "rébecca," which also makes reference to the Jewish woman found dead in the first chapter. In *Du rébecca rue des Rosiers*, the woman is not named Rebecca, but the search for her story leads Burma to an infamous collaborator's hiding spot in an underground cave. Included in *Boulevard . . . Ossements* is a reference to the skeleton of a one-legged dancer, "l'unijambiste," that was sold by a merchant at the Salle des ventes, on the rue Drouot, as well as to other bones disposed of in a questionable manner. *Casse-pipe à la Nation* is set at the annual Foire du Trône, which used to take place at Nation, a round-about in the twelfth *arrondissement*, but has since moved to a larger location in the Bois de Vincennes. A "casse-pipe" is slang for "une action ou situation très dangereuse, surtout en parlant de la guerre," but "pipe" can also mean "visage ou tête," which connects to two pivotal ferris-wheel accidents discussed in the novel: one girl is pushed off the ride and becomes paralyzed from the neck down; the following year the suspect gets into an altercation with Burma, falls off the ride, and is disfigured beyond recognition before he hits the ground, dying instantly. And in a less gruesome interpretation, "pipe" refers to Burma's pipe which is in the shape of a bull's head and never breaks, no matter how badly he loses a fight.

Sometimes Malet subverts the expectations generated by the novels' titles. Bleach water never figures into *Les eaux troubles de Javel* but, given the location of the mystery concerning an illegal arms dealer supplying Algerian rebels at the Javel canal, Malet cannot resist the obvious *jeu de mots* of "eau de javel." The title is even more playful given that Burma is reacquainted with a woman for whom he had arranged a *mariage blanc* before the war. The slang expression "les eaux sont basses" ["l'argent manque"] is another variation on "eaux troubles," significant to the narrative where Burma encounters the arms dealer, who moonlights as an illegal abortionist. While *Pas de bavards à la Muette* is an eye-catching title, juxtaposing "chatty person" and "mute," it is even more telling to know that "bavards" can also mean "avocats" and "armes à feu." In the story, a young woman is accused of shooting her boyfriend with a gun. According to Burma, she could not possibly have fired the gun because she was drugged and unable to focus on a target. In the same vein, "rats" is slang for thieves, but *Les rats de Montsouris* is an even more playful *jeu de mots* given that "mon souris" means "my mouse," and Montsouris is a park in the fourteenth *arrondissement*. Although Malet only wrote one chapter of his tribute to the the eighteenth *arrondissement* "Les neiges de Montmartre," we can expect the standard meaning of snow, subject of so many paintings by resident artists in the first decades of the twentieth century, as well as slang variations of "neiges," such as "fausse identité ou cocaïne." The use of slang in Malet's work renders the process of translation all the more difficult, and has contributed to Malet's obscurity among readers whose knowledge of French does not include the slang of his generation.

Malet's use of slang within a literary form also makes it difficult to situate his production among his contemporaries. In a 1949 interview, five years before the *Nouveaux Mystères*, Malet says, "Je n'écris pas pour faire le moraliste mais uniquement pour *amuser* les gens."[89] Malet's use of slang was clearly a source of amusement for himself and his readers, but was not met with great enthusiasm from critics, who still saw detective fiction as entertainment without intellectual value. One such critic, Armand Hoog, writes of Nestor Burma's differences from the criminal standard:

> On ne se meut pas ici dans la savante logique . . . Nestor Burma, "détective de choc," n'appartient pas à l'école des penseurs qui semblent avoir fait leurs classes policières au Collège de France . . . Nestor Burma cache soigneusement ses connaissances et sa culture.[90]

---

[89] Maurice Renault, "En bavardant avec Léo Malet," *Magazine littéraire* 21 (1949): 109-11.

[90] Armand Hoog, "Mythologie du Pistolet: Romans policiers de Léo Malet," *Carrefour_*07 Sept 1949. Rpt. in Jacques Baudou, ed., *Nestor Burma détective de choc, un monde étrange*. Spec. issue of *Enigmatika* 18 (1981). Paris: Butte-aux-Cailles, 1982: 119-22.

It may not be accurate to say that Burma "cache" his knowledge, as he shares it with the reader whenever possible. The range of his "connaissances," including that of literary figures such as Mallarmé as well as historical *faits-divers*, is both surprising and impressive, as it goes beyond the *culture scolaire* that most French citizens shared. Though they may have bristled at his tone, readers were drawn to Nestor Burma and his choice of vocabulary. In other novels of the *polar* genre, slang had been used primarily in dialogue, as a pejorative means of description. Malet's slang is evocative, often sexist, but rarely vulgar. For Burma, slang provides a way to identify with those he represents or, if his clients are wealthy, serves as a device to set him apart from those he represents. He is a product of the street and speaks in its patois, but he is also a champion of French culture, unaffected by the fallout of the occupation in his sense of national pride.

Nestor Burma is more like Maigret in that he is an ordinary guy, and less like the idiosyncratic Sherlock Holmes or Hercule Poirot. He is an "Everyman," not a gentleman, and as a result has the language of an ordinary man who does not care that his observations are in a less than elegant prose. Burma, who seems to have fallen into his profession by accident, has more in common with an antihero such as Céline's Bardamu than with the great minds of his genre. The antihero is allowed to have moments of incompetence and foolishness, such as when Burma leaves the house without his weapon but remembers his pipe, or moments of shady ethics, such as when he sleeps with a female client. Faithful, trustworthy, heroic Maigret would never enjoy such a luxury. Burma is a man of his appetites, vulnerable to women and culturally adept. He is a new model for a new genre, in that his streetwise detective shakes up the French *roman policier*. He is not, however, what Kristin Ross calls the postwar "new man": "a new construction of (male) subjectivity was proclaimed from all sides, celebrated, analyzed, and debated."[91] She examines "three principle versions of postwar masculinity, each of which occupied a distinct discursive and spatial site: the *maquis* (those inaccessible areas where armed resistance was organized), the university, and the corporation."[92] That Burma does not fit into any of these categories –

---

[91] Ross 158.
[92] Ross 158.

the decolonialized *maquis*, the product of higher education, or the ambitious career-driven *jeune cadre* – makes him an anti-new-man. His unapologetic disdain of progress and reluctance to modernize make him a throwback to an older culture, and an icon of a culture on the verge of disappearance.

Malet further expands the boundaries of detective fiction by including topical issues in his fiction such as postwar renovation, the tension between former collaborationists and resistance fighters, and the beginnings of the end of colonialism. In his Maigret series, Simenon never alludes to either of the World Wars, much less to the occupation. While this omission gives his collective work a more timeless quality than that of Malet, he refuses to acknowledge his readership's reality. Malet's readers had the satisfaction of seeing those who had profited during the occupation come to a violent and painful end. Malet discusses the changing face of Paris, both good and bad, echoing the sentiments of the readers whose neighborhoods were torn down to build skyscrapers. In both *Micmac moche au Boul' Mich'* and *Les eaux troubles de Javel*, Burma reflects the attitude of many French made uncomfortable by the influx of immigrants from former colonies, and he uses slang to express his distaste. He does not object openly to the new citizens living in Paris, but regrets the troubles that their interaction with French society entails. As an example in *Micmac*, Burma cites a "cabaret antillais," where "des Noirs à poil [sont] en train de gambiller uniquement avec de belles Blanches aux cheveux blonds dans la même tenue" (*Enquêtes*, 2: 713). Malet's phonetic slang also distinguishes those whom Burma does not respect, including those who do not use correct grammar. With the Resistance movement, the French freed themselves from the Nazis but they could not stop the times from changing after the war. The end of colonialism provided a new threat to a wobbly French self-esteem. In *Javel*, Malet makes reference to the underground presence of the Algerian FLN, as well as to undercover efforts to subvert the organization's power. When caught spying on an FLN meeting, Burma tells the leader that his identification papers are made with pork, "et vous devez l'avoir en horreur" (*Enquêtes*, 2: 433). His rude and often ignorant comments might not make him more endearing, but they prove him knowledgeable of his times. Malet presents a flawed figure as a literary character, as if to argue that the postwar reality is just as worthy of literary attention as more heroic times. The new detective does not have to be noble, or even free of prejudice; in creating an antiheroic detective concerned with current French issues, Malet opens the door for a generation of French writers eager to change the status quo of detective fiction as well as of literature and of culture in general.

The *roman noir* thus marks a departure from the classic *policier*, not only in its subject matter and body count but also in its choice of language. Malet peppers his characters' speech with *argot*, or Parisian slang, occasionally importing poetical references and literary images. Sometimes the slang is written phonetically. In *Soleil*, Burma repeatedly says "kek chose comme ça" (*Enquêtes*, 1: 437) and his secretary, Hélène Chatelain, has learned to decode his patois. In several novels, she refers to this foreign language she has had to learn in order to understand him. By using the language of the street, Malet invites the reader to become part of the urban landscape and join the ambiance of 1954. In the same way that he renders the American hardboiled tradition culturally accessible to French readers in his use of familiar setting, Malet infuses his text with the language of his era. For his French readers not familiar with Burma's gangsterisms or with the shady milieu in which he operates, Malet provides a glimpse of local exoticism, proving that a detective novel does not have to be set in a foreign country to attract readers. While France was rebuilding and modernizing, Malet was reconceptualizing what detective fiction in France could be. He did so by restoring the notion that popular literature could revolve around French life, and by challenging the status quo without alienating the reading public. Most publishers resisted the marketing of a hardboiled novel with a French sensibility. With Nestor Burma, Malet challenged their expectations. By bringing the *roman noir* home, Malet reestablished a sense of self in those who read his books. French readers could now enjoy a mystery set in their own backyard, featuring their own daily routines intermingled with the exoticism of a literary landscape.

Slippage

Malet further expands the boundaries of the French detective novel by playfully blurring the line between author and "personnage," where "dans l'ombre de ce détective anarcho-surréaliste, on devinait les traits de Léo Malet."[93] The character of Nestor Burma is in part based on the author's own biography, and the character makes reference to the author as if they were friends. Malet thereby finds a way to ensure the legacy of his status as a minor member of the surrealist group when Burma begins to drop names. The 1946 film adaptation of Malet's first novel featuring Burma, *120, rue de la gare*, was well received and helped to make Nestor Burma a more recognizable name than that of Léo Malet. The author makes use of his more famous alter ego to sing the praises of his pre-*polar* work that might otherwise be forgotten. Considering that Malet has been all but omitted from surrealist anthologies, this personal "horn blowing" was a wise decision.

Burma and Malet share many "biographical" traits, including the same birthdate, as revealed in *Du rébecca rue des Rosiers* (*Enquêtes,* 2: 803). Like Malet, Burma came to Paris from Montpellier as a teenager and sought shelter at an anarchist "foyer végetalien" in the thirteenth *arrondissement*. Malet and Burma each sold newspapers on the street as a "crieur professionnel," and both spent time in a German *stalag* during the occupation. Burma was also friendly with the surrealist group, and in *Les rats de Montsouris* he remarks, "je fis mon petit numéro de poète surréaliste"(*Enquêtes*, 1: 931), alluding to his prewar activities which parallel the author's. Also in *Rats*, he visits his old friends Anatole Jakowski, a collector of surrealist objects, and Régis Méssac, a journalist, who are also friends of Malet. In *La nuit de Saint-Germain-des-Près*, Burma has a drink with Paul Boubal, owner of the famous Café de Flore, whom he has known "depuis quinze ans" (*Enquêtes*, 1: 777). Burma is "fidèle aux amitiés de Léo Malet."[94]

Malet's most autobiographical novel, as well as his favorite, is *Brouillard au pont de Tolbiac* in which Burma returns to his old stomping grounds at the "foyer végétalien" when his former mentor dies. The third chapter of the novel, written in italics to indicate Burma's flashback, is a memoir of daily life in an urban commune as well as "la première fois que l'auteur dévoile un chapitre entier de la vie du héros."[95] The narration of this chapter is the only one of the

---

[93] François Bott, "La guinche des antinomies," *Le Monde* 8 Aug. 1975: 7.
[94] Francis Lacassin, *Sous le masque de Léo Malet* (Amiens, Encrage, 1991) 53.
[95] Lacassin, *Masque* 79.

series in third person and speaks of an adolescent we assume to be Burma, but it could just as easily be Malet himself:

> *L'adolescent qui écrasait son visage contre la vitre ne comprenait pas qu'on se soit donné tant de mal . . . pour découvrir un paysage aussi maussade . . . C'était un triste paysage déprimant, mais l'adolescent le contemplait avec une sorte d'avidité.* (*Enquêtes*, 2: 258)

The adolescent is so happy to be in Paris away from "[ses] vieux" that he is willing to overlook the sacrifices he must make in order to stay in the company of disgruntled anarchists. The song that the commune dwellers sing, "Paris, Paris, ô ville infâme et merveilleuse," captures Malet's vision of the French capital: it is at once sordid and marvelous. His novels reflect both elements in Burma's daily life as he stumbles upon "cadavres" in each *arrondissement* but takes the time to appreciate the fantastic moments that the city has to offer.

Malet never gives Burma a physical description. In early publicity photos for *Les nouveaux mystères de Paris*, the author is photographed smoking a pipe and brandishing a gun, perpetuating from the beginning the notion that Burma is based on himself. He seemed to enjoy this confusion, as seen in his autobiography where he says, "Aujourd'hui tous mes amis prétendent que Nestor Burma, c'est moi, les lunettes en moins. C'est flatteur et si mes lectrices le veulent bien, nous nous en tiendrons là pour le moment."[96] Flattered by the attention that his dangerous and provocative character brings him, Malet does nothing to discourage the assumptions that the character is based on his own life. He never fully answers the question so as to ensure that it continues to be asked.

With Burma's voice, Malet comments on the process of writing itself. While searching a man's apartment in *M'as-tu vu cadavre?* Burma stumbles upon a typewriter and says, "et moi, monsieur, si j'avais le temps d'écrire tout ce que j'ai vu au cours de ma vie et si je vous en racontais seulement le quart, etc." (*Enquêtes*, 1: 958). A writer, by professional definition, does have the time to write everything he has ever seen, but chooses which portion to tell or invent. The writing process is also a subplot of *La nuit de Saint-Germain-des-près*, in which a semi-successful writer named Germain St-Germain convinces his friends to commit crimes so that he may

---

[96] Léo Malet, *La vache enragée* (Paris: Hoëbeke, 1988) 177.

write about them, thereby snapping out of his writer's block. When Burma first meets St-Germain, he says, "J'ignorais que vous fussiez un auteur de best-sellers, mais il ne me semble pas que ma réputation soit parvenue jusqu'à vous. Je suis également célèbre, vous savez? Enfin, plus ou moins. Et dans un autre domaine évidemment" (*Enquêtes*, 1: 742). Without the last sentence, reminding us that it is Burma the detective who is speaking, the voice could almost be that of Malet himself, frustrated by his relative anonymity compared to the fame of his own creation or of established writers such as Simenon and Breton. He wants to make sure that he is also remembered. But in the same novel, he takes a swipe at writers who think themselves too important: "La vie est certainement plus compliquée et fertile en péripéties que tout ce que vous pouvez accumuler dans vos livres, dis-je. Mais elle est aussi plus secrète. Alors, n'est-ce pas? Vous, avec votre imagination, vous concluez. La vie ne conclut pas" (*Enquêtes*, 1: 744). If life is more interesting than anything a writer could invent, what is the point of writing? The question that Malet himself must face ultimately stymies him, leaving the series unfinished with five *arrondissements* remaining untreated. Ultimately, St-Germain tells Burma, "ne faites pas attention à ce que je raconte. C'est mon métier de raconter des histoires" (*Enquêtes*, 1:760), advising the reader not to take any writer too seriously.

In a 1989 interview, Malet tells Christophe Driancourt, "J'aime bien qu'on me traite de poète."[97] At least in his own novels, he is referred to as such as well as "chansonnier." In *Micmac moche au boul' Mich*, Burma goes to a nightclub at the Latin Quarter location formerly held by Malet's old cabaret, Le poète pendu, where "Au programme de cette époque lointaine, figuraient Jacques Cathy, Pierre Ferrary, Lucien Lagarde, Léo Malet, etc." (*Enquêtes*, 2: 284). In this casual reference to a time long past, Malet reminds his readers that he has led a life almost as colorful as Burma's. By including them in his novel, he immortalizes his fellow *chansonniers* in the same way that a poet might immortalize a girlfriend in a poem. In a 1958 interview, Gabriel d'Aubarède asked:

> -- Vous aimez l'imprévu et vous comptez sur lui. Comme votre Nestor Burma, dont il est généralement le meilleur inspirateur . . . Au fond, Nestor

---

[97] Christophe Driancourt, "Le charme discret d'un écrivain non-conformiste," *France-Soir Ouest* 8 Dec. 1989: 14.

Burma, n'est-ce pas un peu vous? N'a-t-il pas votre goût du rêve et de la
flânerie fructueuse? Votre côté sentimental, amateur en tout, un peu anar . .
.?
Léo Mallet [sic] reste un moment rêveur. La question lui fut évidemment
souvent posée, mais c'est là un problème embarassant qu'il n'a pas encore
résolu pour lui-même.[98]

At least in his own novels, Malet's name is spelled correctly. This
"problème embarassant" for Malet was neither problematic nor
embarassing but rather part of the game played with the reader. As
cited earlier, Malet says that he writes "pour faire amuser les gens,"
but he also writes to amuse himself, and clearly enjoyed the attention
that the game of slippage garnered for him.[99]

In the same article in which he criticizes Malet's Burma for
infelicitous speech, Hoog praises him for capturing a new energy,
giving a new direction to French literature, an "énergie policière"[100]
that differs from the American "allure" already found in Marcel
Duhamel's *Série Noire*. Due in part to Malet's success with Nestor
Burma, French writers of the *policier* genres were encouraged to write
under their own names, rather than write more strictly formulaic
stories under a pseudonym. *Les Nouveaux Mystères de Paris* have
their place in the history of popular French literature at a time when
the gap between high and low culture is closing and the gap between
literary tastes and class pursuits is narrowing. It is a genre that
novelists and critics alike will try to appraise with the same
seriousness as other literary genres such as poetry and theatre. Malet's
portrait of France after the war appeals to the French and to
francophiles; it is entertaining and informative, but neither universal
nor timeless. His text overflows with familiar Parisians, from cabaret
singers to cleaning women, from café owners to Nazi collaborators.
And once he gained the attention of his readers, he expanded their
appreciation of the genre by infusing this popular reading with the
motifs and images of the avant-garde.

---

[98] Gabriel D'Aubarède, "Je suis contre le roman policier fonctionnant comme un
mécanisme d'horlogerie,' dit Léo Malet." *Nouvelles Littéraires* 20 Mar. 1958: 2.
[99] In the same interview with Driancourt, Malet proudly declares that "trois ou quatre
ont écrit des mémoires universitaires sur moi, j'en suis flatté même si j'en rigole
parfois un peu! Les exigètes me disent que mon personnage fait tel ou tel geste au
chapitre 3 parce qu'il y a eu auparavant 'ceci et cela,' alors que moi je lui ai
simplement fait ce geste pour remplir la ligne" (*Charme*, 14).
[100] Hoog 121.

Chapter Two

Surrealist Traces

When Léo Malet walked past José Corti's bookstore in 1929, he did not have aspirations of joining an infamous literary circle. He passed the bookstore on his way to deliver a toilet, during his "manœuvre" phase. Everywhere in the Quartier Latin, where Malet and his wife co-owned a cabaret, Le Poète Pendu,[101] people had been talking about the surrealists, and when Malet saw the twelfth issue of the journal *La révolution surréaliste* in Corti's window, he decided to see once and for all what all the fuss was about. Surrealism was the latest buzzword, used by the uninitiated, to describe anything that was out of the ordinary. In his autobiography, Malet relates his curiosity:

> Dans les années 1928-30, comme aujourd'hui, quand on ne comprenait pas quelque chose mais on voulait paraître intelligent, on avait l'habitude de dire: "c'est surréaliste!" ou "c'est futuriste!", en ignorant parfaitement le sens de ces mots . . . j'ai tiré mon épingle du jeu très honorablement; mais il était devenu impossible pour moi d'en rester là. Qu'est-ce que c'était que ce putain de surréalisme? Et à qui demander?[102]

With the purchase of the journal, Malet found insight into the group's true philosophy, as well as the address of its leader André Breton. After also buying the *Premier Manifeste*, Malet was inspired to write some poems in the surrealist style,[103] which he mailed to Breton since,

---

[101] In *Micmac moche au boul' Mich'* Malet makes reference to his former cabaret, which in the novel has been turned into a medieval-themed strip club, *A l'Ymage de Nostre-Dame* (*Enquêtes*, 2: 685).

[102] Malet, *Vache* 111.

[103] In his master's thesis, Gaillard establishes points of comparison between Malet's surrealist poetry and his detective fiction. Noé Gaillard, *Du surréalisme au roman policier de Léo Malet*, (Master's Thesis. U Toulouse le Mirail, 1978-79).

in his own words, "J'avais vingt ans . . . et un drôle de culot!"[104] Breton responded to Malet's post with a letter full of praise. Along with his praises, Breton wrote, "Je tiens beaucoup à vous connaître"[105] and, before closing the letter, invited Malet to partake in surrealist meetings at their regular café, Le Cyrano.

The first time he went to the Cyrano, Malet met Breton as well as Yves Tanguy, Paul Eluard, René Char, Alberto Giacommetti, and Louis Aragon, just before the latter's falling out with Breton and subsequent departure from the surrealist group. For the most part, Malet's surrealist production was in the shadow of better-known practitioners. He participated in such infamous activities as the 1936 "Cris dans un théâtre" at a performance of Lillian Hellman's *The Innocents* featuring an actress named Marcelle Géniat. The actress was on the board of a reform school that had been highlighted in a *fait divers*, the only type of news that the surrealists really appreciated, and Breton decided that this woman needed to be taught a lesson. Malet proudly took part in acts of civil disruption such as this:

> Toujours à la pointe du progrès, nous décidâmes au groupe surréaliste d'aller chahuter cette actrice directrice de prison. Au cours de cette soirée houleuse où, en compagnie de Breton, Prévert, Eluard et Bataille, nous avons conspué Marcelle Géniat aux cris de "A bas les bagnes d'enfants!" j'ai été emmené au poste avec Bataille, Rougeul et d'autres, et condamné par le tribunal de police pour "cris dans un théâtre."[106]

One of the surrealists' main objectives was to shock the bourgeoisie. To shock them in their own environment, such as during the production of a respected play, garnered all the more attention and was therefore a successful effort. Another method of provocation was writing political proclamations in texts such as "FIARI" (Fédération internationale de l'art révolutionnaire indépendant) and "Il n'y a pas de liberté pour les ennemis de la liberté." Although he is absent from poetry anthologies, Malet's name on numerous documents provides evidence of his involvement with the group.[107] Because of their

---

[104] Malet, *Vache* 113.

[105] Malet, *Vache* 113.

[106] Malet, *Vache* 116.

[107] Stragliati writes, "Vous vous demanderez bien pourquoi Malet ne figure dans aucune des nombreuses anthologies consacrées ces temps-ci à la poésie française d'aujourd'hui." Roland Stragliati, "Léo Malet, cet autre 'Paysan de Paris'," *Le Monde* 09 May 1975: 10.

signatures on such documents, perceived by the government as anti-French, several minor players, including Malet, were brought in for questioning in 1940, and released as the Nazis approached Paris. The major players, including Breton, had already gone into exile.

One night during the occupation at the Café de Flore, the café frequented by surrealist "dissidents," Louis Chevance proposed a writing job to several of the out-of-work writers who were there. Malet found the writing of detective novels in the American hardboiled style relatively easy. Encouraged by his peers for his work under pseudonym with the character Johnny Metal, he created Nestor Burma, a hardboiled detective with a homegrown Parisian sensibility. His creation was met with great enthusiasm and, without literary pretension, Malet became a pioneer in the genre. When the surrealists returned to Paris at the end of the occupation, Malet knew he would have to choose between life as a writer of popular literature and life among the disdainful avant-gardistes. In an interview with Noël Simsolo, Malet explained:

> Mais les surréalistes n'aimaient pas le roman, en tout cas, c'était un truc édicté par Breton: il n'aimait pas le roman . . . Mais il était établi qu'un poète surréaliste ne peut pas écrire de romans. Le roman, c'est une expression bourgeoise, quelque chose d'élaboré, où il n'y a pas de spontanéïté. D'ailleurs, Philippe Soupault, un des fondateurs du surréalisme, a été exclu en 1925 parce qu'il écrivait des romans . . . Il avait à peine fondé qu'on le fout à la porte![108]

For Breton, and any other surrealist, the writing of novels was an unacceptable concession to commercialism; the writing of popular fiction was an even greater infraction. Not only was the idea of bourgeois commercialism abhorrent to the surrealists, but so was the process of writing novels.[109] The editing and marketing system

---

[108] Léo Malet, "Interview de Léo Malet en 1986," Ed. Noël Simsolo. Rpt. in *Léo Malet: sous pli discret*. Mons (Belgium): Séries B, 1988: 58.

[109] Explaining the politics of avant-garde movements such as surrealism, Williams writes, "To the emphases on creativity and on the rejection of tradition we must add a common factor: that all these movements, implicitly but more often explicitly, claimed to be anti-bourgeois . . . Hostile or indifferent or merely vulgar, the bourgeois was the mass which the creative artist must either ignore and circumvent, or now increasingly, shock, deride, and attack" Raymond Williams, "The Politics of the Avant-garde." Introduction. *Visions and Blueprints: Avant-Garde Culture and Radical Politics in Early Twentieth-Century Europe*. Eds. Edward Timms and Peter Collier. Manchester: Manchester UP, 1988. 5.

removed the traditional production of literary texts from the cultural realm over which the surrealists sought control. For the surrealists, the only authentic cultural act was public and beyond choice. Malet's experience during the war may have alerted him to the very real shocks that harsh reality dealt common people. Likewise, "le détective de choc" meets death in the streets, and "Dynamite" Nestor Burma throws his body and words into an already anarchical situation. A novel focused on the narrative logic of facts and motives cannot be an exercise in automatic writing, and therefore was not "l'automatisme psychique pur."[110] As Malet could not be a commercial surrealist, he had to make a decision.

Malet chose the commercial route. Even without the opportunity to write popular detective novels, Malet likely would have left the surrealists soon after their return, mainly for political reasons: the group had embraced Stalinism and Malet was an anarchist. Nevertheless, when reading Malet's work, we look for residual techniques of his surrealist background. Yvonne Duplessis lists these techniques as: humor, the "merveilleux," dreams, mental alienation, surrealist objects, the "cadavre exquis," and automatic writing.[111] These techniques color Malet's writing, but in a more ironic, self-referential manner than we might expect. The dark humor of the *roman noir*, as cited by Blaha as one of the defining qualities of the genre,[112] easily links to the dark humor favored by the surrealists, as outlined in Breton's *Anthologie de l'humour noir*. Thus Malet's progression from one esthetic to the other is not surprising. Nestor Burma has vivid surrealistic dreams that he recalls and considers the next day. Images of altered states of consciousness, and of being enveloped in smoke and fog, permeate Malet's text, appealing to both literary readers and fans of the *noir* genre. The legacy of the surrealist sensibility, which renders the ordinary *merveilleux*, can be discerned in Malet's writing; objects already fetishized by poetic usage and by the surrealists themselves continue to accumulate poetic meaning. Malet makes the avant-garde and some of its practices accessible through detective fiction and opens the door for readers who might

---

[110] André Breton, *Manifestes du surréalisme* (Paris: Gallimard, 1963) 36.
[111] Yvonne Duplessis, *Le surréalisme* (Paris: PUF, 1995) 22-48.
[112] Blaha 45.

otherwise have been too unlikely to attempt the surrealist texts of Breton and others.[113]

Dream Sequences

Nestor Burma may not be the first detective to have had vivid, sometimes bizarre, dreams, but he is the first narrator of the *polar* genre to want to share them with the reader. Of the fifteen *Nouveaux Mystères*, nine have dream sequences and the others have episodes of unconsciousness after Burma is hit on the head with a variety of blunt objects. The dream sequences serve as a colorful interlude in Malet's text, the avant-garde equivalent of comic relief, rarely advancing the narrative. Though their impact on plot is limited, these interludes provide indirect commentary on the process of postwar modernization. Whereas urban space can be sanitized, the unconscious mind remains a bed of unharnessed and inexplicable psychic activity. As writers such as Robbe-Grillet engage in "redemptive hygiene" in the *nouveau roman*, conducting a "fundamental cleansing of figurative language,"[114] Malet provides insight into the detective's mind where language is unrestrained.

In the course of an investigation, Malet's detective considers all evidence, from physical minutiae to the product of his own psychic processes. Since Burma is always a player in the plot of gathering evidence, his dreams are inherent to the speculative process we might expect from a detective. Along with revealing the exciting, telling, easily analyzed elements of the dream, he unashamedly includes the banalities, without theory as to their significance, countering Robbe-Grillet's "criteria of efficacy."[115] In keeping with the oft-cited Freud quotation, pointedly undermined by Magritte's representation in *Trahison d'images* of a pipe with the caption, "Ceci n'est pas une pipe," sometimes a cigar is just a cigar.

Given that Léo Malet was largely self-taught, even with respect to his knowledge of avant-garde material, it can be reasonably assumed that his knowledge of Freud's theories on dreams was filtered through the surrealist leader André Breton. Though it is true

---

[113] Walz argues that although surrealism "became more preoccupied with its self-defined culture and political rigor, disturbing and provocative tendencies still inhabited the byways of mass culture" (155).

[114] Ross 75.

[115] Ross 76.

that the surrealists owed much to Freud's research, they held him as
neither leader nor founding father. While Breton manipulates certain
Freudian elements in his 1924 *Manifeste du Surréalisme* to justify the
direction of his own artistic movement, "the surrealists did not find
[Freud] as responsive to their work as they had been to his."[116]
Whereas Freud discusses the two stages of the human psyche, of latent
and manifest content, Breton combines the functioning of the waking
dream with the nocturnal dream to form a new absolute reality, or
surreality. In *On Dreams*, Freud discusses three types of dreams: those
that make sense and are intelligible, those that are bewildering, and
those that are meaningless.[117] But for the surrealists, the classification
and analysis of a dream is not as important as the act of documenting
it through automatic writing. The automatic process is more valuable
than the analytic or literary value generated by the end product.
Breton's position, Jacqueline Chénieux-Gendron explains, was that

> il faut refuser le carcan de la logique qui amène dans la vie à dénier au rêve
> sa puissance dérangeante – notons qu'on est ici dans une perspective non-
> freudienne – et dans la littérature à écraser le merveilleux. L'écriture
> automatique fournit une technique à ces fins. Le surréalisme propose une
> nouvelle théorie de l'image, laquelle mène à l'action.[118]

Surrealism expands poetic boundaries imposed by the "carcan" of
logic. Malet brings the same surrealistic concerns to the detective
novel. The recounting and interpretation of dreams, frequent surrealist
activities to which Malet alludes, look for evidence of their "puissance
dérangeante," though the participants often lacked the necessary
psychoanalytic skills. Dreams are not to be discounted, even when
they seem insignificant. The inclusion of Burma's dreams brings a
new layer of narrative to the detective genre, providing insight into the
detective's mental processes through the retelling of the dream itself
as recollected in his *récit*.

In *Les rats de Montsouris*, Malet (through Burma) alludes to
both his and Burma's surrealist past when he says, "Je fis mon petit
numéro de poète surréaliste, en récitant le texte sur la beauté du buste"

---

[116] Anna Balakian, *Surrealism: The Road to the Absolute* (New York: Noonday, 1959)
100.
[117] Sigmund Freud, *On Dreams*, Trans. James Strachey, (New York: Norton, 1952)
30.
[118] Jacqueline Chénieux-Gendron, *Le Surréalisme,* (Paris: PUF, 1984) 58.

(*Enquêtes*, 1: 931), acknowledging that his deference to the surrealist movement is all part of his act, a "numéro." Burma is proud to be called "un poète," and enjoys the distinction of that term in French culture. On the next page, he mentions a dream in which the principal players of the novel are covered in blood, and a red-haired widow is laughing:

> Je rentrai chez moi, me couchai et fus long à trouver le sommeil. Enfin, je sus que je dormais lorsque j'aperçus dans ma chambre Raoul Castellenot, tout rouge du sang de ses victimes. Armand Gaudebert [Burma's client], revêtu de sa tenure d'avocat général, et Henriette [Gaudebert's trophy wife], nue sous la robe de chambre rouge de Marie Courtenay [a known nymphomaniac who commits suicide in a previous chapter] et un voile de veuve, également écarlate, sur ses beaux cheveux roux. Elle riait. (*Enquêtes*, 1: 932)

His dream is in color, but it is still monochromatic in red, the long-wave extreme of the visible spectrum. In Burma's dream, Henriette represents both whore and madonna, juxtaposing the nightgown of a nymphomaniac with "un voile de veuve," as she laughs at the death that surrounds her. This collection of vibrantly blood-stained and blood-colored images grabs the attention of the reader, yet does not affect Burma. A page break follows the sequence, and when we rejoin Burma, he is meeting with Armand and Henriette Gaudebert and his dream is not mentioned again. The dream, occurring on a sleepless night, is momentarily disturbing for him and is quickly forgotten. While the detective is unfazed by this interlude, the reader must switch gears in order to interpret what is going on. Malet challenges his reader to use more than one approach within the same novel.

Entering into Burma's dreams in *L'envahissant cadavre de la Plaine Monceau* is Yolande, a young model who resembles Burma's movie-star client. In the dream, he buys a "publication frivole," and on the pages he sees

> [des] photos animées représentant Yolande en tenue légère, qui court, poursuivie par des bielles, des roues, des soupapes, des pistons, toute une mécanique infernale. Elle disparaît, engloutie par cette ferraille . . . et je m'éveille. Au bout d'un moment, je me rendors et j'achète un magazine frivole à un kiosque. . . . (*Enquêtes*, 2: 937)

Before Burma can wake up, the dream scene begins again and is played over and over until he learns from the mistake of wasting money on a "magazine frivole." In the dream, a beautiful young woman "disparaît" into the "infernale" machine of postwar society. Since he continues to make the same mistakes, such as buying the "magazine frivole" representative of consumerism, Burma is powerless to stop the machine, and the dream always ends in the same way. Malet's inclusion of such dream sequences distinguishes his series from other detective novels as they enrich the text with vivid avant-garde imagery not found in the popular genre.

In *Des kilomètres de linceuls*, Burma encounters a tomcat in the hallway of a building and remarks that it is the only living thing he will run into that day. Later, he dreams of being surrounded by a circle of a thousand cats, and to charm them, "j'entreprenais de leur réciter le poème de Baudelaire," which we assume to be "Les chats." He does not sufficiently charm the cats, however, and is still scratched by one of them:

> Sous l'effet de la douleur, j'étais transporté dans une ville inconnue . . . Les chats étaient à mes trousses. Je fuyais entre eux, mais pas au hasard. Je recherchais un nommé Baudelaire. Je parvenais aussi dans une rue sinistre, étroite, et malodorante où devait demeurer le poète que je cherchais. Et lorsque je fus devant une certaine maison, je sus que c'était là qu'il vivait. Balancée par le vent d'hiver, une enseigne, au bout d'une tringle de fer, rendait le cri d'une girouette . . . Je sautai, échappai aux chats, et saisis à pleines mains l'enseigne gémissante. Les chats avaient disparu. Il ne restait que des oiseaux. (*Enquêtes*, 1: 576)

In this dream Burma is unable to find the Baudelaire he is looking for but, in the process, finds himself in the same "sinistre, étroite, et malordorante" streets that figure in both Baudelaire's poems and Malet's novels. Arriving at what he believes to be the poet's house, he opens his eyes before he can determine the significance of the "enseigne." He wakes up face down on the floor, "nu comme un ver," a target for the "oiseaux" that he might encounter during his continuing investigation, and starts a new day, without further mention of this strange dream. Though he cannot explain what the dream means, Burma shares the experience with the reader as part of the detective's daily process.

In *La nuit de Saint-Germain-des-près*, Burma dreams of being a watch thief in the American West, "selon les lois mystérieuses de l'activité onirique" (*Enquêtes*, 1: 799) when his case revolves around the fictional author of a popular novel called "Un quart d'heure pour s'aimer." In the dream, a "ribambelle" ["a swarm"] of alarm-clocks is set to go off consecutively, provoked by a ringing telephone in Burma's reality.

> C'était un rêve idiot, qui me déplaisait. J'avais la vague sensation qu'à un moment quelconque de mon sommeil il s'y était introduit comme un voleur, lui aussi, chassant un autre rêve, délicieux celui-là, encore qu'imprécis. Impossible de faire taire cette diabolique horlogerie. . . . C'était le téléphone. (*Enquêtes*, 1: 799)

While Burma chases Baudelaire in the cat dream, in this dream he is an observer, but is ultimately frustrated as he, powerless, cannot stop the noise of the clocks. He finds his dream both "délicieux" and "imprécis," though he feels a "vague sensation." Though the contents of the dreams are uncertain, what remains certain is that he will have them. He is awakened by his client's phone call, and a new day begins, counting down the moments until his next dream.

Familiar faces appear in his dreams, and the most familiar face is that of his secretary, Hélène. In *Pas de bavards à la Muette*, Burma has a dream where Hélène, naked, floats down from the sky toward the body of a uniformed man on the ground, "comme un oiseau maléfique," giving Burma a disapproving look while holding a smoking gun in her right hand:

> Un immense désarroi me submergeait. Malgré tout mon désir, je ne pouvais pas sauver Hélène. Elle venait de tuer cet homme sous mes yeux. Une voix ricana sarcastiquement, "Toujours aux premières loges, Nestor Burma! Un don. Ce n'est pas normal. Tu devrais te soigner. Te soigner." (*Enquêtes,* 2: 167)

Again the dream sequence is characterized by his powerlessness. This time, however, his powerlessness is heckled by a familiar voice. When Burma goes into his office later in the day, Hélène uses the familiar expression, "toujours aux premières loges ["being well placed to see an event unfold"]" in conversation. The dream sequences where elements of the fantastic intermingle with feasible dialogue represent a parallel not present in the novels of Malet's contemporaries. Hélène is usually a caregiver, tending to Burma's wounds or helping to cure his hangovers; she is not "maléfique." She is likely, however, to tease Burma about his dalliances and his penchant for getting hurt on the job. Even in his dreams, Burma is always in the wrong place at the right time. He tells Hélène about his dream, and she is more horrified that she was naked in his dream than by the idea of having murdered someone while floating to the ground. She has heard about his dreams before, and is not surprised to hear that she is often a major player in them.

In *Boulevard . . . Ossements*, Hélène is the dreamer instead of the presence in Burma's dream. In textual reality, she and Burma trade places for three chapters, when he is denied access to a lingerie fashion show. The reader has access into Hélène's mind during her undercover *récit* of the Russian lingerie show, as well as the dream she has during her overnight stay with Natacha and Sonia. She is allowed to dream "out loud":

> . . . Je me contemple dans le miroir de l'armoire. L'armoire s'ouvre et il en sort une femme blonde (Natacha?), vêtue d'un uniforme de cosaque. Cet uniforme se transforme en tenue de flic parisien, et la femme blonde prend les traits de Nestor Burma. De son bâton blanc, mon patron heurte le miroir dans lequel je continue à m'admirer. Il se brise dans un fracas épouvantable . . . comme une explosion . . . comme un bruit de tonnere . . . (*Enquêtes*, 2: 491)

She wakes up to a thunderstorm. Hélène has taken Burma's place in the novel's narration, and he displaces her in the dream sequence. When Burma dreams, he sees Hélène in the background; when she is the dreamer, Burma is in the background. Hélène is conflicted in how she sees herself just as Burma is conflicted in how he sees her. Her self-image, reflected in the armoire's mirror, interrupted by what comes out of the armoire, morphs from one "uniforme" to another until it takes on the traits of Burma. Hélène's dream must take on Burma's characteristics in order to fit into the pattern of the other dream sequences which are always Burma's. In *Boulevard*, Burma has several dreams in one evening, but Malet chooses not to relate them to his reader. Instead Burma says, "Entre deux rêves, j'y ai réfléchi" (*Enquêtes*, 2: 470) and offers a glimpse into his notebook, which he keeps during every case for the purpose of testing out leads and theories. Only in this novel are we privy to extended italicized excerpts from his journal:

> *[Goldy] a voulu identifier la victime . . . Pourquoi? . . . Ça c'est une autre question . . . Pour pratiquer le chantage à son tour? . . . Toujours est-il qu'il s'adresse à moi pour remonter, par le maître chanteur, jusqu'à la personne qui chante . . . En fin de compte, Ça ne réussit pas à Goldy . . . Il en meurt .*

> *. . Tué par qui? . . . Le Chinois? . . . Ne pas oublier que, lorsque je me croyais seul dans l'appartement de Tchang-Pou, au-dessus de son restaurant, je me suis imprudemment laissé aller à prononcer à haute voix le nom du diamantaire . . . Tchang-Pou, qui n'était pas loin, a pu l'entendre . . . . (Enquêtes, 2: 470)*

Burma's ellipses illustrate the pauses in his reasoning, which are missing from his usual *récit*. The interrogative nature of the journal thus marks a departure from his usual commentary. The reader sees another side of Burma, that the detective does not always have all the answers. In the other novels, where Burma's is the only narrative voice, we do not have insight into this process of what he does "between dreams."

Burma asks himself in *Du rébecca rue des Rosiers*, "si je rêve ou quoi, j'en ai eu, des clients, depuis que j'exerce ma profession" (*Enquêtes*, 2: 802). And while this is a generic French expression, not necessarily indicative of dream activity, the passage illustrates Burma's feeling of strangeness in response to what he sees every day. Sometimes his reality is stranger than his dream world, for Burma's Paris is a dream turned inside-out. For Breton, "[l]e surréalisme repose sur la croyance . . . à la toute-puissance du rêve, au jeu désintéressé de la pensée."[119] For Malet, dreams are a constant presence in his characters' lives, even if their content seems insignificant. Like automatic writing, where the process is more important than the end result, the act of recording or reporting dreams is more important than the content of the dream itself. Malet's inclusion of a dream in a detective novel is innovative, as no other writer of the genre had previously suggested dream activity in his characters. Like other literary detectives, Burma solves his crimes by using logic and intuition, but he does not entirely dismiss the significance of his sleep-induced visions. Malet's series succeeds in balancing Burma's interaction with his very real surroundings with his subconscious activities.

Altered States

In addition to the dream sequences, there is an episode in every novel where Burma is rendered unconscious as a "matraque inspirante déclenche chez Burma l'habituel flash poético-surréaliste

---

[119] Breton, *Manifestes* 36.

qui constitue pour Malet sa signature infalsifiable,"[120] after which the narrative voice changes. In *Le Soleil naît derrière le Louvre* Burma refers to this phenomenon after which his perception is distorted as "le coup de goumi habituel" (*Enquêtes*, 1: 460). In *Soleil* Burma repeats the phrase, "Je rampais" (*Enquêtes*, 1:461) as he ponders the sharp "pavés" under his fallen body. Though he is surrounded by darkness, "le noir absolu," he can tell that he is near the shimmering light and flowing water of the Seine. While his senses play tricks on him, he is comforted by the familiarity of the ground beneath him. He seems to enjoy these hallucinatory moments and the "frisson" of being in danger like a dreamer who knows he is dreaming. The familiar "coup de goumi" neither upsets him nor intimidates him; and it never convinces him to consider abandoning a case. In *Boulevard . . . Ossements*, Hélène asks him why he is so eager to take on new cases when every case involves a blow to the head:

> -- Ça vous tient donc tant que ça l'envie de recevoir un coup sur le crâne?
> -- Quel coup sur le crâne?
> -- Le coup sur le crâne sans lequel aucune de vos enquêtes n'est complète.
> -- Il n'y aura pas de coup sur le crâne.
> -- Ça serait bien la première fois. (*Enquêtes*, 2:448)

In the context of Malet's plot devices, Hélène's observation helps the reader place the author and his characters within the tradition of the detective genre. Her observation serves as metacommentary in that she makes a comment which the reader cannot: why does Burma persist in his dangerous line of work when he gets more bruises than reward? Burma convinces her that he will be fine, and she concedes: "C'est votre tête, pas la mienne. Et peut-être que vous aimez ça. Que ça vous procure des sensations rares" (*Enquêtes*, 2: 448). Perhaps he does like these episodes, as they provide an escape from his waking state. Her ironic comment draws the reader's attention to Malet's esthetic, derived from surrealism yet occasioned by a *policier* plot device. Burma's mildly obsessive, often fetishistic relationship to objects as well as to certain phenomena of his hardboiled existence binds Malet's innovations to the traditions of the genre.

For Burma, being knocked in the head may be an inconvenience but it also occasions a sort of involuntary dream state,

---

[120] Lacassin, *Masque* 66.

and Malet's surrealist sensibility does not let this aspect of his narrative formula go to waste. As Duplessis explains, when surrealists release control of the subconscious, "l'inconscient se manifeste spontanément et l'écriture automatique permet de transcrire ses messages."[121] In their work, surrealists attempted to exploit the state between dreaming and waking, when control over consciousness is suspended. Truly automatic writing is unedited and is often difficult to follow. Text flowing naturally from the subconscious is rarely coherent or poetic; poetry is, after all, often recognized as such because of rules-based or form-conscious editing. Even Robert Desnos, who had a reputation as surrealism's finest "practitioner," was accused of "editing" his automatic writings to make them more poetic.

Burma enjoys suggesting his potential as a poet, as in *Fièvre au Marais* when, the morning after a "coup de matraque," he proclaims that "ceux qui manient cet ustensible vous rendraient poète!"(*Enquêtes*, 1: 639). He experiences life according to an undeniably literary consciousness. Each novel contains ironic commentary to that effect. Recording Burma's vision from the unconscious is Malet's attempt to narratize the act of automatic writing while at the same time critiquing surrealist pretensions. The act of automatic writing itself is inherently problematic: if a writer tries to write automatically, the effort required to release automatic acts of writing erases the possibility of spontaneity, and the resulting text would seem far from the purity sought by Breton. Lamenting his stupidity, Burma often wonders how he could have been taken off guard yet again, as if his intelligence and experience were supposed to have saved him from surprise. His unconscious appears to crave expression, going so far as to suppress the detective's awareness of danger. Having stretched the logic of spontaneity to its limits, Malet illustrates both the impossibility of automatic writing and the appeal of the mental state that supposedly generates it. Nestor Burma courts death and unconsciousness by virtue of his choice of profession; that Malet placed him in a realm already utilized by poetry gives his professional risks a literariness not readily associated with the American genre.

---

[121] Duplessis 44.

Like in the dream sequences, Malet gives voice to Burma's unconscious mind when he is knocked out. Most frequently, Burma is hit on the head with a blunt object; in *Pas de bavards à la Muette*, it is his own gun that is used to accomplish the deed. We hear the voice of Burma's "inconscient":

> Je restai immobile sur la descente du lit, à écouter le silence nocturne et les battements de mon coeur qui le troublaient, et aussi l'armée de petits lutins qui s'agitaient dans mon crâne. Une voix lointaine, dont j'étais seul à percevoir le son, une voix consolante, la voix de mon inconscient dit: "Tu es emporté sur les montagnes russes. Ça monte et ça descend. Tu as été sûr de la culpabilité de Bénech [an earlier suspect] et puis tu as douté. Et plusieurs fois comme ça. Tu as été sûr de l'existence d'un gang et puis tu as douté. Et plusieurs fois comme ça. A présent, tu ne peux plus douter. Un gang est mêlé à l'affaire et il vient de t'envoyer un ambassadeur. Merci du tuyau . . . Merci beaucoup." (*Enquêtes*, 2: 185-86)

Burma's senses are reprogrammed by a blow to the head, after which he hears the sound of silence and the voice of the unconscious. The voice may be repetitive when it says, "et plusieurs fois comme ça," but it speaks to Burma, and gives him a new lead or "tuyau" that he will follow up on when he wakes up. The unconscious voice coaches him to trust his instincts and break the cycle of doubting which always leads him to physical harm. As these episodes appear in every novel, apparently he does not listen to his own voice. When he comes to his senses, he applies a cold compress and continues, without acknowledging the episode or the voice in his head. Sometimes he hits his head after falling down a flight of stairs, either being pushed or slipping in the dark. In every instance, after regaining consciousness, he makes a few comments, incredulous that he was knocked out once again, and picks himself up again to continue his mission. In *Les rats de Montsouris*, midway down the stairs he tries to fall like a cat, "afin d'éviter à mon crâne un contact trop brutal avec le ciment. Je ne suis pas un chat" (*Enquêtes*, 1: 868). That is to say, he suffers his usual blow to the head (landing on it, rather than on his feet), but before long he is walking around again. Though he has many friends in the medical profession, he is rarely injured badly enough to seek medical attention "chez un toubib." Only in *Corrida aux Champs-Elysées* does he complain of lasting consequences: "pas mal de bruits dans la tête, depuis les coups de matraque" (*Enquêtes*, 2: 87).

In addition to their innovation in the detective genre, the episodes of unconsciousness are notable for the brief change from first-person narration. Often the unconscious Burma refers to himself in the third person, thus disrupting the rhythm of Malet's *roman noir*. After being hit in the head in *Des kilomètres de linceuls*, he remarks, "le bon coup d'instrument contondant, le bon coup de matraques des familles qui attend toujours Nestor à un tournant de ses enquêtes. On allait l'oublier. Il était temps. . . ."(*Enquêtes*, 1: 620). Later he continues, "[j]e revins à moi." The third-person Burma is still Burma, but with a heightened sensibility, able to reason from a broader perspective, as if he were treating his unconscious self as a needy child. The third-person Burma is not omniscient, but he perceives from a double perspective, unlike the first-person Burma, who is confined to conventional reasoning. The unconscious Burma's senses are sharper after a blow to the head, allowing the detective to see more clearly than his unscathed counterpart.

As Burma cannot control the time of his unconscious episode, he cannot control where he will regain consciousness, nor with whom. The detective does not always wake up alone. In some cases, the man who knocks him out awakens him, usually in a different place, for questioning. In *Des kilomètres de linceuls*, he is chained to the body of a prostitute he was questioning, the scene made to look like sadomasochism gone awry (*Enquêtes*, 1: 576). In *Casse-pipe à la Nation*, after being hit from behind, Burma says:

> Je ne pars pas dans les pommes, mais je n'en suis pas moins impuissant. On s'agite autour de moi. Des silhouettes confuses passent devant mes yeux, au-delà d'un voile rouge. Je sens qu'on me fouille et qu'on m'attache guibolles et poignets . . . Puis on me soulève et m'installe plus ou moins confortablement dans un fauteuil. Je reçois une torgnole. Ça m'aide à récupérer. Presque immédiatement, je vois et j'entends aussi parfaitement qu'à tout à l'heure. Seul subsiste un léger mal de cigare. ["head"] (*Enquêtes*, 2: 647)

In this passage, Burma is in a state between full consciousness and unconsciousness, not quite "dans les pommes," but still incapable of conventional reasoning. He is not rattled by his kidnapping experience nor by his momentary unconsciousness. It happens to him so frequently that it approaches the mundane. In *Fièvre au Marais*, he feels the impact of the instrument against the back of his head and is temporarily blinded. He is aware of the process of losing consciousness:

> Et les étoiles, ce n'est certes par [sic] ce qui manqua, la seconde d'après. Au milieu d'une espèce de tremblement de terre en technicolor très réussi, j'entendis une voix intérieure chuchoter doucement, en accompagant ma chute, que "bien mal acquis ne profitait jamais" et que "le crime ne payait pas." Je n'y avais pas pensé, à ces deux-là! (*Enquêtes,* 1: 633)

Even Burma's interior voice speaks in clichés which allow him irony at his own expense, as if he were another ignorant, cliché-spouting criminal. After reading several novels in the series, we begin to wonder when the "coup de crâne" will occur, knowing that Burma will not pull through the novel unscathed. His life must be threatened so that he can laugh in the face of danger, stand up, and brush himself off, thereby proving that he is invincible. His clothes are often "fripés," a suit ruined here, a hat crushed there, but somehow his pipe, shaped like a bull's head, is never broken, even when Burma falls down a long flight of stairs in the Passage des Eaux. It is no coincidence that "la pipe" is slang for "tête." His head may be altered, but the pipe never "breaks." The pipe is always present to remind the reader of what it is and is not: the detective's head.

As surprising as his episodes of unconsciousness may be, Burma can be even more surprised when he wakes up. After being knocked out, Burma comes to in empty hotel rooms, warehouses, under a bridge alongside the Seine, even in a dumpster. His state upon waking up resembles that of a drunk or a drug addict. Woozy, perhaps nauseous, trying to remember the events leading to his passing out, he staggers back to his attacker's trail without a pause in his narrative. Burma has sole narrative authority, rarely ceding the floor to a voice other than his own, and then only twice to Hélène, his most trusted ally, in *Boulevard . . . Ossements* and *M'as-tu vu en cadavre?* In both of those instances, the case requires a female undercover, and since Burma refuses to disguise himself as a woman, Hélène is his only option.

The unconscious state is not always from a blow to the head, as sometimes Burma is drugged. His self-prescribed drug of choice is alcohol and he suffers horribly for it. He is an avid drinker and often wakes up hung over, suffering far more than from one of his "coups de crâne." He is frequently in search of a hangover remedy, "un rince-cochon" (*Enquêtes*, 1: 630) or tobacco for his pipe when he stumbles upon a situation that leads to his next case. When he finds a new packet of tobacco, he often finds a new "micmac" and, with it, a new source of professional inspiration. In some instances, Burma's unconscious episode is due to illicit drugs, which are usually involuntarily ingested. Though certain surrealists, such as Desnos, were known drug users, surrealism as a movement did not glamorize drug use, considering it unnecessary, as Alexandrian explains:

> Ainsi, en principe, par son exploration méthodique du champ de l'inconscient, le surréaliste se flatte de n'avoir pas besoin d'être opiomane, par exemple, pour connaître des sensations analogues à celles de l'opium. Francis Gérard, dans *L'État d'un surréaliste*, s'efforce de définir la stupeur qui s'empare du poète pratiquant l'écriture automatique. Le flux rapide et ininterrompu de l'automatisme produit une somnolence agréable, durant laquelle certaines sensations inconnues acquièrent une acuité extraordinaire.[122]

A true surrealist trusts his mental sharpness and does not need drugs to access his *inconscient*, but the movement does recognize the altered state as a valid source of literary production. In *Micmac moche au Boul' Mich'* Burma has the flu, which he has caught from Hélène. He is feverish and hallucinating, and sees himself sitting at the edge of the bed: "Nestor Burma émergea lentement du fond enténébré de ma chambre et s'assit au pied du plumard" (*Enquêtes*, 2: 710). The two Nestors then proceed to discuss the case. He takes prescribed medication with a glass of whisky, and then dreams of the Russian space dog, Frisette:

> Toute la nuit, je prononçai une conférence en Sorbonne, devant un parterre choisi de savants mondiaux. Frisette, la chienne-cobaye que les Russes, en novembre, avaient embarquée à bord du deuxième satellite artificiel . . . Frisette, le premier être vivant à voyager dans les espaces cosmiques . . . Frisette, que l'on disait morte, eh bien! c'était moi, bien vivant et revenu de ma fantastique randonnée. Et je revivais mes impressions avec une telle ardeur, que je croyais encore y être, dans cette sacrée bon Dieu de bois de boule de fer! (*Enquêtes*, 2: 714)

Burma identifies with the space dog: Frisette is the first animal in space, and Burma is the first detective of his kind in France. And just as she was often thought dead during her mission, Burma is often left

---

[122] Sarane Alexandrian, *Le surréalisme et le rêve*, (Paris: Gallimard, 1974) 162.

for dead by those he encounters. In his delirium, Burma identifies with what he has read in the variety of newspapers that he buys every day, following the surrealists' enthusiasm for the *fait divers*.[123] In his weakened condition, Burma checks out a lead, thinking he is stronger than he is. When he discovers a decapitated body and vomits, "une nausée me submergea" (*Enquêtes*, 2: 730) we know that he must be extremely ill. He often sees mutilated bodies, but never reacts as he does in this novel, in which his defenses are weakened. When Burma's state is altered, whether from a head trauma or from drug or alcohol use, we witness his descent into the unconscious state. Tobacco, which at the time did not have the status of a drug, and his unbreakable pipe are hallmarks of his identity.

Burma's pipe punctuates his conscious life. He never leaves home without it, even when he forgets his gun, and it often defeats an attempt at anonymity. The distinction of a pipe smoker in an age where mass-produced cigarettes are a war-time novelty is compounded by a distinctly recognizable pipe, the pipe "à tête de taureau."[124] This pipe is easily described to the police by witnesses whom Burma has already questioned and harrassed. The pipe leaves a particular odor at crime scenes where he should not be to begin with, leading Commissioner Faroux to remark, "[de] temps en temps, vous devriez vous arrêter de fumer" (*Enquêtes*, 2: 740). When he is caught eavesdropping on members of the Algerian FLN in *Les eaux troubles de Javel*, the rebels spike his pipe with haschish:

> Je parlais, sans même entendre le son (et pas davantage le sens), de mes propres paroles. De plus, je me sentais tout drôle. Je tirai de temps en temps sur ma pipe et continuais à trouver un curieux goût au tabac que je fumais. Mais c'était peut-être ma gueule de bois qui voulait ça! (*Enquêtes*, 2: 433)

Burma eventually realizes he has been drugged and, in his relaxed state, manages to survive the shootout and explosion at the rebels' hiding place. He is taken to the hospital where an intrigued intern

---

[123] Morand writes: "L'écrivain doit compter avec ce public badaud qui préfère à tout le fait-divers ou, ce qui s'en rapproche le plus, le roman policier. D'ailleurs, un fait-divers est à l'origine de bien des policiers." Paul Morand, "Réflexions sur le roman détective," *Revue de Paris* (1934): 483.

[124] Klein studies the representation of smoking and the transition from hand-rolled to mass produced cigarettes in history, literature, and film. Richard Klein, *Cigarettes are Sublime*. Durham: Duke University Press, 1993.

takes down Burma's delirious dictation, which Faroux later describes to a more lucid detective as "[une] théorie qui commence comme un poème et dont certains points ont été vérifiés et confirmés" (*Enquêtes*, 2: 435). He reads the entire statement, but hesitates to analyze it as it comes from Burma's delirium, saying, "[je] n'ai pas le courage de me taper sur ce texte. D'ailleurs, vous le connaissez, puisqu'il sort de votre ciboulot ["head"]. Et c'est par trop entrelardé de phrases incompréhensibles" (*Enquêtes*, 2: 436). Faroux assumes that Burma will be able to interpret the "automatic text," an activity in which the commissioner does not indulge. In this novel, automatic writing is taken by the police as a form of Burma's conscious speech. That Burma is usually evasive in his dealings with the police makes it all the more ironic that Faroux would demand that Burma interpret his own drug-induced babbling. A drugged Burma, they reason, would be too incapacitated to lie as he is known to do, therefore his statement must be credible. The solution to a crime is clearly within the realm of conscious reason. Only a policeman in a Malet novel would take involuntary speech for evidence. The end of this novel supplants sense-making speech with delirium, but it is a poetic red-herring. The episode is of particular value for giving insight into the prewar surrealist movement, and for providing the possibility of a surrealist poet giving an "automatic statement" without knowing it and trying to interpret it at a later date.

Malet finds literary possibility in all aspects of Burma's life, both personal and professional. We see Burma from all sides and, along with the extraordinary events that he encounters, also in moments of monotony. The legacy of surrealism is that interest is to be found in monotony, and beauty in ordinary things. A poetic dream state is at once an accidental and cultivated aspect of Burma's life as a literary character and Malet's challenge to the strictly formulaic *policier* genre. Through his ironic approach to surrealism's love affair with the unconscious, Malet participates in the development of the *policier* genre along novelistic lines.

Ordinary objects and *le merveilleux*

By looking at everyday objects through different, sometimes altered, perspectives, surrealists find new beauty in that which is often overlooked by a popular sensibility. The ordinary and banal become eye-catching and provocative. Even everyday words take on new meaning when they surface in a surrealist context. One of the more infamous surrealist activities was a game of "petits papiers" in which random words on folded slips of paper were drawn out of a hat to form new phrases. This is an extension of a dada game where existing texts were cut into individual words; in the surrealist version, the words were an automatic creation, rather than a reconfiguration of someone else's work. "Petits papiers" is also referred to as "Le cadavre exquis" because the first sentence created read, "Le cadavre – exquis – boira – le vin – nouveau,"[125] and was greeted with wild enthusiasm. Malet takes this image of the cadaver, prominent in surrealist literature, and fuses it with the detective novel's use of a cadaver as the center around which the story of an investigation revolves. However, in Malet's version, the cadaver is no longer the sole focal point; it is rather one of many generative points scattered throughout the novel. Solving the crime is not the only focus of a Malet mystery. For Burma, the sight of a dead body is all too banal, and his psyche is rarely upset by what most detectives would consider extraordinary events. Burma is transfixed and fascinated by ordinary details that another observer in the novel fails to find significant.

For the surrealist, there are different types of objects: "naturels," "perturbés," and "trouvés," where the found object "porte en lui une charge surprenante de hasard objectif".[126] Malet's text is riddled with found objects, sometimes in the form of clues but also in the form of surrealist curiosities. In *Les rats de Montsouris*, Burma encounters two old friends, who also knew a certain Léo Malet: Anatole Jakowski and Ralph Messac, son of Régis Messac, author of the seminal 1929 treatise *Le détective novel et l'influence de la pensée scientifique*.[127] Jakowski is described as a collector of surrealist objects, and he shows Burma and Hélène his latest acquisition, found at the flea market at the Porte de Vanves:

---

[125] Adam Biro and René Passeron, eds, *Dictionnaire général du surréalisme et de ses environs*, (Fribourg, Suisse: Office du Livre, 1982) 74.

[126] Biro 308.

[127] Of this scene, Lacassin writes: "[Burma emmène] Hélène rue des Mariniers, dans l'atelier occupé par le très réel (et alors bien vivant) Anatole Jakowski, auteur de *Paris mes puces*, grand spécialiste de l'art naïf, et dont les collections forment aujourd'hui le Musée de l'Art naïf de Nice. Chez Jakowski, le détective retrouve aussi le très réel et le toujours bien vivant Ralph Messac, longtemps speaker d'*Europe 1* et président du Syndicat National des Journalistes" (Lacassin, *Masque* 87).

Il trônait dans le clair-obscur d'une pièce du fond, encombrée de lanternes magiques et de bronzes 1900. C'était un de ces bustes qui servent, dans les vitrines des boutiques de lingerie, à présenter des soutiens-gorges, mais qu'une imagination délirante a transformé en l'objet poétique le plus étonnant qui se puisse rêver, une sorte d'insolite épave, de tronçon de sirène, on ne savait quelle hallucinante figure de proue de quel vaisseau-fantôme, caressée par les algues visqueuses et où seraient venus se poser, comme des baisers solidifiés, des coquillages rugueux et polychromes. Car, sans bras ni tête, et pathétiquement cambré comme s'il offrait encore sa gorge au couteau sacrificateur, il était recouvert du cou à la taille d'un conglomérat de coquillages marins et d'escargots, agglutinés, se chevauchant, immobiles, mais paraissant grouiller en un permanent assaut. Je ne connaissais pas d'exemple plus typique de ce qu'on a appelé "l'objet bouleversant surréaliste." (*Enquêtes,* 1: 886)

This passage ties together several aspects of Burma's esthetic. First, there is his lingerie fetish, piqued by this bust whose primary function is to display undergarments, and only part of a woman. Second, the bust alludes to Malet's participation in the surrealist movement, which manipulated mannequins for the purpose of shocking passersby. The use of shells, natural objects that mimic the female form, inspires "hallucinating" visions of "sirènes." The eye, trained by society to be more discreet when looking at a woman's chest, is prompted to stare openly at the "buste." Third, the mannequin makes the association between a found object and a "macchabée." Burma's fascination with death is a permanent assault on both the natural and unnatural. He does not see the "buste" as a decorated dressmaker's dummy, but as a decapitated and limbless figure who "offrait encore sa gorge au couteau sacrificateur." Hélène is less than enthusiastic about this creativity and can only offer "[c]'est surprenant" as a reaction to the strange object. The (usually) male surrealist gaze applied to a female object fits into both the tradition of hardboiled misogyny and the tradition of surrealism. Both practitioners of surrealism and detective fiction appreciate that objects are to be observed. While detective fiction expects to find answers in the objects, or clues, surrealism hopes that the object will provoke more questions. Not only does Malet convey an extraordinary description of the object, he also tries to give the reader a lesson in how to appreciate a surrealist object, for those readers uninitiated to the avant-garde.

In the first *Manifeste*, Breton describes the modern mannequin as an object "à remuer la sensibilité humaine durant un temps."[128] One of the more public displays of surrealist activity before World War II was the International Exposition of Surrealism in 1938, where many surrealists, including Malet, displayed individually altered mannequins. Malet's mannequin was pulled from the exposition because Breton did not like Malet's use of a fish in place of the female's genitalia; apparently it was similar to another mannequin already on display. But this incident did not diminish Malet's fascination with mannequins. In *Des kilomètres de linceuls*, which takes place in the garment district of the second arrondissement, Burma compares the sight of a cadaver to a mannequin: "Ce n'étaient pas des chiffons. C'était, aussi, une sorte de mannequin. Pas rose. Mais pas plus vivant" (*Enquêtes*, 1: 601). In *Boulevard . . . Ossements*, flea market finds are pivotal to the plot. A blackmailer, Tchang-Pou, keeps a wax figure of a blond-haired woman in his armoire; Burma mistakes it for a cadaver when it falls onto the floor. Tchang-Pou is not a murderer, only a fetishist like Burma himself. Another man, linked to others in a chain of death, kept the skeleton of a famous Parisian dancer, "l'unijambiste," in his apartment, an object purchased at one of the many Parisian oddity markets. For the purposes of blackmail, the skeleton is altered to include the leg of another body. Burma's awareness of the "unijambiste," celebrated by the surrealists in its *fait-divers* glory, allows him to solve the crime. In Burma's world, the "merveilleux" of the surrealist object and the alterations of the creative act are given a grisly significance. That their playful attitude and Burma's have the effect of damping the horror of misogyny and death is an implicit criticism of prevailing attitudes; Malet tacitly critiques a generation who looked the other way during the occupation. When one is sufficiently distracted, the atrocities of mankind are easily overlooked.

In *Les eaux troubles de Javel*, Burma makes the acquaintance of Jeanne, a charming teenager who lives upstairs from his client. But before we meet her, we encounter her underwear hanging on a clothesline, when Burma notices two boys sitting on a sidewalk, one teaching the other to smoke:

---

[128] Breton, *Manifeste* 26.

Deux mômes, l'un d'eux tousaillant par à-coups, étaient plantés au beau milieu, bravant la fine pluie. Ils levaient les yeux vers un des étages, perdus dans la contemplation d'une culotte bleue à volants qui prenait le frais d'une fenêtre et que la bise humide gonflait par instants ou faisait palpiter comme un coeur. (*Enquêtes,* 2: 340)

Burma is an admitted fetishist of women's lingerie, but of worn lingerie and not lingerie dancing on a line.[129] The sight of hanging underwear is ordinary in a less affluent district of Paris but in this sequence is rendered poetic, something worth "contemplation" while smoking. The boys ask Burma if he has come to see the "joli calcif," referring to the underwear itself, but Burma answers, "Pourquoi? On peut visiter?" (*Enquêtes,* 2: 341) as if Jeanne were entirely defined by the garment, rather than as a human being, to whom one would "rendre visite."

One of the most picturesque images in Malet's corpus is found in the final two lines of *Micmac moche au Boul' Mich,* when Burma is leaving a crime scene alone. He tunes out the sirens of the police cars and the gunfire in the house he has left behind, and focuses his attention on the sound of a snowflake as it falls sizzling into his pipe. Here, the melting of a snowflake is the image of ephemeral things: "Lentement, lentement, quelques flocons de neige dansèrent devant mes yeux. L'un d'eux échoua dans le fourneau de ma pipe et fondit dans un grésillement bref" (*Enquêtes,* 2: 760). Human existence by analogy is as fleeting. A snowflake melting before it lands on the ground is metaphoric in this particular novel where the murders are primarily of university students, who seemed to have their whole lives ahead of them. There is even beauty in death, perhaps especially, in a hardboiled detective novel. The image of the ephemeral snowflake furthers the connection between the poetic sensibility of Nestor Burma and the lyricism in Malet's prose.

For Malet, weather is not a passive element of the decor. Whereas snow is a constant image in *Micmac,* a continuous fog hovers over the city in *Brouillard au pont de Tolbiac,* obscuring and distorting what should be easily visible, and making the living appear like ghosts. He characterizes the fog as "insidieux" (*Enquêtes,* 2: 263) and "sournois" (*Enquêtes,* 2: 265) before remarking, "[le] brouillard

---

[129] In his interview with Simsolo in *L'Organe,* Malet elaborates on his various fetishes. Léo Malet, "Léo Malet: Fétichiste moyen et obsédé sexuel total," Ed. Noël Simsolo, *L'Organe* 2 (1985): 4-6.

qui envahissait la cour se plaqua sur nos épaules comme un linge mouillé." He continues, "La fumée de ma pipe et la buée de nos respirations se mêlaient à la brume fuligineuse"(*Enquêtes*, 2: 283). Fog infiltrates the scene, mixing with both exhaled breath and smoke, obscuring what is right in front of his face. Nature's fog and man-made smoke are an all-enveloping surrealist milieu that actively obscures clear vision. In *M'as-tu vu en cadavre?* cigarette smoke dances and mixes, even when the smokers themselves cannot be as close as they might like. Burma accepts one of his client's cigarettes, though he prefers to smoke his pipe, because he is attracted to her, and he observes, "nous mêlâmes nos fumes" (*Enquêtes*, 1: 965). Smoke mediates the relationship, giving the participants a common ground.

In *M'as-tu vu en cadavre?* Burma compares a large and brightly lit theater marquee to "un gigantesque clin d'oeil"(*Enquêtes*, 1: 996) because it alternates between on and off every other second. The blinking lights call attention to the marquee, but Burma's evocation of its "clin d'oeil" image makes reference to the ironic self-reference implicit in all surrealist images. The scene alludes to the "convulsive" beauty described by Breton in *Nadja* where the batting of eyelids symbolize hope:

> J'ai vu ses yeux de fougère *s'ouvrir* le matin sur un monde où les battements d'ailes de l'espoir immense se distinguent à peine des autres bruits qui sont ceux de la terreur et, sur ce monde, je n'avais vu encore que des yeux se fermer.[130]

Nestor Burma, like Breton's *Nadja*, keeps his (private) eye open, in full observance of the world, though for the detective, blinking registers both ironic winking and the alternation between terror and hope. It is a clue, but for the moment, a "dead letter." The flickering marquee also represents the ephemeral quality of fame: brilliant but fleeting. Burma, trying to keep his own name in the public consciousness, is familiar with this phenomenon. Burma's urges for publicity and his uncanny ability to be party to murder converge and generate the chance-driven plot in Malet's novels.

Some surrealist images aim to shock the observer, such as the vampire imagery appearing in several of Malet's novels. In *M'as-tu vu* Burma tells a woman that her life has been sucked out, and in *Rats* a

---

[130] André Breton, Nadja (Paris: Gallimard, 1930) 130.

moth flutters like Icarus around the slit throat of a cadaver on the floor:

> Un grésillement m'apprit que le papillon de nuit s'était approché trop près de la lampe. Les ailes brûlées, l'insecte tomba au beau milieu de la plaie ouverte dans la gorge de Ferrand. Il y palpita quelques secondes, comme un vampire qui s'abreuve à la source de vie, avant de clamser ["mourir"] à son tour. (*Enquêtes*, 1: 868)

Despite the number of grisly murders in Malet's work, this is one of the rare images that could also be found in an art or a horror film. In *Fièvre au Marais*, the ornate golden handle of the letter opener is in the form of a dancing woman, "qui donnait l'impression de danser sur [la] poitrine" of a dead pawnbroker (*Enquêtes*, 1: 630). Most of the surrealist images in the series function to "livrer de la banale quotidienneté les images finalement les moins vraisemblables."[131] The images serve to shock the reader out of complacency, if only for a moment, providing a brief innovative glimpse of an alternate literary reality. However Malet acknowledges for the novel what Breton avoided pointedly or believed himself exempt from: the commercial implications of novelistic creation itself. Surrealist publications caught Malet's eye through a bookstore display window and brought him into the surrealist movement.

 While Malet winks back at his surrealist background, he follows his nose toward his detective fiction contemporaries. Like that other famous Francophone detective, Simenon's Maigret, Nestor Burma is likely to notice the odor of a scene. Most often it is released by a "cadavre," which can be alleviated by pipe smoking, but other times it is "une odeur indéfinissable [qui] me chatouille les narines" (*Enquêtes*, 2: 884), or "un relent nauséabond me sauta aux narines" (*Enquêtes*, 1: 748). This textual fascination with the sense of smell is given a bizarre twist in *La nuit de Saint-Germain-des-près*. Burma is present for a local bar's beauty pageant for Miss Poubelle, where contestants are asked to adorn themselves with outfits made of discarded vegetable matter. This is another playful representation of the surrealist esthetic. In *M'as-tu vu*, he notices "un drôle de cocktail olfactif" (*Enquêtes*, 1: 986), a mixture of cooking odors and faded flowers, when he visits an apartment building in the tenth

---

[131] Durozoi 174.

arrondissement. His sensitivity to odor, as well as to other literary details which I will discuss in the next chapter, belie the rough exterior of the hardboiled detective, yet they make Burma appealing to his readers and tie him to his more refined literary predecessors.

Léo Malet removed himself from the surrealist group in 1944 without removing the surrealist influence from his writing. In addition to including image-laden dreams, drug experiences, altered states, and found objects, the author comments on postwar French society moving toward significant social change. Culture should not be lobotomized for the sake of hygiene. The psychic activity of dreams and unconsciousness are not to be discounted in Malet's series. The detective can still "met le mystère K.O." when he himself is knocked out.

Though the reader and Hélène come to expect a dream sequence and/or unconscious episode during each mystère, it is always a surprise for Burma. How Burma will react to each episode is what propels the series. With this vivid imagery, Malet challenges the formula of the *policier* and keeps alive the surrealist vision, which will be further exploited by the situationists of the 1960s in "the colonization of everyday life."[132] Malet's innovation sets his series apart from his detective fiction contemporaries and his use of the novel further expands the perimeters of surrealism itself.

---

[132] Ross 7.

Chapter Three

Nestor Burma, comme tu voudras

Nestor Burma, "détective de choc," was introduced to the French reading public in 1943 with the publication of *120, rue de la gare*. Malet wanted his new character to be "un type libre," not to be held accountable to a superior, like the editor to Johnny Metal's journalist or the commanding officer to Maigret's police inspector. The private detective's independence from controlling authority and lack of family ties leave him free to follow his instincts. Malet chose a distinctive, though surprisingly un-French name for this character who would prove to be the first in the French *noir* genre, where for the first time the detective exhibits more qualities of the common man than of the cultural esthete. Malet explained his choice of name in interviews, as well as in his memoir, *La vache enragée*:

> Mais comment en suis-je venu à l'appeler Nestor Burma? Je le dois à Fu Manchu. J'ai pensé à ce type qui se présente, la nuit, tout au début du premier volume des *Exploits du docteur Fu-Manchu*. La scène est la suivante: le docteur Petrie, au travail sous la lampe, est seul dans son cabinet d'un faubourg de Londres, nimbé de brouillard et plongé dans le sommeil et le silence. Soudain, on sonne à la porte. Le docteur va ouvrir. Un homme bien charpenté, engoncé dans un pardessus, se tient sur le palier. "Smith! s'exclame Petrie. Nayland Smith, de Burma!"[133]

Malet was taken with this scene, "absolument dépourvue d'originalité et de sensationnel," and decided his detective should be called Burma. The scene of a Fu-Manchu novel evokes the mysterious fog-filled world of the anglophone hardboiled tradition, and Malet further pays homage to that tradition by naming his detective after a former British

---

[133] Malet, *Vache* 173-75.

colony.[134] As for the name Nestor, Malet claimed not to know why he chose it. It is, despite the question of intention, noteworthy that in Greek, "nestor" means "black" as well as "he who remembers." Nestor was a long-lived warrior, a minor figure in the *Odyssey*. Is it just coincidental that a detective named Nestor would do most of his work in dark places, obsessing on minute *faits-divers* and a pioneer in the French *noir* genre?

The name of Burma's detective agency, Fiat Lux, indicates an elemental play between dark and light. Burma is a man who went through the occupation with his eyes open, who remembers his past and is ready to settle scores when the war is over. He reopens his agency after returning from a POW camp, as if he had only been on an involuntary vacation. Burma takes authority only from himself and thus acts according to *fiat*, according to his own lights. His authority is based on his intelligence, which falters in its struggle with criminality before it triumphs in a coherent account of events. The truth, along with human understanding, is as temporal as a light flickering randomly on and off.

Burma's authority is constantly challenged but is always filtered through the observations of the first-person narration. In *Les eaux troubles de* Javel, a character, not believing that Nestor Burma really is his name, calls it, "trop biscornu pour ne pas être un pseudonyme" (*Enquêtes*, 2: 376). Her observation is valid: his name stands out, calling attention to him when his occupation calls for camouflage. He often begins an assignment with a pseudonym, such as a journalist named Dalor, a play on "d'alors," but before long he reveals his identity, sacrificing his undercover anonymity for the glory of being recognized. The disguise of reporter is aptly chosen as he reports the status of the investigation to the reader, but the reporter's passivity undermines the detective's desire to be the man who precipitates action. When the same character then asks Burma if he works in the circus, he answers, "Plus ou moins. Je suis flic privé"

---

[134] In the Fu Manchu novels where the villian is "Oriental," Eisenzweig writes, "the main focus is on the crime, rather than on the mystery that surrounds it, and the squarely obvious characters are much more dangerous than suspicious." (Uri Eisenzweig, "Madness and the Colonies: French and Anglo-Saxon Versions of the Mysterious Origins of Crime," *L'Esprit créateur* 26.2 (1986):13). Given this tendancy, it is all the more curious that the name of Malet's detective be insprired by such a novel when the mysterious atmosphere of Paris serves as a character.

(*Enquêtes*, 2: 376). His response is a metacommentary in that his work is at times like a circus, with seemingly diverse actions played out in connected rings and a cast of scary clowns he encounters in precarious situations. His narrative authority is frequently undermined in that he is not always the ringleader of the circus around him. He is not in as secure control as he would have the reader believe.

Dispensing with physical description, Malet tells us more about Nestor Burma's character. The reader cannot determine if he is tall or short, fat or thin, handsome or disfigured, or even imposing. We may not know his hair color, eye color, or skin tone, but we know that he begins his day late and well dressed, mainly from the descriptions of his clothes that are damaged by his many scrapes and "coup[s] de crâne." Save for his distinctive pipe, he is an ordinary guy who might fade into a crowd unnoticed. Though he has been told more than once "tu as l'air con" (*Enquêtes*, 1: 1019), he is not offended. In speech and manner, he is not unlike those whose tawdry lives he investigates. He is very much a man of the street and, though the street is a dangerous place, he makes no claim to unusual strengths or martial talents. He is unique among his fellow literary detectives. Compared to the French detectives, he is more brash than Simenon's Maigret or Christie's Belgian Poirot, but more cultured than the American hardboiled icons of Chandler's Marlowe and Hammett's Spade. It is the combination of streetwise abrasiveness and well-read refinement that makes Burma such a compelling character.

In spite of his exotic name, Burma is a champion of French culture. With his anarchist background and use of literary allusion, Burma represents a cultural hybrid. Malet cultivates the irony that the surrealist anarchist came to write formula-bound detective stories through his character, also a former surrealist anarchist. Likewise, Burma is fully aware of the paradox that his profession brings criminals to justice in the name of public order. Burma is an antihero, often arrogant, racist, sexist, and ill-tempered but, rather than turn off readers with his anti-social qualities, he attracts them. The postwar French were ready to celebrate cultural arrogance, to talk tough, and to punish criminals. Nestor Burma embodies the cultural housecleaning necessary in an era where the rules and expectations of authority have changed. He exemplifies an ordinary man who, when empowered, can make a difference in his society. Burma is also a casually literary detective. Proud to cite the more recent works of his culture, Burma brings literary speech to a criminal milieu and carves a new niche in the new postwar order. He is a man with one foot in a larger French mainstream, and the other in a dicier world where crimes occur and where resistance to authority has not lost its post-World-War-II luster.

This chapter will examine Malet as a pioneer in the French *noir* genre whose hero still resonates in modern French popular culture, thanks to the television adaptation starring Guy Marchand, and the *bande-dessinée* adaptation by Jacques Tardi.

The Anarchist Pursuing Order

It is easy to confound Nestor Burma's "biography" with that of Léo Malet, "aventureux, indépendant, libertaire, toujours fauché, Burma empreinte à son créateur jusqu'à sa gouaille, son franc-parler et sa pipe à tête de taureau."[135] Both Malet and Burma arrived in Paris from Montpellier at a young age, befriended an older anarchist mentor, took shelter at the "foyer végétalien," an abandoned artist's studio in the thirteenth *arrondissement*, and sold newspapers on the street as a "crieur professionnel." In *Brouillard au pont de Tolbiac*, Burma faces his anarchist past when his long-lost mentor Albert Lenantais dies, having sent Burma a letter from his deathbed: "Cher camrade, je m'adresse à toi, bien que tu sois devenu un flic, mais tu es un flic un peu spécial, et puis, je t'ai connu tout gamin" (*Enquêtes*, 2: 239). In the italicized flashback of *Brouillard*'s third chapter, "1927. – Les anarchistes du foyer végétalien," Burma remembers his daily routine as a starving *anar* in the late 1920s, a portrait not often found in popular literature nor in the avant-garde writings of those who were affluent enough to spend the period languishing in Parisian cafés. Though Malet himself was disillusioned with politics after the repercussions of Stalinism in the Soviet Union, Burma does not divulge his reasons for leaving the *anar* lifestyle. Burma finds it "marrant," however, to be revisiting his old haunts, "sur les lieux de mes espiègleries malhonnêtes" (*Enquêtes*, 2: 264), riding voluntarily in a police car, with commissioner Florimond Faroux. Did Burma betray his *anar* past by becoming "un flic privé"? Not exactly. Rather than work in the government's hierarchical system, like his friend

---

[135] Michel Abescat, "Léo Malet a quitté pour toujours Nestor Burma," *Le Monde* 09 Mar. 1996: 22.

Faroux, Burma seeks his own version of truth and justice, which shares as much with the rough-and-tumble credo of the streets as with the criminal justice system.

In *Les Nouveaux Mystères de Paris*, the guilty are punished, usually by death, but not because of the death penalty, still in effect in France until 1981. Those who inflict psychic pain receive it in turn, and those who kill are killed, often in a lurid or sensational way. In Burma's world, both the truly evil and a variety of fringe participants "méritent" punishment and often reach a form of justice by killing each other off. For a readership that witnessed horrifying and often unpunished acts in occupied France, Malet provides a satisfying ending. Hungry for heroes, the postwar French readership is willing to accept an imperfect model of justice, observed by an intelligent but not infallible man. In a traditional *roman policier*, the suspect, who for the reader has already been proven guilty by the detective, is arrested by the police and eventually tried and sent to prison to pay his debt to society. In Malet's novels, however, the guilty party rarely lives long enough to spend the night in jail. He either ends up dead at the end of the novel, though Burma does not kill a suspect himself, or the novel ends when the police arrive. If the suspect does not commit suicide when he realizes he has been found out, there may be a shootout, when all interested parties find themselves in the same room, with only Burma left standing in a room full of corpses.

Each type of final scenario is evenly distributed over the fifteen-novel series. In four novels (*Fièvre au Marais*, *Les rats de Montsouris*, *Casse-pipe à la Nation*, *Micmac moche au Boul'Mich'*) the end is marked by suicide. In another four (*Le soleil naît derrière le Louvre*, *Brouillard au pont de Tolbiac*, *Du rébecca rue des Rosiers*, *L'envahissant cadavre de la Plaine Monceau*) the suspects meet their death on the day of their planned getaway. Three (*La nuit de Saint-Germain-des-près*, *M'as-tu vu en cadavre?*, *Les eaux troubles de Javel*) end with a shootout, and four (*Des kilomètres de linceuls*, *Corrida aux Champs-Elysées*, *Pas de bavards à la Muette*, *Boulevard . . . Ossements*) end in "other" circumstances, most commonly with the arrival of the police. The epilogue of *Des kilomètres de linceuls*, is a rare instance where we see Burma paid, though he generously assigns the funds to those left behind in the wave of murders. His involvement with the criminal milieu precipitates violence and sets off a series of events that he seems to guide to a conclusion. In each

scenario, Burma somehow emerges with only a minor scratch or
contusion and delivers to Commissioner Faroux, "ma cargaison
habituelle de cadavers"(*Enquêtes*, 1: 843). Rare is the scene that
follows the arrest of those left standing.

Nestor Burma shows that justice can be served without
invoking a hierarchical system. In addition to clever detectives like
himself, ordinary but observant people like Madame veuve Parmentier
can be very useful in uncovering the truth. A character in *Casse-pipe à
la Nation*, Madame Parmentier is an eccentric reader of the *polar*
genre. Her keen observational skills, honed from years of reading
mysteries,[136] prove to be an asset to Burma when she walks in on a
shootout. She faints at the sight of real action, however, being a rather
frail, 70-year-old woman whose only "experience" has been in books.
But she is fascinated by Burma's quest and tries to play the game. She
even takes on his tone of voice:

> -- Fromentel ne peut vous être d'aucune utilité.
> -- Pourquoi donc?
> -- Il est mort.
> Elle me balance ça comme une héroïne d'Agatha Christie, avec une
> intonation laissant supposer que le Fromentel en question a été pour le
> moins coupé en morceaux et expédié en guise de cadeau d'anniversaire à
> ses divers amis et connaisances. J'entre dans le jeu. Ça flattera son
> innocente manie:
> -- De mort . . . naturelle?
> Le "oui" qu'elle soupire se prononce "hélas!" Toujours les romans
> policiers! (*Enquêtes*, 2: 640)

For the reader of a detective novel, a reader who craves adventure,
natural death is disappointing. Without a murder, there is no novel, but
without a sense of punishment for the crime, whether from the judicial
system or some "karmic" force, the novel cannot come to an end. The
guilty may not realize that he is being punished for his sins, but the
readers are reassured that he will generate no more victims.

Like Malet, Burma is a selective anarchist in that he adopts
some tenets of anarchist doctrine but chooses to ignore others. In an

---

[136] Upon entering Mme Parmentier's apartment, Burma notices "Un roman policier,
qu'elle était en train de lire tout en mangeant, lorsque je me suis annoncé, jette la note
sanglante de sa couverture sur la nappe brodée. D'autres bouquins de la même farine
traînent sur la chaise proche, en compagnie d'un paquet de gauloises" (*Enquêtes*, 2:
639).

interview with *Le Figaro*, Malet calls himself, at the age of 80, an "anar conservateur."[137] In many interviews, he seems more eager to discuss the typewriter he inherited from Rudolf Klement, secretary to Leon Trotsky, on which all of his novels were written, than the political leanings of his youth. The postwar Burma cannot be a true anarchist, as he profits with his own detective agency. We know from *120, rue de la gare* that the agency existed before the war for an indeterminate period. Furthermore, philosophic anarchism repudiates violent methods, a style which Burma's familiarity with his gun would violate. He gives as many *coups de crâne* as he receives. As for the bomb-throwing school of anarchism, Burma wistfully says in *Brouillard*, "Voilà longtemps que je n'ai lancé de bombe"(*Enquêtes*, 2: 248). He looks back on his past with great nostalgia but also enjoys the rewards of being a capitalist. "Burma may condemn the change in himself," writes Teresa Bridgeman, "but the figures in the novel who have attempted to cling to past ideals receive no more favourable treatment."[138] Bridgeman is referring to Burma's mentor Lenantais who, by remaining a pure anarchist, is considered the most dangerous type of anarchist by some and an "imbécile" by others. In the text, Burma and the Inspector Fabre discuss an oft-cited quote of Georges Clemenceau, that "l'homme qui n'a pas été anarchiste à seize ans est un imbécile, mais c'en est un autre s'il l'est à quarante ans"(*Enquêtes*, 2: 248). Burma does not see his formative anarchist experience as a youthful folly, but the lifestyle no longer holds the same cachet as in his youth.

In *Brouillard*, Burma encounters two other former *foyer* residents, one of whom has inherited a factory. Burma can take comfort in seeing that he was not the only one of his *anar* circle to sell out to capitalism. Malet via Burma sees his political needs change as he ages. When asked in a 1988 interview "Mais il y avait une certaine violence et un idéal dans le militantisme anarchiste qui ont disparu aujourd'hui?" Malet responds:

> Les anarchistes avaient deux ennemis pour ainsi dire congénitaux, les royalistes et les communistes. Alors, il y avait continuellement des

---

[137] Jacques Richard, "Malet en verve," *Le Figaro* 01 Mar. 1989: 38.
[138] Teresa Bridgeman, "Paris-Polar in the Fog: Power of Place and Generic Space in Malet's *Brouillard au pont de Tolbiac*," *Australian Journal of French Studies* 35.1 (1998): 66.

échauffourées . . . Je crois que cet idéal anarchiste doit encore exister dans quelques cerveaux, il se traduit par une espèce d'attitude philosophique à l'égard de l'existence plutôt que par le militantisme. On ne peut pas envisager des députés anarchistes, ce serait contraire à l'éthique même du movement (rires). . . .[139]

The priorities of young, angry anarchists change as they become older taxpayers, but the spirit of their youth remains. We learn nothing of the struggles of the period when Malet and Burma changed from anarchist to capitalist, but we see Burma's struggle to justify his more comfortable existence. In *Brouillard* Burma realizes that, although he has sold out to capitalism, he is not as exploitative as he could be, and he can take comfort in that. His employees are also his friends. The former *foyer* residents that he encounters in this novel have profited from their inheritances; they had simply seen anarchism as a way to rebel against their bourgeois parents. For Burma, anarchism was not just a teenage phase and, although he has become a business owner, he can take pride in the knowledge that he made himself who he is and did not ride on someone else's coat-tails. In that sense, he emulates the American dream, likely gleaned from popular literature and film.

In Burma's world, not everyone is equal but, rather than the usual socio-economic gap, the gap is intellectual. Different social classes hold different functions, from the security guard at the gate (to whom Burma always refers as "un cerbère") to the concierge, from the rich model-actress to the blackmailer. Burma values the observations of the working man, who might be overlooked in an elitist society. When he condescends to the people he encounters, he is not looking down on them for the jobs they hold, but rather for their naïveté and/or stupidity in the face of what he sees as common sense. For example, the repetition of civilities, representative of a royalist culture, is presented as both absurd and unnecessary to someone accustomed to the *anar* lifestyle where "on tutoie facilement"(*Enquêtes*, 2: 285).

Burma often encounters such civilities in his exchanges with the domestic help of his clients when he makes house calls. A typical scene is found in *Les rats de Montsouris* when a maid answers the door to Burma.

-- M. Gaudebert, s'il vous plaît?

---

[139] Léo Malet, "Trotsky, Breton, Burma et les autres," Ed. Renaud Monfourny, *Les Inrockuptibles* 13 (1988): 45-48.

-- C'est ici, m'sieu.
-- J'ai rendez-vous avec lui à trois heures et demie. Voici ma carte.
-- Oui, m'sieu. Si Monsieur veut me suivre. (*Enquêtes*, 1: 855)

She leads him to a waiting area. When the maid returns for him, she says, "M. Gaudebert attend Monsieur." By excessive repetition, the word "monsieur" becomes banal and loses its civil cast. Such deference is a vestige of royalist culture rendered irrelevant in the postwar era. The maid relaxes around Burma, a man closer to her working class than her boss, and uses the more casual "m'sieu," until she sees his "bristol." At that point, she must return to her "professional" mode. Having received notification from her boss to bring Burma to his office, she says, "M. Gaudebert attend Monsieur," and no longer uses any informalites. In spite of his relaxed attitude toward *la politesse*, Burma does judge others according to their ability to speak correct French, often depicting dialects and accents, as in the above quotation. Parisian slang, however, is forgiven if it is spoken coherently. Those who experience the unsympathetic side of Burma's personality are often foreign, especially immigrants living in Paris. When familiar ethnic and ideological "configurations" do not return to the "normal" prewar arrangement, Bridgeman writes, many postwar Parisians, like Burma, react with resentment:

> [Burma's] personal ideological compromise is set against the inexorable historical shifts in the political and social configuration of the XIIIe. The dispossessed and anti-institutional group of anarchists who inhabited the arrondissement in the 1920s, with its mixture of ideologues, profiteers and illégalistes, has been replaced in the 1950s by a new dispossessed group, the Arabs of Paris, who are now fighting for Algerian independence, and who comprise a new mixture of idealists, profiteers and illégalistes. That the occupying boot of oppression and invasion has shifted to a French colonialist foot is not, however, presented as any cause for celebration.[140]

Burma's reluctance to embrace the "new dispossessed group" is especially vivid in *Brouillard*, as well as in *Les eaux troubles de Javel* and *Micmac moche au Boul' Mich'*. In spite of Burma's easygoing demeanor, as the series progresses he grows increasingly intolerant of the changing face of Paris and his racist remarks, like those of an older Malet in interviews, may account for his missing presence in academic circles. Within popular literature, however, the French

---

[140] Bridgeman 66.

continue to esteem Nestor Burma as one of their favorite characters of
the late twentieth century.

The Likeable Xenophobe

One of the keys to Nestor Burma's appeal in France is his
resemblance to his readership. Though he is a detached observer, he is
not so removed from the street level he encounters. In spite of his
20,000 franc lottery win with Hélène in *Boulevard . . . Ossements*, he
is not independently wealthy. Like the character Mme Parmentier,
who appeals to the adventure-starved, his lottery win with Hélène
gratifies those who play the lottery to win big. It is recompense for
someone who does his job and rarely sees hefty payment. Burma has
neither a Watson sidekick to record all of his "elementary"
observations nor a Maigret-like sensitivity. And he is not a happily
married member of the police force. Burma is both a man's man and a
ladies' man, but his Everyman qualities also make him susceptible to
the same fears and irrational perceptions of ordinary people, which
include racism and sexism. Such fears and beliefs are representative of
a generation looking to rebuild its status after World War II, only to
find new unrest and instability as colonialism crumbles in the 1950s.
In many ways he is a positive postwar role model; he champions both
French history and literature and encourages the French to take pride
in themselves and their past. But Burma also represents the darker side
of French culture, a "personal ideological compromise [which] is set
against the inexorable historical shifts in the political and social
configuration."[141]

Burma's primary targets are North African Arabs and blacks
from both Africa and the Antilles, but he also takes a swing at the
Japanese and Gypsies. He is an equal-opportunity offender, yet he is
careful about Jews and for that he may be seen as more progressive
than his cohorts. In *Des kilomètres de linceuls*, Burma's ability to
recognize the innocence of an otherwise detestable Jewish factory
owner wins out over the assumptions of his colleagues, who would
have missed the truth out of prejudicial thinking. When Hélène, his
usually sensible secretary, cannot shake the notion that Lévyberg is
guilty, Burma chides her, saying, "Mais, ma parole, vous êtes

---

[141] Bridgeman 66.

antisémite? Laissez donc ce Lévyberg tranquille, une bonne fois pour toutes"(*Enquêtes*, 1: 619). Burma is able to investigate the family's involvement in a crime without prejudice because of his prewar crush on their daughter Esther (then called Alice). The arrogance of the Lévyberg family does not inspire sympathy for very long after the war has stopped providing a theater for personal and political vengeance.

Nestor Burma is not the only likeable antihero of twentieth-century French literature; several parallels exist between Malet's Burma and Louis-Ferdinand Céline's Bardamu. Although both writers see contempt as a way of life, they do not share the same targets. Whereas Céline risked canonical obscurity because of his anti-Semitic collaborationism, Malet, though a racist, was neither a collaborationist nor an overt anti-Semite. Gérard Durozoi asked Malet about his depiction of "le racisme quotidien," using "une langue assez proche de la rue en scrutant la mentalité parisienne des années cinquante."[142] Malet replied that "le racisme existe chez chaque citoyen," including in his own fictional charcter. [143] Burma's xenophobic behavior ultimately goes without reward, as he generally finds himself alone at the end of most novels, a man whose closest contacts are his own employees.

Burma's favorite target is Arabs, in particular, *maghrébins*. Because of their revolutionary involvements, they are cast on the opposite team from Burma, often as gun-runners and cigarette smugglers. Hardly sympathetic to their cause, Burma sees them as a threat to Parisian stability. His anti-Arab attitude is most vivid in *Les eaux troubles de Javel*, set in the fifteenth *arrondissement*, which leads him to a rebel hideout. A police inspector pulls Burma over for a burned-out taillight and asks him to show his "papiers":

> -- Il y a une demi-heure, une voiture a lâché une rafale de mitraillette et une grenade dans un bistrot arabe du secteur.
> -- Ah! Racket noraf [derogatory for "North African"], collecte d'impôts, rivalités politiques et toute la sainte connerie?
> -- Oui.
> -- Eh bien, ce n'est pas moi. Je regrette.

---

[142] Durozoi 9.

[143] In an interview with Casoar, Malet discusses racism in his novels and remarks, "Alors, écoutez, je vais dire une chose: Les Arabes m'emmerdent et je ne les aime pas! Et je les tiens pour des cons!" He also refers to noted racist Jean-Marie Le Pen as "une sorte d'étudiant attardé" (Malet, *Faucon* 30).

-- Vous regrettez?
-- Façon de parler.
-- Hum . . . Faudra améliorer *aussi* votre système d'éclairage, hein?
-- Dès demain. (*Enquêtes*, 2: 380)

By using "le système d'éclairage," the policeman is referring to Burma's car as well as to the detective's mental clarity. Burma is firm in his convictions though they are not always welcome. The style of murder attributed to Arabs in *Javel*, slashed throats, also reflects preconceived notions, that Arab murderers are more sadistic than Christian murderers, who choose to stab their victims elsewhere on the body. When Burma is introduced by Faroux to Inspector Benhamidh, he has to be polite, for this Arab is a "good guy," part of a special brigade to infiltrate the rebels' enclave. About this inspector, Burma concedes, "C'était un Arabe aux traits délicats, à la denture de jeune loup. Rien de marchand de tapis, fichtre non"(*Enquêtes*, 2: 404). His "compliment," however, still compares the inspector to a predatory animal. When Burma is caught spying on the rebels, he is tied up and his pipe drugged with haschish. In his altered state he calls the bespectacled ringleader, "Sidi [derogatory for "Arab"] binoche" and "Sidi Bouffarde," and he is unable to control his inner thoughts, though he generally shares them only with the reader. Fortunately for Burma, the rebels become distracted by the arrival of a police task force and do not have time to react to his comments.

Burma's attitude toward blacks is most vividly demonstrated in *Micmac moche au Boul' Mich'*. He encounters two different black men in the same chapter: one a window washer, the other a medical student. He sees his stereotypes both met and transcended. He asks the first young man to help him find the second, a man named Toussaint Lanouvelle, whose ultimate downfall comes from dating a white woman. When asked about Lanouvelle, the window washer replies, "Tous ces b'aves gens sont aux cou's, à c'tte heu'. Étudiants, Docteu's, P'offeseus. Et m'ssié Lanouvelle, pa'eil. Sans doute. Ah! peut-êt'e non, ap'ès tout . . . Sa voitu' est là, mais ça veut 'ien di', s'pas?"(*Enquêtes*, 2: 716). Burma is put off by this young man's accent, assuming his information will be of little or no use to his investigation. The observant window washer proves to be useful to the police when he successfully describes Burma and his distinctive pipe to an inspector. He might have been useful to Burma as well, had the detective not dismissed him for substandard diction. Walking through the apartment building, looking for Lanouvelle's name card on a door, Burma notices the "odeur particulière" of a building mostly inhabited by blacks. When he finally does meet Lanouvelle, he is surprised to find, "[u]ne voix cultivée . . . [a]ucun accent," which may be the highest compliment a Parisian can pay. Though he is taken with Lanouvelle, he does not argue when the young man says:

> Je suis un nègre, monsieur. Certes, les gens de couleur, en France, sont plus considérés qu'aux États-Unis, mais je suis quand même un nègre . . . Et peut-être encore plus nègre que je ne crois . . . . Vous ne pouvez pas comprendre. (*Enquêtes*, 2: 718)

When asked if he is racist, Burma unapologetically answers, "Ça dépend des jours"(*Enquêtes*, 2: 713), as if his feelings were a controllable urge, something within the frame of reason. With each xenophobic comment, however, he proves that he is unable to control those urges and is ultimately just as irrational as the criminals he investigates.

Burma's racism also targets the Japanese. When he is attacked by a judo expert in *Pas de bavards à la Muette*, Burma rants about the source of judo, even though his attacker is not Asian:

> Ces vaches de Japonais! ils vous rendraient racistes, avec leur saloperies d'inventions, leur jichidsu et leur judo. Je comprends qu'on ait employé la bombe atomique contre eux. Impossible d'en venir à bout autrement. (*Enquêtes*, 2: 185)

Considering his attitude toward both the Japanese and their culture, it is ironic that in the 1946 film adaptation of *120, rue de la gare*, released before the publication of the *Nouveaux mystères*, Burma is provided with an Asian valet who doubles as his judo coach. The unsettling nature of racist thinking is more sharply represented in *Brouillard au pont de Tolbiac*. After falling for and sleeping with a beautiful young gypsy, Burma has an altercation with her brother Salvador, who does not approve of his sister's choice of lover. Now that the racist shoe is on the other foot, Burma says:

> Maintenant que le Salvador savait que je couchais avec la Gitane, il n'allait pas falloir s'éterniser dans le coinsto. Le Salvador reviendrait certainement et pas seul. Quelle bande de cloches, avec leurs histoires de race! Je me demande ce qu'on a reproché à Hitler. (*Enquêtes*, 2: 291)

Here is the racist's cry of reverse discrimination, also present in *Des kilomètres de linceuls*, when the Jewish Lévyberg family is portrayed as racist for having shunned their daughter's non-Jewish lover. Does the reader see any irony in Burma's words, or do Burma's remarks read like an advertisment for white supremacy? Or as a criticism of clannish behavior among Jews and gypsies? Burma sees his racist leanings as a viewpoint he is entitled to maintain. When someone speculates that a Nazi collaborationist murdered a Jewish jeweler in *Bavards*, Burma says, "Si nous faisons intervenir des sentiments politiques ou racistes, nous n'en sortirons pas"(*Enquêtes*, 2: 212). Ironically, Burma does "[faire] intervenir" these sentiments without assistance from any other party; there is no "nous" in his action, only "je." He is able to "s'en sortir" because he does not allow the other side of the argument to rebut. In general, Burma's racist remarks are scattered and short lived. These are bilious outbursts from a usually cool-headed man, taking the reader by surprise. Burma makes a quick remark and leaves the scene without waiting to witness any resulting consequences.

He is at once likeable and hateful. Though not the *gentleman-cambrioleur* of Arsène Lupin, Burma can be a genuinely good guy, sometimes generous, very loyal to both friends and employees, often funny, and always unpredictable.[144] Upon his release from the *stalag*, Burma reopens his agency with its original staff, including Réboul, an investigator who returns to his job missing one arm, and therefore a more conspicuous bystander. His loyalty does not, however, always extend to his clients. In *Le soleil naît derrière le Louvre*, Burma uses a stolen car to run over his client in order to obstruct the man's illegal activities. By hospitalizing the ironically named Lheureux, Burma guarantees that his client stay in Paris. In *Linceuls*, he works for Esther Levyberg, who he knows is obsessive (to the point that she would betray her family), and easily concludes the worst about her. Her murder does not end Burma's investigation, and he manages to keep the secret of her lurid betrayal.

Burma often refers to himself in the third person, such as "Nestor Burma. C'est un type qui va vite quand il ne va pas

---

[144] Because of his likeability and lack of the "dégoût" present in other French noir detectives, "Burma, qui semble parfaitement bien dans sap eau, et plein d'énergie pour remettre le monde à l'endroit, n'y fait guère figure de torturé existential. Peut-être conviendrait-il de parler de roman 'gris'?" (Verdaguer 8).

lentement"(*Enquêtes*, 1: 828). He makes fun of himself in *Casse-pipe* after his car is stolen by a young girl: "Le détective de choc s'est fait barboter la voiture. Ça la fout mal"(*Enquêtes*, 2: 605). He is the first to admit he is not perfect, refreshing in a genre with seemingly infallible heroes. His flaws bring an element of humanity as well as self-deprecating humor to the detective genre which had been absent in Malet's French contemporaries. Burma says in *Les rats de Montsouris*, "Je suis là pour amuser les gens"(*Enquêtes*, 1: 854), and though his humor is not always sophisticated, he exploits even the most racist of *jeu de mots* in the surrealist tradition of provocation. Though their content may not be amusing, the plays on words add comic relief between murders. Malet's *jeu de mots* also reflects his intellectual side, such as in *Micmac moche* when he remarks "Je suspense donc j'essuie"(*Enquêtes*, 1: 721) as he wipes sweat off his brow. This might have been Malet's credo as he cranked out playful novels to make his living. Such a literary reference is not an isolated incident. Just when we think we have Burma figured out, he quotes Baudelaire and other masters of French literary culture. Burma's unpredictability contributes to the allure of the series.

The Literary Detective

Nestor Burma appeals to the common man, though his personality quirks give depth to his Everyman status. In addition to having an anarchist background and misanthropic tendencies, Burma is a champion of literary culture, "[le] détective privé le plus lettré de toute l'histoire du roman policier."[145] Since he cannot read during surveillance missions, it must be during his down time between cases that he reads the great works that he cites. Burma is happy to share his findings with the autoworkers and chauffeurs he meets at the corner café, dropping reference to everyone from Villon to Verlaine at any given time, never altering his diction to suit the audience of the moment. Burma's tendency to confuse his fellow café-dwellers leaves a lasting impression. This is not the best strategy for a man whose occupation requires silence, discretion and sneaking about unnoticed.

Burma is a walking contradiction, full of conflicting agendas. Bringing the high brow to popular culture, he cites friends and mentors from the Café de Flore along with the great masters of

---

[145] Lacassin, *Masque* 55.

literature. He frequently drops the name of Jacques Prévert, who was a witness to Malet's wedding to Paulette Doucet and lived in the same apartment building as the newlyweds. Malet mentions this connection in *Les rats de Montsouris* (*Enquêtes*, 1: 880). In *Casse-pipe à la Nation*, Malet alludes to one of Prévert's most famous poems, *Déjeuner du matin*: "Un peu de café? Volontiers. Elle me passe une tasse. Je me la tasse. Ça fait du bien ou ça passé"(*Enquêtes*, 2: 577). He also honors his literary heroes, including Guillaume Apollinaire. Malet evokes *Le pont Mirabeau* in *Les eaux troubles de Javel*, with a description of the area near the Citroën factory:

> . . . entre le quai de Javel et la Seine, qui, elle, coulait doucement sous le pont Mirabeau, avec un tas d'autres choses, si l'on en croit le poète. Bref, l'endroit était plutôt mélancolique. (*Enquêtes*, 2: 386)

Malet suggests the poem again in *Casse-pipe à la Nation*, when he says, "Et les jours passent. Et les semaines. Et les mois"(*Enquêtes*, 2: 586). Apollinaire is one of several poets that Burma alludes to as "le poète," as if his status were common knowledge, expecting from his reader a general knowledge of cultural history. In *Pas de bavards à la Muette*, Burma alludes to Dumas (comparing himself to D'Artagnan), Flaubert (referring to a young woman's "éducation éErotico-sentimentale"), and Jarry, when Burma bets on a horse named Ubu V. The horse loses – being too literary does not pay after all – but Burma wins for getting the horse owner's joke.

The writer that Malet most identifies with is Baudelaire, whom he credits via Burma for inspiring him to become a writer. In *Micmac Moche au Boul' Mich'*, he says, "Oui. Je me retrempe dans Baudelaire, depuis hier. C'est un bon bouquin. Sans lui, je me demande ce que je serais devenu"(*Enquêtes*, 2: 750). The *bouquin* in question is *Les Fleurs du Mal*, which in Malet's 1957 *Micmac* leads Burma to discover the crime of a doctor who killed his wife by infecting her with typhoid. When he first sees the poems on the table, Burma says,

> Pauvre Baudelaire! Où étais-tu tombé? Tu serais donc toujours victime de l'incompréhension! D'abord de ces abrutis de chats-fourrés, voici un siècle, et, depuis, de ceux qui s'imaginent de tes vers douloureux sont prétexte à imagerie graveleuse. Je ne suis pas contre l'érotisme, au contraire, mais j'estime que les poèmes de Baudelaire se suffisent à eux-mêmes. (*Enquêtes*, 2: 729)

He feels a personal connection with the poet of modernity, addressing him with "tu" and relating to his having been misunderstood. Burma reads through the book for old times' sake and finds that the poem *Une martyre, dessein d'un maître inconnu*, about a "cadavre sans tête," has been underlined by a fingernail. He remarks, "Il était dit qu'un livre jouerait un rôle, dans cette affaire. (Forcément! dans le quartier des Écoles!)"(*Enquêtes*, 2: 744). Burma cannot imagine his fellow characters sharing his connection with his favorite poet, never considering that perhaps he is also guilty of misinterpretation.

That Malet should look to Baudelaire is not surprising, given that Baudelaire wrote of the isolated poet in Paris, the *flâneur* in an overcrowded metropolis. As Baudelaire evokes images to appeal to all five senses, Malet aptly renders the sights, sounds, and even at times the smells of the modern city. Other references include the dream where Burma is looking for a cat named Baudelaire (beatnik *avant la lettre*) in *Des kilomètres de linceuls*, inspired by Baudelaire's *Les chats*, discussed in chapter two. In *La nuit de Saint-Germain-des-Près* he quotes Baudelaire's "les charmes d'horreur n'enivrent que les forts" in the same paragraph in which he refers to Simenon's *La Tête d'un homme* as "de la connerie"(*Enquêtes*, 1: 782). Malet thus credits his readership with appreciation of Baudelairian imagery while expecting readers to share his disdain for the worn-out clichés of classic French detective fiction. As Baudelaire writes nostalgically of his youth, so Malet longs for the Paris of his own youth, of prewar innocence. And like Baudelaire, Malet seeks to evoke a place between the real and the surreal, choosing the poem, *Une martyre, dessein d'un maître inconnu*, where the word "cadavre" figures prominently. Burma emulates Baudelaire's penchant for frequenting the undesirable strata of urban life. Never would Simenon's Maigret know a prostitute on a first-name basis, whereas Burma considers her a credible source.

Burma acknowledges his *policier* predecessors, but his references are not necessarily intended to honor them. When introducing himself in *La nuit de Saint-Germain-des-près*, he says, "Philip Marlowe, Hercule Poirot ou Nestor Burma, comme tu voudras"(*Enquêtes*, 1: 780), placing himself in illustrious company. Though Burma is presented as real and the genre predecessors are presented as fictional, he shows that he has learned from Malet's literary colleagues. He admires Sherlock Holmes's attention to detail, describing a difficult situation as "[t]ravail délicat, subtil et fin. À la Sherlock Holmes"(*Enquêtes*, 2: 938). In *Pas de bavards à la Muette* he is also in awe of Holmes's sense of intuition:

> Je secouai les cendres de ma pipe, me levai et allai voir de plus près les mégots éparpillés entre la table et la commode. Une demi-douzaine de bouts de cibiches, de longeurs variables, jetés là depuis . . . Vraiment d'une importance capitale, n'est-ce pas? Sherlock Holmes aurait su le dire, depuis qu'ils gisaient là, ainsi que l'âge respectif des fumeurs. Je n'étais pas Sherlock Holmes et tout ça, c'était peigner la girafe. (*Enquêtes*, 2: 152).

He repeats "[j]e ne suis pas Sherlock Holmes" (*Enquêtes*, 1: 902) in *Les rats de Montsouris*, as if to say that Holmes is a fictional character who is infallible but that he, Burma, is real because he makes mistakes.

Though he is not as attentive as Holmes, Burma is more like Maigret than he cares to admit. Often enough, like the inspector, Burma is known to follow his nose, as in *Boulevard . . . Ossements* when he remarks, "Je me laisse guider par mon nez" (*Enquêtes*, 2: 507). Burma's nose is rather sensitive to the familiar "drôle de cocktail olfactif"(*Enquêtes*, 1: 986) he encounters, which usually contains a mixture of food, urban exhaust, tobacco, and sometimes even the smell of death. He is also attentive to both perfumes and their wearers. In *Brouillard au pont de Tolbiac*, Burma recognizes the "odeur de ce parfum bon marché"(*Enquêtes*, 2: 243) on the letter from Lenantais as the same worn by a gypsy he had earlier passed in the metro. Likewise, in *Les eaux troubles de Javel*, the owner of a unique vial of perfume turns out to be the victim of a recently murdered blackmailer. In *Du rébecca rue des Rosiers*, following his nose gets him into trouble; after the inevitable coup de crâne, Burma wakes up in a dumpster and remarks, "La dernière fois, je me suis réveillé parmi les parfums. Aujourd'hui, ce n'est pas le cas. Ça schlingue ["ça pue"]"(*Enquêtes*, 2: 830).

In general, Malet (via Burma) is not so favorable in his allusions to Simenon's work. Burma is complimentary of Madame Parmentier for being a well-read fan of the *polar* genre, but he never classifies her as a Simenon enthusiast. In *La nuit de Saint-Germain-des-près* Burma advises a hotel concierge that the Maigret novel he is reading is "de la connerie"(*Enquêtes*, 1: 781) and adds that he should not read too much of the genre. Malet resents the fictional representation of detective life, a life depicted as glamorous, and chooses to recite details both scintillating and banal. Burma gives as much importance to an afternoon of uneventful surveillance as to an armed chase through a dark alley. Not content to denigrate only Simenon, Malet also gives a sarcastic representation of the traditional American hardboiled novel in *Casse-pipe à la Nation*:

> Il faudra que j'aille m'installer en Amérique. Là-bas, les flics privés, si j'en crois les bouquins, n'arrêtent pas de siffler du whisky de marque, en compagnie de gens tout ce qu'il y a de distingué, riche à millions, et de gonzesses modèle cinéma. (*Enquêtes*, 2: 593)

Burma alludes to the "bouquins" that Malet used to write under pseudonym. The image of America as a land of "flics privés" drinking "whisky de marque" and surrounded by "gonzesses" is perpetuated in both popular fiction and on screen, but is a promise ultimately as empty as Malet's postwar French reality. Whereas Maigret solves a mystery in New York, Burma never leaves France. In Malet's first novels to feature Burma, the detective crosses into the unoccupied zone at least once per novel. In *Les Nouveaux Mystères de Paris*, however, he never leaves the capital. In *Corrida aux Champs-Elysées*, he even spends his vacation in the eighth *arrondissement*, knowing that the view from the other side of town is completely different from his own.

Nestor Burma is an innovative figure in French detective fiction with as much streetwise sensibility as cultural refinement. His brash persona is balanced by an appreciation for literary culture, which Malet successfully integrates into the criminal milieu. His multifaceted personality and eclectic opinions lend to his popularity. He appeals to a well-rounded reader who expands his horizons by reading many genres. As a cultural hybrid, Burma espouses both the mainstream of popular culture and the avant-garde of surrealism, while appealing to the fringe interests of both anarchism and xenophobia.

A character full of surprises, Burma is an ideal choice for a series, as the readers will tune in for the next installment to see the detective's unpredictability within the frame of a formulaic genre.

Chapter Four

Supporting Players

Nestor Burma does not work alone, and the cast of Burma's supporting players remains unchanged even as the locale of each *mystère* changes according to the *arrondissement*. In addition to having the traits outlined in the previous chapter – the anarchist seeking order, the likeable xenophobe, and the champion of literary culture – Burma is further defined by his choice of company, found in three *policier* archetypes. Marc Covet, Burma's link to the press corps, is the cowardly version of Johnny Metal; Florimond Faroux, an inspector in *120, rue de la gare* later promoted to police commissioner, is the tough-talking street version of Jules Maigret; and Hélène Chatelain, Burma's faithful secretary, embodies the unattainable ideal woman while evoking Hammett's Effie Perrine and Gardner's Della Street. Throughout the fifteen-novel series, we rarely encounter these now-familiar faces outside of their element, seeing them only through Burma's eyes and apropos of his situation. This chapter will analyze the narrative balance that these supporting players bring to Burma's brash persona. The balance is affected as the supporting players provide Burma with information as well as a support network for when he feels lonely or needs help. They have accepted the terms of Burma's friendship: not only will they frequently receive half-truths instead of reasonable explanation, but they must also be prepared to be proved wrong by the detective's superior professional logic. The detective's interactions with Covet, Faroux, and Chatelain are as vital to the narrative as the discovery of yet another "macchabée," and their absence is significant in the few novels in which they do not appear.

Marc Covet, star crime reporter for the fictional newspaper *Le Crépuscule* ("le *Crépu*"), is Burma's public voice, and functions "comme auxiliaire et informateur de Nestor Burma."[146] Living vicariously through the detective's adventures, "le journaliste-éponge," as Burma calls him, soaks up the stories around him in addition to numerous alcoholic beverages throughout the series. Given Covet's penchant for indulgence, the question arises as to his reliability as a source, though Burma does not seem to mind as long as his own name appears in the daily publication. Burma, drunk with his own fame, expects instant recognition upon uttering his infamous name. Though annoyed by Covet's journalistic persistence and obligation to deadlines, he dares not offend the reporter because he needs him for access to archival information, both print and photographic. Burma is only as successful as his most recent triumph, and needs Covet to keep the flame of his glory burning.

As police commissioner, Florimond Faroux is Burma's most influential friend as well as the looming paternal authority in Burma's life. When embroiled in conflict with the police in various Parisian districts, Burma immediately drops Faroux's name and waits for special treatment. In any given meeting with the commissioner or his "sous-verges" (*Enquêtes*, 2: 890-91), inspectors Fabre and Grégoire, the detective hesitates to disclose all that he knows. He conceals his involvement in the crimes under Faroux's investigation until he can no longer do so; the "understanding parent" expects Burma to lie about how much he really knows. After all, if the police solve the case before the detective does, there is no newspaper glory for Burma. Faroux and Burma are antagonistic friends; their mutual desire to see justice served outweighs their clashing personalities. And now and then, the detective's unusual methods prove useful to the police department's particular needs.

Though they enjoy a mutual flirtation, Hélène Chatelain is the woman whom Burma can never have. Whereas Faroux is the paternal presence of Burma's sphere, Hélène is the maternal presence. She cares for his wounds and keeps his office running smoothly while he is on an investigation or distracted by a new girlfriend. The reader may wonder if they will ever get together, but is relieved that they do not since the women in Burma's lovelife, following hardboiled tradition, never survive to return in the next installment. Hélène is on a pedestal, referred to by Burma in *M'as-tu vu en cadavre?* as "la seule,

---

[146] Lits 148.

la vraie" (*Enquêtes*, 1: 1000), when he tries to distinguish her from another woman in the same novel also named Hélène. She is further honored by Malet in being the only character other than Burma to provide a narrative voice, in the form of the *récit*, in two novels of the series.

Burma's friendships serve his own needs and provide him with support during the down time between cases, but his intentions are not entirely self-centered as he goes to movies with Hélène, to dinner with Faroux, and to bars with Covet. His friends keep him grounded when his name appears prominently in the newspaper, and his dependence on their services reminds him that he cannot maintain his success on his own.

Informative Symbiosis

The recurring characters in *Les nouveaux mystères de Paris* are allowed to return because they are irreplaceable: they provide Burma with information necessary to help him solve his case, but have the courtesy not to beat him to the punch. They are players in a game in which information is a commodity to be exchanged, hoarded, stolen, and fabricated.[147] Burma always wins the game by knowing more and hiding more, but the others continue to play with this friend of whom they often expect the worst and whom they cannot really trust.

Marc Covet gives Nestor Burma access both to the past, via the *Crépuscule* archives that Burma regularly consults, and to a future legacy, thanks to the articles that Covet writes about the "détective de choc." Respectfully addressing each other as "vous," Covet and Burma enjoy a symbiotic friendship in that Covet needs a good story to retain his "star reporter" status just as much as Burma needs to appear on the front page from time to time to keep his "dynamite" nickname. Burma is Covet's journalistic jewel, and the reporter does

---

[147] Moran's data for his analysis of question formation in French comes from "written representations of spoken language" (135) found in the detective fiction of Malet and Simenon. He writes, "These detective novels were chosen not only for their high frequency of quoted dialogue . . . but also because the authors represent characters from all walks of life . . . in a wide variety of settings (rural and city) and a great number of subsettings such as cafés and homes" (136). (John Moran, "How to Ask: Question Formation in Written Representations of Spoken French," *Georgetown University Roundtable on Languages and Linguistics* (1992): 135-46.)

not take kindly to his "exclusivité" being threatened. In *Corrida aux Champs-Elysées* another reporter, Rabastens, tries to angle in on Burma at a party that the detective attended because of Covet's connection. Rabastens says, "Je suis correspondant criminel pour quelques canards ["newspapers"] de province. Je sais bien que Covet a une sorte d'exclusivité envers vous, mais bon sang! . . . Il pourrait désormais, sans inconvénient, laisser des miettes aux copains" (*Enquêtes*, 2: 7). Covet, however, does not see the situation in the same manner: "Et voilà comment est la nouvelle génération, gronda Marc Covet. Ambitieuse. Démésurement ambitieuse et prête à enlever le pain de la bouche des aînés pour arriver" (*Enquêtes*, 2: 8). Information is the source of life for the reporter. Like Hansel and Gretel's crumbs in the forest, this "pain" leaves behind a trail that is easily picked up by others. But Covet need not feel threatened for long, as Rabastens is soon killed off while trailing a dangerous story not involving Burma. More typical of the journalistic community's understanding is that of a photographer, Fred, who remarks, "Covet . . . . Burma . . . Les deux font la paire, hein?" The pair benefits from each other in finding more information and getting the most out of its crumbs. Burma goes to Covet before any other Parisian reporter and, in exchange, he has access to the archives and special services of *Le Crépu* at all hours of the day and night. Thanks to Covet, Burma can use the newpaper's resident artist to retouch a photo of an unidentifiably disfigured man in *Casse-pipe à la Nation* (*Enquêtes*, 2: 562). This information gives Burma an advantage over the police in the race to solve the mystery of the armed man who fell off a roller coaster.

Covet's articles are as useful to Burma as is his friendship. When he is afraid to admit to Faroux that he knows about a murder, Burma waits for the newspaper article to appear so that he can claim to have just read about it. In *Boulevard . . . Ossements*, Burma anticipates Covet's latest edition to provide him with "des informations supplémentaires" (*Enquêtes*, 2: 513), because he himself cannot get closer to the crime scene without arousing suspicion. In *L'envahissant cadavre de la plaine Monceau*, Covet's investigative reporting uncovers a trans-Mediterranean, cigarette-smuggling ring (*Enquêtes*, 2: 893) and in *Les Rats de Montsouris*, it is Marc Covet's article that names the jewel thieves of the novel's title. In this novel, Burma proudly says to a client, "C'est mon copain Marc Covet . . . le journaliste du *Crépuscule*, qui les a baptisés ainsi, dans son canard" (*Enquêtes*, 1: 864).

In order for their information exchange to succeed, the two men have to abide by a mutual understanding: Burma will continue to give exclusives to Covet if the reporter will keep the information out of the newspaper until the time is right. Otherwise, the police could solve the case before Burma. In *Pas de bavards à la Muette*, Covet respects Burma's wishes to "aller mollo ["easily or quietly"] dans le mesure du possible" (*Enquêtes*, 2: 166), understanding the detective's needs to keep certain information secret until the final story. But Burma does not have complete control over his friend. In *L'envahissant cadavre de la plaine Monceau* the reporter calls the detective's bluff. Burma tries to convince Covet that he was in the seventeenth *arrondissement* "par hasard" and not because of a new case:

> -- C'est vrai ce mensonge? poursuivit Marc Covet, soupçonneux comme pas un.
> -- Oui.
> -- Vous êtes dehors de si bonne heure?
> -- Je profite des belles matinées d'un printemps précoce.
> -- Mais pas tous les jours. Aujourd'hui par exemple . . .
> -- J'ai peur de tomber encore sur des macchabées.
> -- Comme si ça vous faisait quelque chose!
> -- Quand ils ne sont là que pour me faire créer des emmerdements et me faire soupçonner de je ne sais quoi, oui.
> Il frétille.
> -- On vous soupçonne? (*Enquêtes*, 2: 894)

Covet has known Burma long enough to recognize his work habits and when the detective is lying. He knows that the only reason for Burma to be so far from his office at such an early hour is to meet a client. In this passage, he hopes to trick Burma into revealing more than he had intended. But Burma knows that Covet plays this game well, and carefully chooses his words in order to retain the upper hand.

Burma also understands the power of the press, and happily drops the name of his friend Covet when it serves his purpose. Covet understands the power of his pen as well, and carefully chooses his words in order to keep Burma happy with his public image. In *Casse-pipe à la Nation*, he offers to make the story more interesting: "Est-ce que vous voulez que je l'assaisonne de commentaires particuliers?

demande Marc Covet, qui a l'esprit compliqué" (*Enquêtes*, 2: 559).
Covet knows that sensational stories sell more newspapers, resulting
in more *gloire* for both subject and writer. At press time they decide to
keep this story, which had not yet been solved, as simple as possible
until more concrete evidence is available. In *Pas de bavards à la
Muette*, Covet's article on Burma is strategically placed next to an
article featuring Brigitte Bardot. The names of Burma's clients are
represented by initials, whereas Burma's own name is spelled out:

> [Mon nom], par contre, s'étalait en toutes lettres et, en trente lignes, Marc
> Covet a réussi à le mentionner trois fois. Ce qui me donnait un léger
> avantage sur Brigitte Bardot, dont on parlait à la colonne voisine, en ne
> citant son nom que deux fois. Il est vrai que l'actrice bénéficiait de la
> reproduction de sa photo, chose qui m'était refusée. Les lecteurs ne
> perdaient pas au change, mais enfin! (*Enquêtes*, 2: 168)

Covet's article is sure to be noticed next to Bardot's glamorous photo,
which is guaranteed to please Covet's subject. If Burma is kept happy
with his press coverage, he is less likely to defect to another
newspaper. Thanks to Covet's press pass, Burma can frequently tag
along to high-profile events, such as the film premiere in *Corrida aux
Champs-Elysées*, which leads the detective to his next mystery.
Whereas the relationship between Covet and Burma is based on
mutual back-scratching, the one between Faroux and Burma is
friendly yet antagonistic, "une agressivité rhétorique."[148]

Burma and Faroux share a mutual respect, but their
professional relationship is based on hiding what they know. To the
commissioner's irritation, they frequently cross paths, usually at a
crime scene. He typically greets the detective with a chagrined, "Vous
voilà une nouvelle fois dans le bain, Nestor Burma" (*Enquêtes*, 1:
694) in *Fièvre au Marais*, when Burma finds himself at the Palais de
Justice, also known as "la P.J." or "la Tour Pointue." Faroux has
known Burma long enough to be aware of the detective's talent for
finding himself where he should not be and to know that when he is
brought in for questioning he will be released before the night is over.
Burma recognizes this as well and takes full advantage of his
relationship with the commissioner. Burma hesitates to admit that he

---

[148] Lacassin, *Masque* 74.

is on a particular case, knowing that Faroux, in his thoroughness, will soon figure out this information on his own.

With respect to professional ethics, Faroux invites comparison to Jules Maigret. Whereas Maigret faithfully follows police procedure, Faroux will resort to shady tactics to get his job done. In *Le soleil naît derrière le Louvre*, he asks Burma for a professional favor:

> -- Beaucoup de boulot en ce moment?
> -- Pas des masses.
> -- Très bien, répéta-t-il. Je disais donc que je vous crois. Et tellement, même, que je prends sous mon bonnet de vous charger d'un petit travail confidentiel, que je vous apporte en guise de petit déjeuner . . . Hum . . . Les flics officiels ne peuvent pas tout faire. Vous le savez. Ils sont parfois gênés aux entournures. Bref, des fois, ils sont bien contents d'avoir un privé sous la main . . .
> -- . . . pour certains boulots délicats?
> -- Tout juste. (*Enquêtes*, 1: 440)

Faroux explains to Burma that he wants him to seduce Geneviève Levasseur, the girlfriend of a gangster under surveillance.[149] Faroux hopes that Burma can get more information in a more intimate setting and, in the end, is not disappointed. In their symbiotic relationship, Burma can depend on Faroux to get him out of a jam and Faroux can depend on Burma to do his dirty work when necessary. Though Faroux does not always approve of Burma's line of work, the two men do enjoy a constant exchange of witty banter. He cannot be too familiar with Burma in a public setting where duty calls, but on the telephone they are free to converse as longtime friends.

When Burma is taken into custody at a crime scene, usually because of the suspicious gun in his pocket, he is quick to invoke the name of his influential friend. In *Des kilomètres de linceuls*, he is arrogantly confident of Faroux's influence:

> Je demandai alors la permission de téléphoner à mon vieil ami le commissaire de la P.J. Florimond Faroux. M. Grandjean me dit que c'était inutile. Faroux n'allait pas tarder à arriver, certaines particularités de ce règlement de comptes laissant supposer qu'il était lié à une affaire dont s'occupait déjà le Quai d'Orfèvres, en la personne de mon ami, justement.

---

[149] Of this arrangement Lacassin writes, "Le détective est chargé . . . de surveiller de près un mannequin de la rue de la Paix. Burma la suit de si près qu'il tombe dans son lit, et en ressort amoureux" (Lacassin, *Masque* 46).

J'attendis. Florimond Faroux vint bientôt me sortir du pétrin ["difficult situation"]. (*Enquêtes*, 1: 532)

Burma understands the power of his friend's name and makes the most of his connection. Faroux is familiar with Burma's work habits and work ethic. When he makes his regular call to Burma in *Les Rats de Montsouris*, he says, ". . . j'espère que vous avez préparé suffisamment de mensonges pour faire mon bonheur. Vous savez que je les adore" (*Enquêtes*, 1: 906). Just as Burma expects Faroux to call at anytime, Faroux expects Burma to prepare a well-spun lie to cover up his latest *enquête*. In *Pas de bavards à la Muette*, the two men disagree about a man's mustache. Looking at a photo, Burma begins:

> -- Il n'a pas toujours son embryon de moustache à la Charlot, dis-je, histoire de parler.
> -- A la Hitler.
> -- Si vous voulez. A la Hitler ou à la Charlot, c'est du kif ["the same"].
> -- Pas tout à fait.
> Je haussai les épaules.
> -- Alors, vous, vous cherchez la petite bête.
> -- Ça nous fait parfois trouver les grosses. (*Enquêtes*, 2: 210)

While the title, *Pas de bavards à la Muette*, is a play on words given that Chaussée de la Muette is a street in the sixteenth *arrondissement*, in this case the chatty *bavards* of the title also makes reference to Burma and Faroux, who can talk for hours, finally agreeing to disagree. Though Burma is privileged enough to have the commissioner's home phone number (*Enquêtes*, 2: 155-56), clearly a certain level of mistrust exists when the commissioner teases Burma in *Corrida aux Champs-Elysées* that "Le huitième . . . c'était un arrondissement plutôt tranquille, avant que vous ne décidiez d'y demeurer" (*Enquêtes*, 2: 45).

Between Burma and Hélène, antagonism is replaced by flirtation. Hélène is sometimes sent on assignment in Burma's place as a reward for completing menial tasks. As Burma's proxy source of information, Hélène serves as an undercover investigator where Burma himself cannot or will not go. Her assignments range from archival research at the Bibliothèque Nationale (*Enquêtes*, 1: 891) to spending an entire day shopping at jewelers' boutiques for a perfume vial similar to one carried by a suspect (*Enquêtes*, 2: 409). Her most frequent disguise is as Burma's partner, in situations requiring them to appear as a couple. In *Fièvre au Marais*, they go to the circus (*Enquêtes*, 1: 711); in *La nuit de Saint-Germain-des-près*, they pretend to be tourists (*Enquêtes*, 1: 811); and in *Les rats de Montsouris*, they pretend to be lovers in search of a "nid d'amour" in a seedy area of town (*Enquêtes*, 1: 876). More than a mere decoration, Hélène always has a mission during the assignment. For example, in *Boulevard . . . Ossements* she is responsible for the getaway car at the Chinese restaurant (*Enquêtes*, 2: 454). She is quick on her feet and usually capable of taking care of herself when sent on assignment alone, avoiding the *coups de crâne* that sideline Burma, except in *Du rébecca rue des Rosiers* where she is briefly kidnapped.

Hélène is the only one of the recurring supporting characters for whom Malet submits narrative of what happens during her "heures supplémentaires" (*Enquêtes*, 1: 973). Her first lengthy *récit* occurs in two non-consecutive chapters of *M'as-tu vu en cadavre?* when she infiltrates a fan club for Gil Andréa, the latest teen-idol. Since Burma himself could not have gone to this meeting for female fans, Hélène takes on the role of undercover detective. She provides an interesting narrative function, as the reader gets a glimpse of how other people view the "détective de choc." We learn that Hélène never refers to her boss as "Monsieur Burma," but as "Nestor Burma," using both names at once, or "mon patron." In spite of their flirtation, she refers to him as respectfully as an employee in any "entreprise," yet the lack of "monsieur" suggests a degree of informality. Her *récit* includes an indication of her tastes in regard to women's fashion, in comparison to what Burma prefers. Before the fan club meeting begins, she has time to do some window shopping and comes across a display window for a shoestore specializing in high-heeled boots. Hélène hopes that Burma does not see this window himself for fear that he might offer her yet another (physically) uncomfortable gift, as he has done in the past.

> Je le connais, mon patron. Il serait capable de lui demander une paire d'échasses qu'il m'offrirait pour le jour de l'An. J'avais eu droit à un cadeau semblable, déjà, une fois. Je ne sais pas si c'est du fétichisme, mais les hauts talons, il aime ça. Ça le botte, c'est le cas de le dire. "Mais je ne pourrai jamais marcher avec ça, avais-je protesté. Je ne vais jamais pouvoir tenir debout." Il avait repliqué que lorsqu'on mettait ce genre de chaussures ce n'était pas pour rester debout. J'avais fait celle qui ne comprend pas, mais n'avais pu m'empêcher de rougir. Je me pose un peu là comme hypocrite, moi des fois. (*Enquêtes*, 1: 975)

Though Burma has not yet seen this particular display, Hélène knows her boss well enough to know what his reaction would be, and chooses to hide this information from him. Her *récit* has a special quality because it is written for the reader, and not written for Burma and passed on to us. So the reader becomes a co-conspirator in a secret on Burma, turning the tables on the detective who is usually the clandestine one.

Hélène is defined by her occupation, with few indications as to her life outside the office. For example, we do not know anything about her love life and, given her description by Burma as smart, attractive, and good company, it is hard to imagine that she would be alone. She never seems to be dating anyone and, when in Paris, is always available to respond to Burma's requests. The agency is her life and, as seen in her *récit*, we see that she takes her assignment seriously, even when it involves coming up with an exotic pseudonym to use among the other fan club members. She calls herself "Lotus pensif," when the name "Coeur brisé" is already taken by another member (*Enquêtes*, 1: 979), but continues to introduce herself by her own name because she finds the pseudonym does not suit her.

In the second chapter of her first *récit*, Hélène puts herself in danger by going to a "modeling agency" that recruits members of Gil Andréa's fan club for its prostitution ring servicing Argentina. As it is a seedy establishment, she encounters two men in the hallway who make catcalls at her. She tells them that they could be more polite, remarking to the reader, "Ils ne me faisaient pas peur. J'étais la secrétaire de Nestor Burma. En mission"(*Enquêtes*, 1: 1003). Hélène enters the club as a prospective employee, but is able to escape the man's roaming hands by stepping on his foot with her high heel. As she escapes the room, she cannot help laughing at the man, whose toupée has since fallen off. Her fit of giggling, however, is short-lived when a bloodstained man grabs her in the stairwell until he falls, having been shot in the back. Hélène provides Burma with the information he needs but in the process leaves a trace behind at the man's office, which will later be uncovered by Faroux. So while she is capable and has learned much from Burma, she has not quite learned, in this novel, how to leave a scene without leaving behind evidence. However, Burma himself has not mastered that particular technique either.

Hélène's episodes mark a departure from the hardboiled style, reading like a diary of her outer-office adventure.[150] By the time she engages her next *récit*, in *Boulevard . . . Ossements*, Hélène is slightly more experienced but still concerned that the required femininity will be a drawback to her assignment. She lectures herself to be more Burma-like:

> Aussitôt, je me sermonne: "Ma fille, si tu ne peux controler ton émotivité, si tu perds aussi facilement ton sang-froid, tu n'as pas beaucoup de chance de mener ta mission à bien." Mais j'ai beau me sermonner, l'inquiétude subsiste. (*Enquêtes*, 2: 478)

Hélène wants to "mener [sa] mission à bien" and the only way to accomplish her goal is to "controler [son] émotivité." To succeed, she must be more like her boss "qui met K.O. le mystère" (*Enquêtes*, 1: viii). Disguising herself as an intern for *Le Crépuscule*, akin to Burma's favorite disguise as a *Crépu* reporter named Dalor, Hélène infiltrates a lingerie show attended only by women. Burma is beside himself with jealousy. She makes friends with the "target," a pair of Russian sisters who own the store providing the fashion show, one of whom has a suspicious past. Hélène congratulates herself on a job well done when she is invited to spend the night at the sisters' house in Châtillon, but quickly realizes that she drew attention to herself upon her arrival at the fashion show because of a suspect piece of paper in her purse, which was noticed at the security check. Her pride at the invitation distracts her from the idea that she might have blown her cover. As the same thing could have easily happened to Burma, the reader is never disappointed in Hélène and, when she safely escapes the situation, cheers for her as for the detective himself. After once again putting herself in danger, as the suspected sister confronts Hélène with a gun, she gets the information Burma needs. She successfully completes her mission, but her confidence is shaken and she does not provide any other *récits* in the series. As for what information Burma shares with Hélène, he will claim to have brought his secretary up to speed upon his return to the office. Often he keeps

---

[150] Though Hélène's textual voice is feminine, she represents Malet's perception of how a female detective, or a secretary "en mission" would react. A study of female writers with female detectives can be found in Deborah Hamilton's dissertation.

Hélène in the dark to "protect" her from the criminals he is pursuing as well as from the inquiry of Faroux.

Burma thus enjoys a mutually beneficial relationship with the three most important recurring characters of the series. Covet remains the star crime reporter of *Le Crépuscule* by retaining exclusive coverage of Burma's *enquêtes*; Burma makes use of Covet's archives and press pass to solve crimes before the police, thereby giving Covet an exclusive. Faroux is promoted to police commissioner because of the criminals he has arraigned, many of whom he arrested thanks to Burma's investigations; because of his association with Faroux, Burma never spends more than a few hours in police custody. Hélène is Burma's most loyal supporter and faithfully completes her assignments, even when there is no financial incentive; Burma gives her a potentially dangerous assignment, risking her life, but also giving her the same adrenaline rush that he experiences on an almost daily basis. Burma's friends, however, do more than serve his professional needs. They also fill a void in his personal life, providing Burma with the sense of family that he never had.

Surrogate Family

Nestor Burma's biography is similar to Léo Malet's in that both men, orphans, left Montpellier at a young age to live in Paris. Both lived in an anarchist commune before becoming cabaret singers in the Montmartre district, and both fell into the surrealist group before the outbreak of the war. Here is where the similarities end. Malet found a family when he married and became a father, while Burma became a detective and remained a bachelor, with the recurring characters of the series, Hélène, Faroux, Covet, as well as his freelance investigators, Roger Zavatter and Louis Reboul, serving as his surrogate family.

Faroux is the father figure of Burma's world who serves as both a disciplinarian and protector. The commissioner is the one character whose respect Burma tries to earn and whose wrath he fears the most. A Nestor Burma mystery does not feel complete without a scene where Faroux scolds Burma for doing his job. In *L'envahissant cadavre de la plaine Monceau*, Faroux says, "Voilà. Ça m'embête, Burma, que vous soyez encore mêlé à un micmac" (*Enquêtes*, 2: 957), sounding like a disappointed but not surprised parent. After speaking with Marc Covet on the telephone to arrange a meeting, Burma says,

"Je ne tiens pas à ce que Faroux vienne me casser les pieds avant que j'aie eu une explication avec Mme Souldre" (*Enquêtes*, 1: 1013). Burma subverts Faroux's authority, hiding (in *Des kilomètres de linceuls*, at Hélène's apartment) unsuccessfully when he wants to avoid being caught and ignoring the phone calls. Faroux knows of Burma's talent for finding trouble, but still berates him for it. When Burma offers his "intuition" as an excuse for being at the scene of a crime, Faroux responds, "Je n'aime pas vos intuitions" (*Enquêtes*, 1: 694), because they always lead to trouble. Faroux does not trust Burma's excuses, knowing that the detective will only reveal so much at a time, and reminds Burma, "Je ne veux pas d'emmerdements avec vous, vous comprenez?" to which Burma replies, "Vous n'en aurez pas" (*Enquêtes*, 1: 907), yet another promise that he is unable to keep. Despite his disapproval of the detective's behavior, Faroux is there when Burma needs him.

When Burma wakes up in the hospital in *Les eaux troubles de Javel* (*Enquêtes*, 2: 435), Faroux is at his bedside, after saving Burma from a ring of angry Algerian rebels. In *Boulevard . . . Ossements*, Faroux and his men arrive in time to disarm Natacha, who shot at Burma and missed. In the way that Burma is in the wrong place at the wrong time, Faroux is in the right place at the right time, saving Burma when necessary and taking over when the case is too complicated. As rebellious and evasive as Burma can be, Faroux is always available to step in, evoking both *deus ex machina* and *in loco parentis*, to save the detective from serious harm. Burma is allowed to take credit for solving the mystery, but the police still have a job to do when it is time for arraignment.

Like a parent, whom Burma jokingly refers to as "grand-père" (*Enquêtes*, 1: 440), which is a slang "surnom donné au directeur du Palais de Justice à Paris," Faroux is suspicious when his "child" is too clean or too quiet. In *Corrida aux Champs-Elysées*, he runs into Burma and Covet at a crime scene following a black-tie engagement:

> -- Et alors? tonna le commissaire. Vous êtes encore en plein bain, on dirait? Et Marc Covet est avec vous? Ça va simplifier les choses. Qu'est-ce que vous faites, en smoking?
> -- Vous emballez pas, dis-je. Le noir convient aux enterrements.
> -- Ouais. Alors? Que se passe-t-il? (*Enquêtes*, 2: 23)

Seeing the working class Burma in a tuxedo arouses suspicion in the commissioner. As the detective is out of his element at the upscale party, he must be on a case. Faroux is not in the mood to listen to Burma's quips, and cuts him off to get down to business. Faroux's professional obligations override his personal interests. In order to maintain his professional authority, he must at times be the authoritative disciplinarian of their friendship.

Meanwhile, Hélène Chatelain is the consistent female presence in Burma's life. As the secretary of the Fiat Lux agency, she is faithful to a fault; in *Fièvre au Marais* she even allows a two-month lapse in her salary. Her absence is significant in the three novels in which she does not appear: in *Corrida aux Champs-Elysées*, she is vacationing at her parents' house, while Burma vacations in the eighth *arrondissement* of Paris; in *Casse-pipe à la Nation*, she is to return from a vacation in the south of France, only to miss her train because of a sprained ankle; and in *Micmac moche au Boul' Mich* she is absent for most of the novel because of a bout with the flu, which she then transmits to Burma.

The language Burma exchanges with Hélène is chastely flirtatious. Burma is certainly attracted to his secretary, to whom he often refers as "la poupée jolie" (*Enquêtes*, 1: 809), but he chooses not to pursue anything beyond their flirtation. On slow office days, he is easily distracted by her legs (*Enquêtes*, 2: 447) or by her cleavage (*Enquêtes*, 1: 852), depending on what she is wearing. But a great deal of the attraction between Nestor and Hélène is on an intellectual level, as they match wits and vie to produce the most accurate and coherent narrative of the crime scenario for the benefit of both the detective agency and the reader. They conduct themselves like a comfortable married couple. Considering the fate of Burma's other lovers throughout the series, Hélène would not survive from installment to installment if she did not keep a degree of professional distance between her and her "patron." While they respectfully address each other with "vous," Hélène is not afraid to tell her boss, when he stumbles in the office after a late night out in *Le soleil naît derrière le Louvre*, "Je croyais que vous étiez tombé dans une cuve de Chanel . . . Faudra faire désinfecter votre costume!" (*Enquêtes*, 1: 493) In *Les rats de Montsouris*, when Burma returns to the office after one of his many scrapes, she remarks, "On ne peut pas vous laisser sortir seul. Vous ne changerez jamais" (*Enquêtes*, 1: 871). Having worked for him since before the occupation, she knows Burma better than he knows himself, and rare is the occasion where he can surprise her.[151]

She is also familiar with his taste in women, which tends to run toward the younger type. In *Brouillard au pont de Tolbiac* Burma falls in love with the gypsy companion to his recently deceased *anar* mentor Lenantais, resulting in his frequent absence from the office. When Hélène calls him at home, the woman, Bélita, answers the phone when Burma steps out for coffee. When she calls again, this time she reaches Burma directly:

> -- Tiens, bonjour patron, fit-elle. Dites-donc, j'ai essayé de vous avoir, il y a cinq minutes. J'ai dû tomber sur un faux numéro.
> -- Ah! Pourquoi?
> -- C'est une femme qui m'a répondu. Une très jolie femme, à en juger par sa voix. Pas une voix très jolie, mais jeune. (*Enquêtes*, 2: 304)

And soon after, she remarks, "Je m'explique pourquoi on ne vous voit plus au bureau, maintenant" (*Enquêtes*, 2: 305). Revealing her jealous side is part of the game they enjoy.

The voice of reason in Burma's life, Hélène asks him why he chooses not to abandon the case in *Boulevard . . . Ossements* when the client who paid him, Goldy, dies. Earlier in the same novel, she protests when Burma agrees to take Goldy's case at all, wanting herself to enjoy a well-deserved vacation after winning at the lottery, but Burma convinces her otherwise, "Un peu plus tard, Hélène se calme. Ses colères de petite fille capricieuse ne durent jamais bien longtemps" (*Enquêtes*, 2: 449). She asks Burma the types of questions that lead him to self-evaluation: why does he continue this line of work when he is constantly being hit in the head? Obviously concerned for Burma's safety, in *L'envahissant cadavre de la plaine Monceau*, she asks him "Quand cesserez-vous de me faire peur comme ça?" (*Enquêtes*, 2: 977) after another of his brushes with death. She herself could go into a safer line of work, especially after being kidnapped in *Du rébecca rue des Rosiers*, but remains faithful

---

[151] At the end of *L'envahissant cadavre de la Plaine Monceau*, the final novel of the series, Burma comes into possession of three large diamonds, which he lifted from a crime scene. He keeps one for himself, one for Régine (who had been victimized in the novel), and one for Hélène. He delivers this gift to his secretary by slipping the diamond down the front of her shirt, which leaves her stammering with excitement (*Enquêtes*, 2: 1000).

to her job and to her boss. She cares for his wounds when he can avoid a doctor's office, and offers him good company when he is lonely.

At the beginning of *Corrida aux Champs-Elysées*, Burma is licking his wounds after his love interest, an American actress named Grace Stanford, has left Paris to return to Hollywood. Though she is Burma's only girlfriend to leave him without dying, in Burma's world, departing from Paris is synonymous with death. This indication of a legitimate love life, unconnected to his professional activities (though they met when he served as her bodyguard during a film festival), is a rare "off camera" adjustment to his character. Malet teases the reader by suggesting that Burma is having adventures with beautiful women between novels, raising suspicion as to what other stories he is withholding. The fatality associated with his women is a consequence of his profession, and that is clearly what interests Malet and his readers. Grace is dispatched to reassure us that Burma has a "healthy" side, but, as she has already left Paris when the novel opens, she is sure not to interfere with the formula. As Burma recovers from his heartache, Covet is there to take him to celebrity parties, looking for a new case, and reacclimating him to his professional life.

Burma's friends thus serve as a support network and the detective will support them in return. While Faroux might be considered Burma's overbearing parent for always scolding him and trying to keep him from murder investigations, Burma will refer to the commissioner as his good friend. Though he sometimes puts Hélène in dangerous situations, when she is kidnapped in *Du rébecca rue des Rosiers* he considers the act a personal attack, as his surrogate family is an extension of himself. He and Covet keep each other in business, though Burma sometimes resents Covet's journalistic persistence. But more than supporting Burma personally, these friends provide a narrative balance to the "détective de choc." The next section will demonstrate how the supporting players give Burma feedback when he presents his theories and give the reader a break from the violence of the series.

Narrative Balance

Malet's supporting characters lend balance to Burma's narrative. Sharing Burma's sense of humor, Covet, Faroux, and Hélène provide opportunities for witty banter and comic relief from the violence and frequent "macchabées" of his investigations. Along with Burma, the supporting players encounter the underbelly of Paris which, along with other realistic films and novels of the period, refutes the postwar portrait of prosperity. Malet's cast of characters represents a slice of everyday postwar life that would be ignored by other fiction of the 1950s, seeking to represent French society as "streamlined and fast-moving."[152]

In addition to having multiple crimes, a *roman noir* features a dark sense of humor, including questionable, even inappropriate irreverence in the face of what might be a grisly death. As cited by Franz Blaha, Marcel Duhamel's introduction to the *Série Noire* characterizes dark humor as the one constant element of a genre where policemen are often corrupt and where a tangible mystery or even the detective himself may be absent.[153] In Malet's case, in the tradition of American hardboiled writers, the narration is first-person and the detached observer is the detective himself, whose seen-it-all-before narration is filled with dark laughs. Burma shares this gallows humor with his friends and close associates who also strive to cope with the professions they have each chosen.

Burma's detached remark at the end of *La nuit de Saint-Germain-des-près* "J'avais à livrer à Florimond Faroux ma cargaison habituelle de cadavres" (*Enquêtes*, 1: 843) is one example of reducing the body count to a running joke. Referring to the "cadavres" as if they were this week's trash to be dropped off evokes the *danse macabre* and removes any sense of individuality or personal history from the scene; one cadaver is as dead as any other. Likewise, in *Pas de bavards à la Muette*, Burma refers to a "macchabée" he finds as "le premier de la saison" (*Enquêtes*, 2: 155). In *Brouillard au Pont de Tolbiac*, Burma has a conversation with Faroux and his men when they converge at the morgue at the same time. Faroux is the first to suggest that they go to an "endroit plus gai" (*Enquêtes*, 2: 257) where they can pursue their discussion of tattoos and noses in a more appropriate venue, but only after they have been standing around for quite a while. When he says, "Changeons de crémerie . . . Vous n'en avez pas marre, de cet amphithéâtre? Je déteste le genre vampire, moi" (*Enquêtes*, 2: 257). Burma jokes that Faroux's office is not much more pleasant than the morgue itself, and the others agree. To these

---

[152] Ross 3.
[153] Blaha 45.

men, the morgue is just any other place that they might have to visit on a typical day, and their detachment is oddly comic.

Though Burma does not engage in gallows humor with Hélène, their flirtatious conversations provide a narrative distraction from the investigation. One such exchange is in *Boulevard . . . Ossements*; when Burma gives Hélène her assignment to go undercover at the lingerie show. To show her appreciation, Hélène winks and says, "Si vous étiez un peu mieux rasé, je vous aurais embrassé," to which Burma responds, "Je n'ai pas de poils aux lèvres" (*Enquêtes*, 2: 478). Their flirtation is tender at times and shows the softer side of Burma, who makes such remarks because he knows that "Ça la fait rire et c'est tout" (*Enquêtes*, 2: 478); this is not the same Burma who hits one client with a car in *Le soleil naît derrière le Louvre*, or slaps a woman in *L'envahissant cadavre de la Plaine Monceau* who had taken away his gun. With Hélène, Burma cultivates a brand of gentle machismo which gives him the confidence to go out on the street and tackle tough guys.

Hélène is accustomed to Burma's short-term liaisons, but allows their flirtation to continue, with episodes scattered throughout Malet's series. In *Pas de bavards à la Muette*, Burma checks into a hotel in the sixteenth *arrondissement* to be closer to his case. When he gets lonely, he calls Hélène, who comes to visit. As he tells her about the day's findings he strokes her hair, "Machinalement, [il] lui caress[a] les cheveux," until she tires of the gesture and says, "Vous m'avez assez dépeignée comme ça" (*Enquêtes*, 2: 203). In a gesture of her own, when he asks her to send over a suitcase for him, to make him look more like a hotel tourist, she wraps a gun in a pair of lacy panties (*Enquêtes*, 2: 127). She is as aware of his fetish as is the reader, and enjoys teasing him whenever the situation allows, thereby breaking the tension in an office where death is rendered a commodity.

The everyday interactions of Burma and his associates present a portrait of everyday postwar life which contradicts the notion of universal prosperity during modernization and renovation. Kristin Ross writes, "In the postwar period realist fiction offered a critique of official representations of a uniformly prosperous France, surging forward into American-style patterns of consumption and mass culture."[154] While detective fiction is not necessarily realist fiction, Malet's portrait of the postwar period contributes to the "critique of official representations." Burma's France is hardly "uniformly prosperous" as the detective encounters characters from all walks of life, from high-powered businessmen and movie executives to auto-factory workers and prostitutes, with professional criminals (gun runners, art forgers, and blackmailers) in between. Burma himself is a private businessman without a reliable source of income; Faroux is a governmental official; Covet is a reporter; Hélène is a secretary dependent on Burma's wages. None of them represents the upwardly mobile appliance and automobile consumers depicted in 1950s advertising. Many of the criminals Burma tracks are those who want to pursue the "American-style patterns of consumption,"[155] but must resort to criminal ways in order to achieve the goals of the *nouveau riche*.

By 1947, writes Ross, "American films had overrun [France]"[156] with images of prosperity. She adds, "The postwar screens of Europe were filled with an illustrated catalog of the joys and rewards of American capitalism."[157] These material rewards are satirized in the films of Jacques Tati, such as *Mon Oncle*, where the machines that are supposed to make life more efficient and "automatic" only serve to create more problems for a traditional Frenchman like Monsieur Hulot. In Malet's novels, the pursuit of such prosperity leads to greed, which leads to murder. In *Casse-pipe à la Nation*, a wine-producer conspires with his partner's unhappy wife to rub out her husband; the co-conspirators marry but they are eventually caught. Their plan to make more money ultimately fails them. In *Brouillard au pont de Tolbiac*, Burma reunites with two men he had known at the "foyer végétalien" who had since renounced anarchism, received their sizeable inheritances, and taken over the family businesses. Their greed to expand their holdings leads them to their deaths, as they turn against each other. In general, characters in Malet's series who try to follow this French version of the American Dream do not survive to enjoy the payoff of their scheming. As a former anarchist, Burma himself does not buy into consumerist

---

[154] Ross 13.
[155] Ross 13.
[156] Ross 33.
[157] Ross 38.

enthusiasm, but he does buy a car between *La nuit de Saint-Germain-des-près* and *Les rats de Montsouris*. In his thriftiness, however, he buys a used car which frequently strands him, forcing him to return to public transportation.

Postwar modernization is characterized by new industry, including engineers and the *jeune cadre*, or technocrat (also satirized in Tati's *Mon Oncle*), who bring the same efficiency to the blossoming French industry that they had brought to the colonies. This is not the French society that Burma and his associates encounter. Rather, they are more familiar with the lawless outcasts of Paris, who had been pushed out of the spotlight during the post-occupation *épurations* when, among other reforms, at least 177 brothels were closed by De Gaulle. Malet's series suggests that those elements were alive and well during this era. Burma has several prostitute acquaintences, usually for information rather than for services. The first person he encounters in *Le soleil naît derrière le Louvre*, the first novel of the *Nouveaux Mystères*, is a prostitute whom he trusts as a reliable source. In *Fièvre au Marais*, he passes out in a brothel and awakens chained to a dead prostitute who had been his informant. Burma learns the etiquette of the pick-up near the Hôtel de Ville in *Du rébecca rue des Rosiers*. Malet's inclusion of a thriving brothel and "successful" prostitutes undermines the presumption that this industry had been eliminated during the campaign for national cleanliness, raising the question of what other criminal activities were also covered up.

Burma's interactions with his friends and associates balance the narrative of his investigations, while the characters' interaction with the underbelly of postwar life balances the official representation of the era. As in the occupation, there were victims of the postwar renovation, with criminals preying on their victims to pursue dreams of a more prosperous life. Covet, Faroux, and Hélène represent ordinary people working regular jobs and living from paycheck to paycheck. They resemble the readership of detective fiction rather than the conspicuous consumers associated with the 1950s.

Burma proves his loyalty to his agency when he reopens it in *120, rue de la gare* upon being released from the P.O.W. camp, reassembling the same players: Hélène, Zavatter, and even Reboul, who returns with only one arm. Though "le manchot" is now more conspicuous than before his accident, Burma remains confident in

Reboul's abilities and does not hesitate to send him out on surveillance and reconnaissance missions. The employees, in turn, return the favor, remaining faithful to Burma even when the agency's finances are less than fluid. Faroux keeps an often suspect Burma out of jail, allowing the agency to remain operational. Covet, serving as Burma's publicist, keeps new clients coming to the detective's office. All of the characters do their part to maintain the environment on which they have come to depend. Each is an integral part of a well-running, if sometimes squeaky, machine. Burma's repeated interactions with these supporting players help to fashion him as the character he is: a postwar icon accurately representing what it truly meant to be in Paris after the occupation.

Chapter Five

"Paris est Paris, voyez-vous." [158]

Léo Malet left his mark on French literature and popular culture with his decision to set an American-style harboiled novel in the city of Paris. As detective fiction is generally an urbanized form, Malet's contribution lies in bringing this particular style to a city heretofore monopolized by the classic *polar* of Christie, Holmes, and Simenon. Malet's Paris falls somewhere between the mob-run Chicago of the American tradition and the strictly European city of his detective fiction contemporaries. His city is modern, with modern preoccupations and concerns that extend beyond its historical role. Nestor Burma is the reader's tour guide, highlighting points of historical interest that litter the trail of his investigation as "[il] feuillette pour nous le Tout Paris de l'époque." [159] Even for the Parisian reader, Burma is likely to point out something new as, according to the detective, most Parisians are lacking in the history of their own city, and he intends to pique their curiosity.

Various biographical articles suggest that Malet left his *Nouveaux mystères de Paris* series unfinished, with the stories of five *arrondissements* unwritten, because he was depressed by the changing face of Paris in the post-occupation renovation, even though, like other European capitals, Paris has always constantly evolved. The Paris of Malet's youth, by French standards, had not been finished for very long with the well-planned avenues of Haussman only about 100 years old by the outbreak of the Second World War. Prendergast

---

[158] As cited by Prendergast, this is the remark of "the chief of police at the moment of unmasking the master criminal, Vautrin, in Balzac's *Le Père Goriot*." (Christopher Prendergast, "Framing the City: Two Parisian Windows," *City Images: Perspectives from Literature, Philosophy, and Film,* Ed. Mary Ann Caws, (New York: Gordon and Breach, 1991) 179.

[159] Lacassin, *Masque* 91.

studies Haussmann's significant changes to Paris, in particular the addition of gas (followed by electric) street lamps. Light was rendered as yet another commodity of the industrial age. He writes:

> On its public surface Paris seemed altered beyond recognition, supplying at once the promise of excitement and the reasssurance of security, as the place where it was safe to look at, and for, what you wanted. More lights meant more tourists and less crime . . . the project of the illuminated city became cognate of the enlightened city.[160]

The addition of street lights provided a false sense of security, as the crime rate hardly dropped in the latter half of the nineteenth century. Even if there was no change in the actual rate of criminal activity, its documentation was increased due to the advances in the printing industry and the rise of newspaper culture. The genre of detective fiction became more popular and more readily available, as newspapers began to include *feuilleton* mysteries to increase circulation, and as cheaper books and higher literacy rates produced a market for popular fiction. Both newspapers and *feuilletons* are sources of crime stories; where journalism records the crime after the fact, for detective fiction, the story is found in the intrinsic shadows and fog.

The false sense of security provided by street lights brought unsuspecting people out of their homes after dark, leading to more petty crime. The surrealists, including Malet, were among those suspicious of such "progress."[161] The focal point of Aragon's *Le paysan de Paris* is the musings of a narrator wandering about the soon-to-be torn down Passage de l'Opéra. As he explores the city in pursuit of information, Burma resembles Aragon's narrator. Even after buying a car with a sizable payment at the end of *La nuit de Saint-Germain-des-près*, a Dugat 12 with "un grand coffre arrière, de quoi contenir deux macchabées, le cas échéant" (*Enquêtes*, 1: 854), Burma remains a Parisian pedestrian. Throughout the series, this car proves to be less than reliable, forcing Burma to continue to take the metro or

---

[160] Prendergast 183.

[161] Melly notes, "It is, in fact, surprising how little modern life impinged on the Surrealist imagination. Science and technology were alien to it. The cinema was welcomed, certainly, but for the hypnagogic effect of its imagery alone. In general, the Surrealists chose to look backwards, over their shoulders." (George Melly, *Paris and the Surrealists*, (London: Thames & Hudson, 1991) 80).

the occasional taxi, which also allows him to keep his man-of-the-street credibility.[162]

Though, Vilar claims, "Le Paris décrit par Léo Malet, avec toutes ses petites touches sensibles, tous ses parfums des rues, sa violence et sa séduction définitive (fatale, pour tout dire) n'a jamais été, bizarrement, un Paris 'réaliste'," [163] Malet's portrait of Paris suggests details of everyday French life. The side of Paris that he chooses to portray is not the city of the gentleman-cambrioleur, or even the city of the *flâneur*, but the dark corners, back alleys, and banal habits that most writers of popular fiction were choosing to ignore. Inspired by Baudelaire, for whom any subject was worthy of poetic praise, Burma frequents both prostitutes and societal outcasts, holding them as credible sources. Burma may share the traits of a *flâneur*, the "protagonist of modern metropolitan traffic [which] Baudelaire describes . . . as the leisurely collector of diverse, evanescent impressions of modern urban street life,"[164] but Malet's armed *flâneur* notates these impressions for his surveillance report. With the *flâneur* comes a "corresponding notion of the city as a special kind of visual and social space, peculiarly open to the random gaze and the unforseen encounter." [165] For Burma, however, the random and unforseen always lead to murder.

As tour guide, Burma emphasizes the points of the city that he finds most interesting, including many descendants of the surrealist-favored *fait-divers*. Choosing to ignore the more prominent sites of the French capital, such as the Tour Eiffel, Montmartre, and the Bastille, he prefers to focus on overlooked sidestreets and bridges as he carries the torch for the Paris of the past. In 1989, Malet told *France-Soir*, "Je ne voulais pas faire de guide touristique. J'aurais pu choisir les catacombes, j'ai préféré les réservoirs de Montsouris, plus

---

[162] Analyzing Malet's "monde ferroviaire," Chlastacz focuses on the scenes which take place in métro and train stations. In Malet's *Nouveaux Mystères*, he writes "une série noire bien parisienne commence et les enquêtes du détective de choc sont autant de parcourus dans le métro ou d'échappées dans les gares." (Michel Chlastacz, "Les Trains de Nestor Burma," *La vie du Rail* 2356 (1992): 10.)

[163] Jean-François Vilar, "Les pas perdus de Nestor Burma," *Le Monde* 01 Aug 1986: 9.

[164] Rolf Goebel, "Paris, Capital of Modernity: Kafka and Benjamin," *Monatshefte* 90.4 (1998): 455.

[165] Prendergast 180.

mystérieux." [166] Providing an alternative to a typical bus tour, he highlights areas forgotten by both tourists and Parisians. Malet, Jonzac writes, "en promenant son héros d'un arrondissement à l'autre, nous en apprend plus que n'importe quel guide sur la capitale." He also provides insight, though fictional, to the Paris of (his) present, 1954-1957, citing popular movie stars as well as contemporary issues, including the end of colonialism and the post-war fate of collaborationists. Finally, Burma illustrates the discomfort of many Parisians in the face of renovation, and paints a portrait of a Paris that in many ways no longer exists. Especially vivid is the portait of the thirteenth *arrondissement*, painted in *Brouillard au pont de Tolbiac*, a district that has been completely remodeled in the wake of Mitterand's "Grands Projets." The bridge immortalized by the title was dismantled in 1996, ironically, two months after Malet's death. [167]

This chapter will look at Malet's use of Paris. The city serves as both a setting and a character, and even "le véritable héros de Malet," [168] since Burma himself is an antihero:

> Mais le vrai héros de ces quinze enquêtes, celui qui est onmiprésent à chaque page, c'est bien sûr Paris, "Paris, Paris, ô ville infâme et merveilleuse." Paris qui s'éveille vers minuit, alors que les êtres courent dans les rues, à la rencontre de leur destin. Destin parfois tragique. Cet univers populaire, ce Paris de Malet, c'est celui des films de Marcel Carné . . . et les photos de Robert Doisneau. C'est un Paris où l'on vole, où l'on tue, où l'on s'aime . . . . [169]

Malet's Paris is both "infâme" and "merveilleuse," as well as "étouffante et sèche" (*Enquêtes*, 1: 847). He presents the city from all sides, including those that are less than flattering. This is perhaps not so innovative in canonical literature, where the naturalist movement displayed the warts of the newly industrialized city, but for popular

---

[166] Valérie Marin La Meslée, "Léo Malet ne reconnaît plus le Paris de Nestor Burma," *France-Soir* 11 Dec. 1989: 29.

[167] The caption underneath *Le Parisien*'s photograph of the dismantled bridge read: "Quelques semaines après Léo Malet, le viaduc de Tolbiac s'en est allé pour une autre vie et se fondre dans un autre brouillard" ("Au revoir au pont de Tolbiac," *Le Parisien* 06 May 1996: 4).

[168] Michel Le Bris, "Les malheurs de Malet," *Le Nouvel Observateur* 18 June 1979: 80.

[169] Johnny Fric-frac, "Léo Mallet [sic]: le mal de Paris," *Le Bien-Public* 12 Mar. 1985. N. pag.

literature Malet's choice and focalization of setting is groundbreaking. For French readers of detective fiction, this dark Gotham is no longer a fantasy on the other side of the ocean; it is in their own backyard.[170]

Parisian Curiosities as Cultural Literacy

The beginning of each of the *Nouveaux Mystères* introduces the spotlighted *arrondissement*. After the third installment, *Fièvre au Marais*, Malet began to include a map of the area to be featured, facing the first page, with captions serving to bait the reader into starting the novel such as "Au Diderot-Hôtel, on louait des chambres pour l'éternité," and "Rue Blaise-Desgoffes, une vieille dame s'inquiétait pour sa niece" (*Enquêtes*, 1: 736). Once the novel has begun, it does not take long for Burma to find himself at a historic crossroads, a moment he can only share with the reader, as he is usually alone during his wanderings. In *Fièvre au Marais*, he says:

> C'est souvent que, dans ce coin de Paris, des touristes se plantent devant les vieux palais historiques respectés, jusqu'à nouvel ordre, par le pic des démolisseurs. Et justement, devant moi, à l'angle des rues Francs-Bourgeois et Vieille-du-Temple, se dressait un élancé alibi de pierre construit depuis des siècles. La Tour Barbette, sauf erreur, dernier vestige d'un hôtel ayant appartenu à Isabeau de Bavière. (*Enquêtes*, 1: 635)

This is one of many "coins" in Paris with its own story that has fallen out of touristic interest, much to the disdain of history buffs like Burma. While tourists flock to castles and monuments of extraordinary figures of history,[171] for Burma, the real history lies in the daily struggle of ordinary people, like the people who read

---

[170] Pinçonnat's article compares Simenon and Malet's use of New York as a narrative locus. Her focus on Malet is limited to his Johnny Metal series under pseudonym. She writes, "Tandis que Malet imite une esthétique 'made in the USA' et joue avec elle pour créer une poésie urbaine et onirique, Simenon, pour sa part, semblant rejeter en bloc la mythologie américaine, la prend systématiquement en fait à contre pied" (Crystal Pinçonnat, "Maigret contre Metal: Georges Simenon et Léo Malet face à la tradition américaine du roman noir," *Études Littéraires* 29.2 (1996): 111). I maintain that Malet's frustration with the limitations of the "Made in the USA" esthetic is what led him to set his novels in France.

[171] In a joint interview between Malet and Robert Doisneau, the photographer asserts, "Nos quartiers favoris sont ceux qui ne sont pas parcourus par les autocars de Japonais" (Robert Doisneau and Léo Malet, Interview, "Paris et autres aventures," Ed. France Debray, *Leitmotiv* 1 (1988): 34) Malet agrees, but gives the Tour Eiffel as an exception to the rule, even though the structure never appears in his series.

detective novels. For Burma's inner anarchist, the New Order will include restratification of historical sites. Burma is a tour guide leading his readers; they are a captive audience because they want to see how the mystery ends. Through the narrative process, he tries to teach his audience something in addition to entertaining them.

Malet's fascination with the city's past suggests that Parisian life was somehow easier before the war changed everything, giving Paris "le décor d'une aventure quotidien."[172] The twentieth-century imagination is less optimistic than its nineteenth-century predecessor:

> The idea of Paris as an endless adventure and feast for the eyes, a vast and inexhaustibly interesting catalogue of *choses vues* (in the title of Hugo's collection of note-books), is basic to the more optimistic side of the nineteenth-century urban imagination.[173]

Though Paris is still an "endless adventure," many of the "*choses vues*" that remain after the war constitute a nightmarish "feast for the eyes." Malet keeps his nostalgic vision of the past alive by inserting historical anecdotes into Burma's narrative. He treats these forgotten corners of the city as venerable veterans in the evolution of France. Burma's memory may be selective, as the past is never as rosy as it is remembered to be, but it is preferable to the present, where "[d]epuis deux guerres et quelques révolutions ont rendu tocbombes ["un peu dérangé mentalement"] les gens honnêtes, ou réputés tels, ce sont ceux-ci qui abusent des armes offensives" (*Enquêtes*, 1: 1039). As attitudes toward the futility of war are questioned in the twentieth century, memories of past wars that seemed to "make sense" are glorified.

As a fan of the *fait-divers*, Malet will conveniently drop everyday stories or informative tidbits into Burma's investigation. In some cases, the seemingly trivial factoid will prove to be the pivotal missing link, rendering the *fait-divers* itself more relevant than it is generally allowed to be on the back pages of daily newspapers. Through *faits-divers*, newspapers record the vanishing quotidian which will never be the same after the *trentes glorieuses*. In *Micmac-moche au Boul' Mich*, Burma's suspicion is aroused when he meets a doctor whose wife mysteriously died from typhoid in the 1950s. He

---

[172] Rivière, *Noir Jeu* 62.
[173] Prendergast 183.

soon remembers a 1920s *fait-divers* about a doctor who poisoned his
patients with typhoid. When he follows up on his hunch that the two
stories are somehow related, the doctor eventually confesses. Burma's
recollection of this throw-away story brings to justice a doctor who
would never have been caught. Malet's moral is to read the daily
newspaper carefully, for today's seemingly insignificant story may
eventually return as the seed of a larger story. At the beginning of
each new case, in the hope of finding such seeds, Burma scours
Covet's *Crépuscule* archives in search of pertinent *faits-divers* of that
particular *arrondissement*. In *Les rats de Montsouris*, Burma has an
appointment on rue Blottière, and digresses, "La dernière fois que
j'avais entendu parler de la rue Blottière, c'était en 1938. On y avait
découvert trois morceaux de viande impropre à la consommation,"
when the cuts of meat were identified as an elderly woman's headless
"tronc, le bras droit et la cuisse gauche" (*Enquêtes*, 1: 861). While this
attention-grabbing anecdote in no way connects to the mystery at
hand, it serves as a reminder that grisly crime is not limited to
detective fiction.

In some cases, the *fait-divers* relates to Malet's own agenda,
bringing a slice of his politics to his readers. In *M'as-tu vu en
cadavre?*, he mentions the name of Philippe Daudet (son of prominent
anarchist Léon Daudet) who died of a gunshot wound to the head in a
taxicab in 1923, during the period in which Malet was selling
anarchist newspapers. The event divided the anarchist circle – was his
death a suicide, or a homicide? – but was largely ignored by the
French mainstream. While looking for a professional blackmailer,
Burma finds himself in the same area as the incident.

> . . . j'arrivai à la hauteur de l'immeuble cossu où demeurait le chanteur. Il
> s'élévait non loin de l'endroit où, par un après-midi brumeux de novembre
> 1923, vers quatre heures et demie, était né un des plus troublants mystères
> de Paris, en admettant que, pour certains, le mystère subsiste encore. Ce
> samedi-là, un taxi, piloté par le chauffeur Bajot, s'était arrêté devant le
> numéro 126. Les flics, alertés, avaient extrait de la voiture un adolescent
> mortellement frappé d'une balle à la tempe. Transporté à Lariboisière, le
> blessé y décédait deux heures plus tard, sans avoir repris connaissance. Cet
> adolescent au front étoilé se nommait Philippe Daudet, fils du directeur de
> *L'Action française*. Je me demande pourquoi je songeais à ce drame, en
> examinant, du trottoir opposé, la façade de la maison qu'habitait Gil
> Andréa. Au lieu de penser à l'affaire Daudet, je ferais mieux de m'intéresser
> à celle dans laquelle j'étais présentement embringué. (*Enquêtes*, 1: 1016)

The story of Philippe Daudet has no apparent connection to the novel, other than the shared location of the 1923 incident and Burma's case. The novel's title, *M'as-tu vu en cadavre*, takes on another meaning, however, when the case of Daudet is considered. The case's controversy stems from whether Daudet was shot in the taxicab or inside the building to which he was driven; apparently no one could recollect seeing what actually happened. Malet uses his novel as a platform to shed light on a real mystery which "subsiste encore" in the midst of his readers. The detective remembers the Paris of recent past, losing sight of what he is being paid to observe. He is on an assignment in the tenth *arrondissement* which does not involve taking a trip down the memory lane of unresolved stories. As his mind wanders, his narration follows, and the reader becomes involved in the sidestory as well. Burma preaches his lesson to anyone who will listen.

Malet's activistic platform is also didactic. In *La nuit de Saint-Germain-des-près*, Hélène says of the famous café Les Deux Magots, "C'est plutôt bizarre, comme un nom de café. Pourquoi s'appelle-t-il ainsi?" to which Burma replies, "C'est bien simple . . . C'est à cause de l'enseigne de la boutique de bonneterie qui existait jadis, je ne sais quand, sur le même emplacement" (*Enquêtes*, 1: 813). Malet creates Hélène to represent most Parisians who do not know the history behind some of the city's lasting landmarks. Of the handful of French literary detectives, Burma may not be the most refined, but he is certainly culturally literate and expects other Parisians to aspire to the same level of knowledge about their city, even the "curiosités parisiennes" (*Enquêtes*, 2: 517), such as the "squelette unijambiste" for sale in *Boulevard . . . Ossements*. In *Les rats de Montsouris*, Burma remarks, "On en apprend tous les jours sur la topographie parisienne" (*Enquêtes*, 1: 880), and each "balade" through the city is likely to produce new sights. A city of infinite possibilities, Paris possesses history and significance that is usually stumbled upon.

Like any urban metropolis, the history of Paris is multifaceted, containing political, social, economic, artistic, and philosphical memories. Bridgeman writes:

> Paris becomes the source of allusions to a vast wealth of Parisian texts, narrative and poetic, fictional and non-fictional, realistic and fantastic, triggered through association with the streets explored by Burma.[174]

The culture of Paris figures into other artistic works, with paintings, novels, poems, and films becoming part of the common cultural landscape. The advent of mass media distributes this culture to a larger audience, which then molds it to suit individual needs. The city is represented, writes Rifkin, "as a means for the elaboration of identity, an identity for a reader or of a writer, worked into both stable and changing images of the City."[175] When the city evolves without Burma, the detective loses part of his identity. He considers the city's history his own and interprets the cultural ignorance of its inhabitants as a personal insult. In addition to setting up a mystery to be solved, Malet presents a guided tour through the French capital in order to promote cultural literacy.

"À battre les pavés de Paris, on s'instruit."[176]

Within the frame of the detective novel, Malet depicts the Paris of the 1950s, a city where "depuis 15 ans le monstrueux est quotidien" (*Enquêtes*, 1: 563). In the same way that he brought the *noir* style to a French setting, he brings an "immense Frenchness"[177] to the detective genre with the inclusion of ordinary elements of daily French life from the postwar era which he recasts "en lieu poétique."[178]

In his wanderings, Burma finds the "beauté inhérente au quotidien parisien."[179] Like any conversationalist, he often begins a novel with a comment, generally unfavorable, about the weather, such as "Il faisait trop beau, depuis quelques jours. Ça ne pouvait pas durer. Ça ne dure jamais, dans cette sacrée bon Dieu d'Ile de France!"

---

[174] Bridgeman 61.

[175] Cited in Bridgeman 61.

[176] In *L'envahissant cadavre de la Plaine Monceau*, Burma offers "À battre les pavés de Paris on s'instruit" (*Enquêtes*, 2: 903) as explanation for his vast knowledge of Parisian curiosities.

[177] Bridgeman 61.

[178] Peter Schulman, "Paris en jeu de l'oie: Les fantômes de Nestor Burma," *The French Review* 73.6 (May 2000): 1156.

[179] Schulman, *Paris* 1162.

(*Enquêtes*, 1: 897)[180] In *Brouillard au pont de Tolbiac*, the weather remains poor throughout the novel, hampering Burma's visibility, causing him to ask, "Je n'y viendrai donc jamais un jour où il y aura du soleil?" (*Enquêtes*, 2: 265) With this comment, he suggests that the weather differs from one district to another as he travels back and forth from his apartment in the center of Paris to the thirteenth *arrondissement* across town, as if each district has its own weather system in addition to its own set of rules and local customs. Paris is diverse enough to be like more than one city, prompting both Burma and Reboul to spend their respective vacations in less familiar *arrondissements*. In *Corrida aux Champs-Elysées*, Burma takes a holiday in the same upscale hotel where he had been a bodyguard for the film star Grace Stanford, since the room had been paid for through the end of the month. In other novels, he rents hotel rooms in the same *arrondissement* of his investigation, immersing himself in the culture of the neighborhood.

Another prominent Parisian feature in Malet's series is the metro. The first line of *La nuit de Saint-Germain-des-Près*, "Le métro me cracha à Saint-Germain-des-Près" (*Enquêtes*, 1: 737) evokes the image of a disgruntled monster, contrasting with the impression of the subway as an underground dungeon from which one must escape. With the more violent image of being spit out, the metro easily blends in with violence in Burma's world. In *Du rébecca rue des Rosiers*, the pursuit of a reviled collaborationist leads to a shootout in the metro station at La Râpée. The subway system provides another set of mysterious tunnels and hallways, an underground parallel to the catacombes. In *Brouillard au pont de Tolbiac*, another pursuit ends in death when the man whom Burma is chasing tries to cross the tracks before it is safe:

> J'atteignis la voie du métro comme une rame passait, dans le roulement de tonnerre. Je fus balayé par les chaudes lumières du wagon et manquai de l'être plus proprement par le vent qu'elle déplaça. Sur le viaduc, minuscule auprès de l'arc gigantesque, Baurénot courait . . . vers la morgue . . . Exactement vers la morgue. Le brouillard s'empara bientôt de lui. (*Enquêtes*, 2: 331)

---

[180] Ezine remarks that the novels of the series "s'ouvraient toujours par deux sortes de considérations au choix: le métro ou la météo" (Léo Malet, "Léo Malet," Ed. Jean-Louis Ezine, *Lire* 105 (1984): 90).

By running across the tracks in the direction of the morgue in order to escape Burma, Baurénot runs into the path of an oncoming subway train, resulting in his death. He still goes to the morgue, but in a body bag in a police car. This ending links back to the novel's beginning where, at the morgue, Burma meets up with Faroux and Inspectors Fabre and Gregoire in order to examine the body of Burma's anarchist mentor. The death of Baurénot is another example, as discussed in chapter three, of a criminal who dies in Burma's presence before he can brought before the judicial system.

When not in the metro, Burma drives his car and, like most Parisians, must park his car where he can and walk to his destination. He complains in *Boulevard . . . Ossements*:

> Je n'apprends rien à personne. Les bagnoles, c'est très joli, mais quand on circule dans Paris, pas question qu'elles vous conduisent à l'endroit exact où l'on veut aller. Il faut les parquer parfois à un kilomètre du point exact où l'on se rend. (*Enquêtes*, 2: 462)

Parking in Paris was becoming problematic in the 1950s, with the number of cars in the capital increasing from 500,000 on the eve of World War II to a million by 1960. This sharp increase, Ross explains, led to the construction of the Périphérique in 1956.[181] In *Casse-pipe à la Nation*, Burma proclaims the joy of a good parking space and the sense of pride provided by an automatic ticket dispenser: "Je me procure un beau ticket de quai, flambant neuf, au distributeur automatique et – vlan! – voilà que ça me fait tout drôle, de sentir ce carton de quinze centimètres carrés en ma possession" (*Enquêtes*, 2: 541). Because Burma is often forced to walk where he had not intended, he learns more about the city, as he is always alert to his surroundings. Ever the observant detective, he creates a mental inventory of "choses vues" that may prove pertinent at a later date. Burma makes use of this inventory when in *Du rébecca rue des Rosiers* he is kidnapped by a carload of thugs and taken to an abandoned warehouse for questioning. When the interrogation is over, they take him back to where he had been, trying unsuccessfully to drive in a zigzag manner to confuse the detective's sense of direction.

> Je n'ai pas eu énormément le loisir de voir quoi que ce soit du décor, mais je connais Paris. Mes zigotos n'ont peut-être pas pensé à ça. Ils en sont pour

---

[181] Ross 53.

> leurs zigzags. Sauf erreur, nous sommes passage du Prévôt, un boyau qui
> relie la rue Charlemagne à la rue Saint-Antoine. (*Enquêtes*, 2: 801)

Knowing the city's topography inside out comes to his advantage
against those whose familiarity is confined to their own
neighborhoods.

In his appreciation of the *quotidien*, Malet immortalizes the
details of Parisian life. He writes of the quintessentially French *heure
apéritive* (*Enquêtes*, 1: 984), the annual P.T.T. calendars "qu'un
facteur souriant et peut-être facétieux m'avait . . . offert avec ses
meilleurs voeux" (*Enquêtes*, 1: 960), and even pigeons (*Enquêtes*, 2:
353). He eats at the chain of Café Batifol (*Enquêtes*, 1: 951), the
Greek restaurants on the rue de la Harpe in the Quartier Latin
(*Enquêtes*, 2: 743), and enjoys the comfort of *choucroute maison* at
the Brasserie Alsacienne (*Enquêtes*, 2: 374). The discount chain
Prisunic is mentioned twice in the series. The first time is in *M'as-tu
vu en cadavre?* when he condescendingly refers to the small scale
matinée idol Gil Andréa as "notre Don Juan de Prisunic" (*Enquêtes*, 1:
985); the second time is in *Casse-pipe à la Nation*, when he describes
a well-dressed young woman, whom we assume to be from a wealthy
family because Burma remarks, "[s]es chaussures, un peu esquintées
par des promenades dans le terrain vague, ne sortent certainement pas
de Prisunic. Fichtre non" (*Enquêtes*, 2: 596). And to represent the anti-
Prisunic crowd, Malet alludes to Fouquet's (*Enquêtes*, 2: 84), where
movie stars and glitterati wine and dine, in *Corrida aux Champs-
Elysées*. Malet also writes of the sirens tested at noon on Thursdays
(*Enquêtes*, 2: 915), and complains when trashcans are not used, "Il y a
des gens comme ça, à Paris, qui ignorent l'existence des poubelles"
(*Enquêtes*, 2: 915) though Burma appreciates the presence of
"mégots" at a crime scene. In *Pas de bavards à la Muette*, Burma
notices

> une demi-douzaine de bouts de cibiches, de longeurs variables, jetés là
> depuis . . . Vraiment d'une importance capitale, n'est-ce pas? Sherlock
> Holmes aurait su le dire, depuis quand ils gisaient là, ainsi que l'âge
> respectif des fumeurs. Je n'étais pas Sherlock Holmes et tout ça, c'était
> peigner la girafe. (*Enquêtes*, 2: 152)

While he lacks the skills of Holmes, Burma is capable of discerning
whether the smoke is stale or fresh, an indication of how long ago the
perpetrators were at the scene. Though he wants his city to be as clean

as possible, if it is too clean, no clues are left behind, making his assignments more difficult.[182]

Malet presents a gritty picture of postwar Paris, sprinkled with some of the more pleasant moments from daily life. Albert Simonin notes, "[Malet], ce qu'il aime à la vérité, c'est le côté extrêmement humain de la capitale; il aime ses personnages, il aime aussi les quartiers et il veut les faire vivre."[183] Malet goes beneath the touristic façade to portray the everyday side of 1950s Paris as he saw it. He crafts each *arrondissement* as if it were a character that he seeks to "faire vivre." Simonin is so impressed by Malet's efforts that he continues, "J'ai l'impression que les historiens de mœurs dans un siècle voulant avoir une idée précise de ce qu'étaient ces quartiers de Paris . . . pourront et devront se référer . . . aux livres de Léo Malet." [184] In the interest of fiction, some of Malet's details are fabricated, but the atmosphere he renders is both vivid and accurate. Having learned much about Paris from his *flânerie*, he declares, "j'aime ça, moi, baguenauder dans Paris" (*Enquêtes*, 1: 1015). When his familiar city changes in the path of renovation, Burma is as unfamiliar with Paris as the tourists he complains about.

Paris Under Renovation

Malet began his *Nouveaux Mystères* series in 1954 in the first *arrondissement* with *Le soleil naît derrière le Louvre*. Though the subsequent two novels are situated in the second and third *arrondissements*, the series does not follow a chronological pattern for long, following instead an order of the districts with which the author was most familiar. Toward the end of the 1950s, however, Malet's familiarity with Paris was beginning to wane, as the postwar process of modernization and renovation was already underway. In his autobiography, *La vache enragée*, Malet writes:

---

[182] Rivière maintains that it is Malet's description of the sullied capital that make the series memorable: "Devenu par hasard auteur de romans policiers, c'est dans la description souvent hallucinée des ruelles ténébreuses, des passages malodorants et des cités en cul-de-sac qu'il s'approprie enfin en 'service commandée' que le poète de *J'arbre comme cadavre* nourrit sa fiction" (Rivière, *Noir Jeu* 62).

[183] Albert Simonin, "Conseils aux futurs historiens de moeurs," *Les Cahiers du Silence: Léo Malet*, Ed. Daniel Mallerin, (Paris: Kesselring, 1974) 105.

[184] Simonin 105.

> Je connais bien Paris, mais enfin, comme je n'avais pas mis les pieds dans
> certains endroits depuis dix ou quinze ans, j'allais m'imprégner de
> l'atmosphère du quartier, de son architecture. Le Paris de 1954 était encore
> celui de 1925. Mais qui aurait pu prévoir qu'il se transformerait aussi
> rapidement, à partir de 1960?[185]

The "unusual swiftness of French postwar modernization"[186] surprised
many residents who found themselves displaced as dilapidated houses
were torn down. Ross compares this process to the Hausmannian
projects of the nineteenth century, calling it the "second wave of
expulsions."[187] She writes:

> Modernity and hygiene served as pretext for the demolition of entire
> *quartiers*: Montparnasse, Italie, Belleville, Bercy . . . Under the second
> wave of expulsions, between 1954 and 1974, Paris proper lost 19 percent of
> its population – about 550,000 people, or approximately the population of
> Lyon . . . were dispersed to the outlying suburbs.[188]

Malet himself was one of the thousands "dispersed" to newly
constructed suburban HLMs. As industry moved away from
intramural Paris, the working class followed, unable to pay their
increased rent. In turn, renovated houses and apartments were rented
by the new middle class of *jeunes cadres*. This recently formed class
also purchased *hôtels particuliers*, inexpensive because of their
disrepair. In *Les Rats de Montsouris*, Malet, speaking through an
article written by Covet that Burma is reading, laments the situation:

> Le journaliste se permettait une digression sur la crise du logement,
> exposant qu'il existait des quantités de maisons [en ruine], dans Paris, où les
> citoyens les plus honorables ne sont pas en règle, parce qu'ils ont
> emménagé dans les lieux cédés par des amis lesquels jouissaient déjà de ces
> lieux par la grâce du locataire au nom duquel les quittances continuent à être
> établies. (*Enquêtes*, 1: 908)

The *jeunes cadres* of industrial middle-management purchased *hôtels
particuliers*, only to let them fall further into ruin by not maintaining
the buildings. In *Fièvre au Marais* Burma finds himself sandwiched

---

[185] Malet, *Vache* 208.
[186] Ross 4.
[187] Ross 151.
[188] Ross 151.

between two such *hôtels*; one, the Hôtel Salé, is well maintained,[189] but the other is not so well maintained, having "souffert des ans et des ânes, je veux dire des homes" (*Enquêtes*, 1: 676). Burma sees the negligent behavior of the "ânes" as a criminal activity. A building is demolished, along with its memories, and eventually forgotten, unless a plaque is erected in its place. Burma comments on the abundance of plaques in Paris which give a cold, cemetery quality to places such as the Palais-Royal. In *Le soleil naît derrière le Louvre*, he ponders "ce qu'ils y trouvent de séduisant, les gens, à ce coin," incredulous that a writer such as Cocteau or Colette could be inspired to anything artistic while living there, as "même les souvenirs qu'on peut évoquer, là-dedans, . . . ne sont pas bien gais" (*Enquêtes*, 1: 506). For Burma, the daily violence that he sees on the streets of Paris pales in comparison to the "souvenirs sanglants, voluptueux et sordides" (*Enquêtes*, 1: 506) of the French monarchy. In his series, however, prominent historical dates are not as significant as the smaller, everyday stories of ordinary people.

Renovation "as Manuel Castells defines it, and as Christiane Rochefort and others lived it, is always aggressive."[190] Burma speaks of the aggressive "urbanistes" as if they were a new army invading the recently liberated Paris. In *Du rébecca rue des Rosiers*, Burma stops in front of the demolition site of a boarded-up house in the Marais, "le spectacle d'un chantier de démolition. La maison aveugle doit faire partie d'un îlot voué au pic des urbanistes" (*Enquêtes*, 2: 860). He assumes that the house is slated for demolition for being part of an "îlot insalubre," which Ross describes as:

> densely populated city blocks that had received their name in the 1930s by virtue of their high tuberculosis mortality rate. In 1954, the *îlots* were still largely intact; more than 100,000 people lived in them, but tuberculosis was no longer a problem. This did not, however, prevent the use of hygiene and sanitation by developers and promoters as the major justification for launching urban renewal operations.[191]

Opponents of renovation saw the demolition of the *îlots* as an excuse to push the poor and working classes out of the city and into the

---

[189] In Malet's novel, the Hôtel Salé "abrite aujourd'hui je ne sais plus quelle école technique" (*Enquêtes*, 1: 676) but now serves as the Musée Picasso.
[190] Ross 153.
[191] Ross 154.

suburbs, which lead to further racial tensions at the end of the century as immigrant clusters formed in the surrounding *banlieues*. As Ross further explains, the same justification of "hygiene and sanitation" is given for the removal of Les Halles from the center of Paris, in order to protect the city from the "armies of rats" and other filth lurking beneath the surface.[192] In *Casse-pipe à la Nation*, while in the twelfth *arrondissement*, near the Bois de Vincennes, Burma wonders how far this renovation will go:

> J'ignore si c'est la proximité du Bois de Vincennes qui veut ça, mais c'est certainement l'arrondissement de Paris où il y a le plus d'arbres. Et des beaux. Pourvu que ça dure. Avec leur urbanisme et leurs problèmes de circulation, *ils* sont bien capables d'abattre tout ça, un de ces quatre. (*Enquêtes*, 2: 606)

With the italicization of "ils" and the repetition of "leurs," Burma compares the urbanists to looting Nazis. Instead of seeing any possible benefits of modernization, he envisions new France as a concrete slab.[193]

In *Boulevard . . . Ossements*, Burma says, "[Il] n'y a que Paris qui m'inspire" (*Enquêtes*, 2: 532), but, in the face of unfamiliar surroundings, Malet leaves his series unfinished. When asked in an interview about the new neighborhoods of Paris, including La Défense, considered by many as the twenty-first *arrondissement*, Malet responds, "Je ne vois pas ce qui peut arriver dans ces endroits-là."[194] The fast pace of modernized life and space-age concerns are no longer compatible with Malet's *flâneur*. The vision of 1950s France, as seen by Jules Romains, was of

> a country with the same fever; a country that would self-inject enthusiasm as its daily drug; that would envisage its future not with optimism . . . but with a profound necessity . . . A whole nation where the joy of working

---

[192] Thanks to the renovation which eventually led to the construction of the underground shopping district known as Le Forum des Halles, the "armies of rats" feared by the government have given way to "mallrats."

[193] Lacassin also laments the concretization of Paris: "Mais, avant la destruction du XIIIe arrondissement par le cancer du ciment-armé propagé par les prophètes de l'urbanisme concentrationnaire, *Brouillard au pont de Tolbiac* – au moment où Malet l'écrivait, en 1956 – était déjà un voyage au 'paradis des mémoires rétros'" (Lacassin, *Masque* 76).

[194] Jean-Paul Morel, "Le retour de Nestor Burma," *Le Matin* 14-15 July 1979: 21

together at a great common project would replace the bitter pleasures of discord.[195]

Romains's sentiment was not shared by all of France's citizens, including Malet. "Working together at a great common [government dictated] project" did not comply with Malet's anarchist foundation. Rather than adapt his series to reflect the new Paris, he abandons the project.

In his series *Les nouveaux mystères de Paris*, Malet depicts "le Paris gouailleur, le Paris canaille, le Paris tendresse."[196] His portrait is neither completely dark, nor completely cheerful.[197] Malet celebrates what France should be proud of while at the same time lamenting the new direction after the war in the face of "une urbanisation galopante."[198] Like the supporting characters of Covet, Faroux, and Hélène, the city of Paris is a constant presence in the series. Unlike his detective fiction contemporaries, whose mysteries could easily be transplanted into another urbanized zone, Malet's series could only take place in Paris. In the novels prior to the *Nouveaux Mystères*, Malet's Burma ventures into the unoccupied zone of southern France,[199] but only as an interlude, always returning to Paris and to his office in the second *arrondissement*. Le Bris sees Malet as "à la fois le contemporain de Chase et le dernier rejeton de la grande famille des feuilletonistes populaires anarchos et rebelles."[200] While his style was innovative for its time, his tone was becoming *démodé* with each successive publication. Le Bris adds, "c'est probablement son malheur d'avoir été ainsi à la fois en retard d'une

---

[195] Ross 23.

[196] Jean-Claude Lamy, "Léo Malet, chroniqueur du pavé parisien," *Le Figaro* 08 Mar. 1996: 16.

[197] Sheringham writes of Paris and the "connection between urban experience and individual self-discovery or attunement to the sprit of the age" in the works of surrealists (including Breton), Benjamin, and Réda. (Michael Sheringham, "City Space, Mental Space, Poetic Space: Paris in Breton, Benjamin, and Réda," *Parisian Fields*, Ed. Michael Sheringham (London: Reaktion, 1999) 87.)

[198] Lamy 16.

[199] *Le cinquième procédé* (1948), the sixth Burma mystery, takes place mostly in Marseille, exceptional to the other early novels, which have Burma finding new ways to acquire passes to cross the demarcation line.

[200] Le Bris 80.

époque et en avance d'une autre," but concludes, "il faut lire Léo Malet."[201]

---

[201] Le Bris 80.

Chapter Six

The Apparent Heirs

By 1959, Léo Malet had completed fifteen of the intended twenty *Nouveaux Mystères de Paris*, but lost interest in the project as the city around him started to dramatically change. He and his wife Paulette relocated their apartment to an HLM in Châtillon-sous-Bagneux, a suburb south of Paris, coinciding with an immigration surge in the *métropole* resulting from the decolonization of French territories. Changing his home and neighborhood, while witnessing a nationwide postwar renovation, led to Malet's writer's block beginning in the early 1960s and, with the exception of the occasional magazine short story, lasting until his death in 1996.

Meanwhile, the genre that he helped to develop in France continued to evolve and splinter. By 1966, the year of Tzvetan Todorov's *Poétique de la prose*, not only had the *roman policier* split into subgenres such as *noir* and *espionnage*, but the *roman noir* was finding its own voice as well. Malet's innovations of using the familiar location of Paris, introducing an antiheroic French detective, and mixing slang with literary form were taken even further by the writers Jean Amila, Jean-Patrick Manchette, and Didier Daeninckx. Each took the *roman noir* outside the *peripherique*, and all but abandoned the need for a detective. Amila, a contemporary of Malet, came to prominence in the genre with his involvement in Gallimard's *Série Noire*, a series concurrent with *Les Nouveaux Mystères de Paris*. As Malet had an agreement with the publisher Robert Laffont, he did not participate in the Gallimard series. Amila and Malet share a number of characteristics, including an anarchist background. Manchette, who helped to develop the *néo-polar* of the 1970s, experiments with narrative structure, bringing elements of *la série blanche* to the *roman noir*, in the tradition of Malet's use of surrealist imagery. In *Meutres pour mémoire*, Daeninckx establishes a historical *roman noir*, evoking Malet's streets in his scenes set in 1960, and goes beyond the politics of Amila and Manchette to bring political activism to the genre.

This chapter will examine Malet's legacy and the progression of the French *roman noir* as evidenced in Jean Amila's *La Lune d'Omaha*, Jean-Patrick Manchette's *Le Petit bleu de la côte ouest*, and Didier Daeninckx's *Meutres pour mémoire*.

Jean Amila, *La lune d'Omaha*

Jean Amila, under his patronym of Jean Meckert, had originally started his literary career in the anti-establishment, maverick style of Céline. Bored with his work as a *fonctionnaire*, Meckert was inspired to write *Les Coups* in 1942, based on his experiences at home which had led to a life of anarchism. Despite the support of his editor and such writers as Gide and Martin du Gard, he had little following. In his forties, Meckert, recruited by Marcel Duhamel, turned to the more profitable Série Noire and, like other French writers choosing the American style of hardboiled fiction, chose the American-sounding name John Amila, publishing *Y a pas de Bon Dieu!* in 1950. But before long, he was publishing as Jean Amila, a compromise of his own name and "Amilanar", a hybrid of "Ami l'anar", which Duhamel had deemed too long. Before his death in 1995, Amila had written around 20 novels for the Série, including *La lune d'Omaha* in 1964, *Le boucher des Hurlus* in 1982, and *Au balcon d'Hiroshima* in 1985. Like Léo Malet, Amila achieved "le mariage d'une littérature populiste à la française et du roman noir à l'américaine des Hammett ou des Cain."[202] Unlike Malet, Amila remained an anarchist for most of his life, and his distrust of authority and institutions such as the military, church, family, and State are found in his novels.

Born in 1910, one year after Malet, Amila "avait, très tôt, trouvé quelques motifs de nourrir sa révolte."[203] In 1917, his father was shot "pour l'exemple, lors des grandes mutineries qui secouèrent l'armée française,"[204] leading his mother to spend the next two years in a mental hospital. He began to work in a factory at the age of

---

[202] Bertrand Audusse, "Jean Amila: un écrivain réfractaire," *Le Monde* 11 Mar 1995. N. pag.

[203] Audusse, *Amila*.

[204] Audusse, *Amila*.

thirteen[205], and, like Malet, held a series of odd jobs before officially becoming a writer, after first taking a desk job as a *fonctionnaire* so he could learn to use a typewriter. He wrote his first novel, *Les Coups*, while an "interné militaire" in Switzerland for nine months.

Despite their similar childhoods and mutual embrace of anarchism in their teens, Amila and Malet's life experiences do not color their writings in the same way in terms of style. Unlike Malet, who disappeared from the French literary scene in the 1960s due to a depressive writer's block, Amila's eight-year absence from publishing was due to an attack he suffered in 1973 in Tahiti, provoked by his anticolonialist writings,[206] which left him in a coma for twelve hours, unable to write again until 1981, and amnesiac and epileptic for the rest of his life. "Il m'a fallu tout réapprendre," he told Jean-Paul Morel, "jusqu'au sens des mots."[207]

  Amila was not interested in writing a *noir* series with a recurring character, such as Nestor Burma, or even a detective. He preferred to use his fiction as a political platform, with themes such as "l'humiliation et la violence, l'antagonisme des sexes – dont les difficultés du couple – l'anti-intellectualisme et l'anti-hypocrisie, le rêve et l'évasion opposés aux contraintes de la civilization."[208] The dream sequences in Amila's fiction may lack the surrealist imagery of Nestor Burma's dreams, but Amila shares Malet's compulsion to shake the status quo of a formulaic genre. Amila's *La lune d'Omaha*, an installment of Duhamel's *Série Noire*, turns the *policier* formula on its head. Where the classic *policier* has a murder in the first chapter that the rest of the novel tries to solve, and the *roman noir* has a

---

[205] "A treize ans, j'ai eu mon certif et on m'a tout de suite foutu en usine. C'est ça les milieux populaires" (Jean-Paul Morel, "Amila l'anar de la Série Noire," *Le Matin* 26-27 Oct. 1985: 25).

[206] Commissioned to write an "anti-James Bond" screenplay for André Cayatte, Amila went to Tahiti to write what would become *La vierge et le taureau*. While writing, however, "j'ai vu là-bas des choses qui ne m'ont pas du tout plu: des Polynésiens traits comme des esclaves, entre les mains de militaires et de fonctionnaires. Quand [Sven Nielsen of Presses de la Cité] a vu ce que je lui ramenais, il a plutôt fait la gueule, Cayatte aussi d'ailleurs. Mais le livre est sorti. ... Et puis un jour, [three years after publication] j'ai reçu un coup de telephone, naturellement anonyme: «On va te foutre la gueule au carré.» J'ai trouvé l'expression marrante, mais c'est ce qui m'est arrive: un soir que je rentrais chez moi, deux hommes m'attendaient, et je me suis reveille à la Salpé après douze ou quinze heures de coma" (Morel, *Amila* 25).

[207] Morel, *Amila* 25.

[208] Michel Lebrun, *Almanach du crime, 1982*, (Paris: Veyrier?, 1981) 36.

murder in the first chapter which leads to more murders in the subsequent chapters, Amila's *Lune* saves the murder until the final scenes, though a death by natural causes in Chapter Three leads to a series of revelations. Because it is a Série Noire, however, the reader waits for the murder in every chapter, and stays with the narrative until the end to see the expectation met.

Amila also has the innovation of bringing the American style to the French *roman noir* by setting the novel at the American cemetery in Normandy twenty years after D-Day, and focusing on a handful of Americans who now live in France. Rather than write as an American under pseudonym, as in *Y a pas de Bon Dieu!*, Amila writes of an American, George Hutchins, deserting the U.S. Army by pretending to be French after taking on the identity of a Frenchman who died on the day of the invasion. Also struggling to adapt to French society is Steve Reilly, caretaker of the American cemetery, whose much younger French wife, Claudine, leaves him early in the novel. *Lune* evokes similar themes as Malet's *Nouveaux mystères*, such as French identity and reconstruction in the postwar era, but by setting the novel in Normandy rather than in Paris, Amila gives the genre a provincial perspective that will also be used by both Manchette and Daeninckx.

Léo Malet peppered his text with slang in an effort to make his detective, Nestor Burma, a man of the street, a detective not afraid to get his hands dirty. Instead of slang, the Americanized French of Steve Reilly in *La lune d'Omaha* is written phonetically, rendering him alien to the France around him. This is not the case when he is "speaking English" to his fellow soldiers on an American boat on its way to the Normandy coast for the D-Day invasion – represented as grammatically correct French in Amila's text – but when Reilly first speaks outside of his interior monologue, it is clear that he still speaks French incorrectly after more than twelve years of living in France.

> Il dit, dans son français élémentaire à fort accent de plouc des collines du Kansas:
> -- J'espère il se porte mieux demain.
> -- Faut pas trop y compter, dit Tronelle.
> -- Très dommage, dit Reilly avec gravité. Peut-être le "monmontannement" remplacère?
> -- Ce serait raisonnable, approuva Tronelle.[209]

---

[209] Jean Amila, *La lune d'Omaha* (Paris: Gallimard, 1964. 2003.) 34.

The use of the word "approuva" suggests that Reilly makes an effort, much like a child or a student, and seeks the approval of those around him, even when he is their supervisor. This dynamic undermines his authority and colors his relationships at both work and home. Reilly says "pâ'ler" (Amila 35) instead of *parler*, and his insecurities about his language ability, as well as the departure of Claudine, contribute to his general impression that everyone is making fun of him (Amila 62). In an argument with "Claodine," who does not want to raise a family in a *nécropole*, he cries, "Pas peurmise blaguère les maorts et dire je souis paôv type! Pas peurmise!" (Amila 42) George Hutchins, however, has achieved a near-native French accent in order to assume the identity of a deceased French soldier and assimilate into French culture as Georges Delouis. In conversations with his French wife Janine, there is no trace of "Americanisms." But when he reveals his true self to Fernand Amedée, son of the recently deceased man who had sold George his new identity, to be "Djôdj Ray Hutchins, Niou Djeuzé" (Amila 120), meaning, "George Ray Hutchins, New Jersey," his American accent is displayed phonetically as almost incomprehensible, though the reader has been exposed to the name "Hutchins" since the first chapter. Later, when he makes the same revelation to Captain Mason and his wife, Norah, he speaks in italicized English, "*My name is George Ray Hutchins*" (Amila 189), which startles Norah, not expecting to hear an American accent. Like in Malet's text, Amila's phonetic rendering of non-native or incorrect French is almost always pejorative, to alienate the reader from identifying with the character. Where a French accent in an anglophone novel or film can be seductive, in French that is hardly the case.

The language barrier leads to comic relief when George and Janine, staying at Reilly's house on the cemetery grounds, scheme to blackmail Fernand Amedée, in an attempt to recover some of Janine's money paid to the père Amedée over the years to keep the secret of George's true identity:

> [George] -- Depuis seize ans qu'on arrose le père Delouis, [Janine] a tout donné ce qu'elle avait! Tout!
> -- Comprends arrose, fit Steve. Comprends vieux saligaud demande argent pour fermer son guiole?

> -- Des millions! dit Georges avec fureur. Et nous assez cons pour cracher comme des broques!
> -- ... branques! rectifia Janine. Mais c'est fini, mon grand, n'en parlons plus!
> -- Des millions? s'exclama Reilly. Vous verse des millions à ce vieux saligaud? Je voudrais ressuscitation des morts pour lui mettre mon pied la fesse!
> -- Pour ça, dit Georges, ressuscité, il l'est bien! Toute la famille dans le même sac!
> -- Fils Isigny prend aussi vous pour des braques?
> -- Branques! rectifia inlassablement la petite femme. (Amila 163)

Along with the misappropriation of the words *broques-braques-branques*, Reilly's stilted, grammatically incorrect speech makes him sound like a child, or a mentally retarded man, when that is not the case. Though the words are phonetically very close, "branques" is slang for "un homme incensé ou fou; se dit quelque chose de stupide", while "broques", a derivitive of "brocante," can be slang for both "centime" and "pénis", and "braques" is a type of hunting dog, though it can also mean "un peu fou". Amila's sense of humor is characteristic of the *roman noir* style, also including an inside joke in the community around Omaha Beach: that the locals often pronounce Omaha as "Omeuheuuu!"(Amila 62) because hundreds of cows were buried in the mass grave at the cemetery as well as soldiers. The extended phonetic rendering by the local *curé* startles Reilly, and sets off his temper. As defensive as he is of his own shortcomings, he knows first-hand that the mass grave includes thousands of his friends and countrymen who he could have easily joined twenty years earlier.

The exchange is also indicative of Amila's distrust of church officials. The local *curé* delights in taunting Reilly, who had submitted to a "conversion-express" (Amila 53) in order to marry his French (Catholic) wife four years earlier. Reilly gives the *curé* a ride on his way to pay his respects to père Amedée, who had called out to him on his deathbed, though Reilly did not arrive in time. Since he does not attend church regularly, yet another way, in addition to language, that Reilly alienates himself from his wife's community, he is at a loss as to what to say to the *curé* while in the car.

> Il ne savait pas quoi dire au curé. C'était un homme aux cheveux blancs, trapu, pas très propre, mais au regard candide et franchement bon, devant qui il avait toujours éprouvé la vague répulsion qu'on réserve aux crapauds... (Amila 54-55)

The reader, however, mistrusts the *curé* almost immediately, primarily because he tells Reilly, who has just said "Je reuspecte les maorts," that he has made "des progrès immenses! On voit que vous avez épousé une Française! Vous vous exprimez presque sans accent!"(Amila 56) The pleasantries of conversation do not last long, however, and soon the *curé* is pressing Reilly's buttons with stories of how the Americans Army "se foutait ben des morts" (Amila 58) using a bulldozer to clean up the bodies after the D-Day invasion. But before allowing Reilly to respond to this accusation, the *curé* changes the subject, and asks Reilly to forgive Amedée for whatever transgressions led him to call for the American from his deathbed, since Amedée did not confess before dying, "et le bon Dieu n'a pas pu lui pardonner, pour les grosses saloperies qu'il a faites" (Amila 59). Reilly is reluctant at first, since he does not know what these transgressions might be, but the *curé* is convinced that they are related to the activities of the post-invasion cleanup, which included burying livestock with humans. We later piece together that Amedée had probably wanted to confess his blackmailing of George and Janine. Instead of forgiving Amedée, or the *curé*, however, Reilly lashes out. Though he had known about the bulldozers, he had not known about the livestock:

> Mais le coup des vaches, il ne l'avait jamais soupçonné. Et, parce qu'il éprouvait du ressentiment pour Claudine, ce matin-là il trouva cela aussi normand, aussi français, aussi dégoûtant que le croissant trempé dans du café au lait. Il eut un raclement de gorge écoeuré et balaya d'un geste de main...
> -- Beuah!
> -- Vous pardonnez, n'est-ce pas? Sergent Reilly, priez avec moi pour une âme qui se débat aux portes d'Enfer.
> -- Pas envie prière, envie foutre pied au cul saligaud, tant mieux qu'il est crévé!
> Le curé leva le doigt:
> -- ...Comme je pardonne à ceux qui m'ont offensé! N'oubliez pas, mon fils. La loi divine! Ce n'est pas nous de juger les hommes.
> -- Je juge pas, je pâdonne pas! Cria Reilly en violaçant. Bien meilleur que soldats am'ricains mélangés de vaches, ploutôt mélangés personnes déguélasses! (Amila 61-62)

In refusing to forgive Amedée for his sins, Reilly rejects the Catholic convention, and to some extent, French culture. He returns to the cemetery, very upset, and confronts his supervisor, Captain Mason, who does not deny the potential existence of a "contaminated" gravesite, but refers to the *curé* as a "farceur" who cannot be trusted. One institution questions the authority of the other, and vice versa. Whose version of events should be trusted? Or should either be trusted?

The institution of marriage and family is challenged in the relationship of George and Janine, whose relationship unravels when George chooses to come clean about his past, after seeing the white cross at the cemetery with his name, rank, and hometown carved into the stone. However, the potential social consequence of any revelations of their wartime activities is more than Janine is willing to bear. Though she knew he was a deserter, Janine married George with the condition that he keep his true identity hidden. Complicit in his assimilation to French language and culture, she had used her own money to pay Amedée's blackmail in order to keep the secret. She begs George not to admit to anything in front of his former peers, but he ignores her. When George finds solace in revealing his true self, she cannot cope with the change in her husband, nor the change in how others might perceive her, and kills him on the same moonlit beach where he had arrived with his compatriots, not because he was frolicking in the water with a topless Claudine, but because, as she tells Captain Mason, "il allait me quitter" (Amila 230). Janine could perhaps live with the shame of having her husband leave her for another woman, but not the shame of having everyone know of her collaboration in his plan to assume the identity of a man who should have been mourned, and to have their children think of their father as the *déserteur* that he was. She does not cry when she is next to his naked corpse on the beach, having already formed the lie that she will tell their children, but cries when she finds his clothes on the shore. The man is not as important as the illusion. Even Mason does not understand why George would turn himself in when his lie is working so well.

> -- Besoin de me faire une opinion, dit Mason. Vos papiers sont au nom de Delouis?
> -- Georges Delouis, né à Saint-Lô.
> -- Vous êtes mariés civilement sous ce nom, et vous avez trois enfants?
> -- Exact.
> -- Vous vous conduisez honorablement, vous avez du travail et bonne réputation?

> -- Oui.
> Mason engloutit d'un coup le contenu de sa petite moque, fit claquer sa langue.
> -- Alors, mon vieux, qu'est-ce que vous désirez de mieux? Les États-Unis ne sont pas à court des citoyens.
> -- Je m'appelle Hutchins, New Jersey, s'obstina l'ex-P.V.T. (Amila 190-91)

George, however, dismisses his wife's concerns and Mason's suspicions, and is relieved to be free of the burden of carrying the secret of his identity for another twenty years. "Je suis moi. Je veux être moi. Je suis déguisé depuis vingt ans. J'en ai assez! J'ai déserté, qu'on me punisse! Mais j'ai le droit d'être moi, même au fond d'une cellule" (Amila 190). In revealing himself to Mason who, as *gardien de cimetière*, represents authority in the novel though he is not officially Military Police, George selfishly takes charge of his destiny, with little thought to the implications for those around him, including Janine, his children, and even Reilly, who had also recently learned of his secret. George and Janine's marriage does not recover from this incident. In the remainder of the novel, Janine becomes increasingly distant to her husband, her face described as "diaphane et osseux" (Amila 210) like a "cadavre." The lie that she lived with her husband has ended, and as George re-reinvents himself to return to his American identity, Janine reinvents herself in the final chapter as a woman who resorts to murder.

The institution of marriage is further challenged in the case of Reilly and Claudine, where the implications of marrying someone twenty years younger means that Claudine was a mere child during the war. She cannot appreciate her husband's struggle, except through stories passed down to her.

> Il m'a eue avec ça quand j'avais dix-sept ans... Le débarquement, les hommes de sa patrouille, le premier Américain à percer les lignes... Les citations, les coupures de journaux, la photo où Eisenhower lui serre la main... C'est flatteur pour une gosse, vous comprenez. Mais maintenant je suis majeure, je vois les choses autrement. Je vois seulement que je suis la femme d'un sergent de carrière, enfermée dans un cimetière, avec un bonhomme qui est trop bête pour passer seulement adjudant, depuis vingt ans! (Amila 154-55)

She has no war memories of her own, but has reached an age of wanting to question for herself. The American that she has chosen is not a "great liberator," but rather keeps her confined to a cemetery, where she can hardly imagine starting a family, though that is still preferable to going back to Reilly's home in Topeka, Kansas. She tells George of "des gros ploucs"(Amila 213) there who do not know how to eat, drink, or have fun. As much as Paris may look down on *la province*, Norman culture is still superior to that of Kansas. In taking refuge from Reilly at her mother's flower shop, Claudine cannot completely escape the culture of death, as she must still contend with funereal arrangements, some of which go to the American cemetery. Norah Mason, the American wife of Captain Mason, suggests that perhaps having a baby would help her marriage, if Reilly could transition from the role of "war hero" to that of father. Claudine dismisses the idea, at the risk of becoming "une mitrailleuse... Pan, pan pan! Un petit Américain tous les ans!" (Amila 155) Claudine espouses a controversial view of family: that she does not seem to want children, even if it is what is expected of her. Despite the reconstruction and recovery around her, Claudine holds on to a romantic notion of love, and does not want to be tied down to her husband by starting a family. When Norah tells Claudine that she must accept the fact that she has married her husband as well as his career, Claudine replies, "j'aimerais savoir si Steve est marié avec ses morts ou avec moi?" (Amila 157) Soon after returning to Steve, Claudine throws herself at the first man she can, George, who then dies on the beach. Though it is not clear what becomes of the Reilly household, it is already better than what would have been her fate in a Malet novel. She is neither *femme fatale* nor *femme victime*:

> Rejetant tout idyllisme, tout manichéisme, Amila fait de ses personnages des êtres de chair et de sang, qu'ils soient masculins ou féminins. Il ne pose pas la femme sur un piédestal; il ne la craint pas non plus, comme le bon misogyne classique. Il la fait évoluer dans ses romans, comme évolue l'homme. Toutes ses femmes sont décrites sans complaisance, mais avec le même respect qu'il accorde aux personnages masculins.[210]

Lebrun's assessment is certainly true of Claudine, but not necessarily of Janine, who does eventually kill her husband. But the role of woman in the *roman noir* evolves from Hélène's sidekick to a complex portrait of women struggling to find their place in then-contemporary France.

---

[210] Lebrun, *Almanach* 141.

Amila sets *La lune d'Omaha* in 1964, the same year as its publication, twenty years after the D-Day invasion of Normandy, and five years after what would be Malet's final *Nouveaux Mystères*. In this region, the modernization of postwar France, illustrated by Kristin Ross, is a welcome effort, cleaning up after the annihilation of the war. Amila does not see the reconstruction as a cultural threat, as did Malet, but rather as a way to make life more comfortable.

> Isigny avait été entièrement détruit. Ça donnait l'immense avantage, dix-neuf ans plus tard, d'habiter une petite ville aux maisons neuves et confortables. Et finalement, pour les Normands, la guerre resterait moins le souvenir d'un massacre que l'avènement du bidet, de l'eau chaude sur l'évier et de la cuvette à chasse d'eau. (Amila 105)

While convenience and hygiene help to erase the pain of war and destruction, there can be no gratitude for the arrival of such progress, nor is there nostalgia for prewar Normandy. While the Americans see themselves as having liberated France from the Nazi occupation, those who survived the crossfire wonder if liberation could have been more on target. When Hutchins the deserter takes refuge on a Norman farm,

> ... ils me regardaient comme une sale bête. La bonne femme m'a montré la pièce où ils avaient leurs morts. Elle m'a demandé si c'était nécessaire de tuer les civils. Elle m'a dit que toutes les villes de Normandie étaient anéanties... On entendait que ça cognait vers la côte. Elle m'a dit que l'armée américaine en bavait peut-être, mais que ça lui apprendrait à faire la guerre. Parce que, ce qu'ils avaient fait là, massacrer les civils, c'était pas la guerre. (Amila 205)

The reaction that George receives is typical: while the French were appreciative of the Allied efforts, they would have preferred less destruction of their population and resources. Amila uses the popular forum of the *roman noir* to make a political statement that others of his generation might have been hesitant to make at the risk of sounding ungrateful to the Americans. While this position is, at times, different from that of Malet, who used his novels to promote cultural nostalgia and France's literary heritage, the forum of using popular genre fiction to expose the reading public to something they might not have seen otherwise is not so different.

Though Amila's *roman noir* differs wildly from Malet's Nestor Burma series, the intent is the same: to use the format of popular fiction to espouse radical, or non-traditional arguments.

Where Malet introduced surrealist imagery and a nostalgia for France's literary legacy, Amila challenges cultural institutions such as the family, the church, and the military. Even if his example in *La lune d'Omaha* is of the American military, the struggles of career officers in the aftermath of war and reconstruction are still relevant to the French experience. Though he eschews the traditional format of the *roman noir*, by saving the murder for the final chapter, Amila takes Malet's innovation of setting the American-style mystery in France one step further, before handing the baton to the next generation of writers, the *néo-noir*. Stylistically, Amila's distrust of authority and institutions greatly influence the work of Jean-Patrick Manchette, who also avoids the detective's presence in his *roman noir*.

Jean-Patrick Manchette, *Le petit bleu de la côte ouest*

Despite the efforts of Amila and writers such as Pierre Siniac and Francis Ryck, the *roman noir* in France in the 1960s remained stagnant, recycling the old clichés of the American hardboiled style, including the iconic detective and the *femme fatale*. Further progression of the genre did not occur until a new generation of writers, who had grown up reading both Malet and Amila, and were influenced by concurrent movements in literature and politics culminating with the events in Paris of May and June 1968, forming a new style in the early 1970s known as *néo polar*. "Revendiquant Léo Malet comme leur précurseur," writes Lits, "de jeunes auteurs vont se rassembler derrière le plus doué d'entre eux, Jean-Patrick Manchette, sous l'étiquette du néo-polar."[211] The term is also used in reference to works by Jean-François Vilar, Frédéric Farjardie, and Thierry Jonquet, all writers who were left-wing activists and had been influenced by the Situationists. As the radicals of the late 1960s were rebelling against the conformism and repressive capitalist society of their parents, embodied in the advent of an "Americanized" consumer culture and rise of the upper-middle class[212], the *néo polar* used popular genre fiction to attack "the French State and the complacency

---

[211] Lits 63.

[212] Gorrara explains how the "advent of consumer culture was to revolutionize urban living in the 1960s," with previously unaffordable luxury items available on a large scale to a "new generation of middle-class professionals (*les cadres*)," creating both tension and anxiety for those trying to live better than their parents. (55)

of the dominant bourgeois order."[213] From this perspective, crimes are committed by the State against the individual as often as the individual commits crimes against society. Most of the individual crimes committed in this new style are by those consumed by their desire to conform to the new, materialistic, bourgeois ideal, who will do anything to achieve or maintain their social or economic status. The *néo polar* is characterized by its political stance as well as the disillusionment of its protagonists. The figure of the detective, without which Malet's series would be non-existent, is all but absent in the *néo polar*, which instead prefers characters which are

> ... far more implicated in the social and political reality of their times: terrorists, former left-wing militants, the unemployed, disaffected youth, and, at the extreme end of social alienation, the mentally disturbed. These characters are presented as both victims and perpetrators, often living in the suburbs or on large council estates and holding down dead-end jobs with little hope of change.[214]

In the *néo polar*, the criminal element is no longer mysterious, with motives to be revealed at the end of a novel, but is as prominent in the narrative as the victim. In Manchette's *Le petit bleu de la côte ouest*, the reader follows the story of the hitmen Carlo and Bastien, and their *patron* Alonso Emerich y Emerich, with as much interest as their target, Georges Gerfaut. With these new characters comes experimentation with narrative style and form, borrowing as much from *la série blanche* as from its *noir* predecessors.

Like Malet and Amila, Manchette did not set out to write *romans noirs*. Born in Marseille in 1942, Manchette seemed destined to be an English teacher. Without a diploma, however, he used his English skills to teach French in an English school for the blind, and to work as a freelance translator, mostly of American crime fiction. In 1967, he took up screenwriting, writing for both television and grade "Z" films for a few years before turning to the Série Noire in 1971. Manchette said:

> Je voulais faire du cinéma, je me suis mis à écrire parce que les producteurs ne lisaient pas mes scénarios. Et j'ai fait des traductions pour avoir le temps

---

[213] Gorrara 58.
[214] Gorrara 59.

d'écrire. Finalement, je suis meilleur traducteur que romancier et meilleur romancier que scénariste.[215]

After an initial novel, *Laisse bronzer les cadavres*, co-written with Jean-Pierre Bastid, Manchette went solo, publishing *L'Affaire N'Gustro* in the same year. In the *roman noir*, Manchette found the freedom to incorporate his politics, fueled by the events of May 1968, into the same genre that even his Scottish grandmother enjoyed reading.

> Ainsi, Manchette développe-t-il, juste après les évènements de 1968, la notion d'un roman policier ancré tout autant dans le genre que dans le temps et l'histoire, autrement dit ce «monde où les salopards et la Contre Révolution sont au pouvoir.» Un roman policier *nécessairement* politique, réaliste, critique et acerbe, humoristique par touches précises, dans une langue toujours effilée et solidement stylée.[216]

Despite his politicized style, Manchette takes extreme caution to keep his narration practically free of slang, resulting in a more "literary" *roman noir*. His prose is as influenced by Flaubert as by Hammett. Manchette, considered the *renovateur* of the French *roman noir* that Malet "fathered", wrote nine novels for the Série Noire before retiring in 1981, at the age of 40, when he began to suffer from agoraphobia. He continued to write occasional magazine articles, mostly crime fiction reviews for the journals *Charlie Mensuel* and *Polar*, until his death in 1995 from lung cancer at the age of 53, having already survived a bout of pancreatic cancer. Writing about Malet, Manchette claimed, "La ruse du roman noir était de porter la critique et la rébellion en plein milieu de la littérature la plus commerciale et la plus vulgaire."[217] Continuing this legacy in his own fiction, "Manchette stands out as a figure who united a radical social critique of contemporary France with a formidable reworking of *noir* style and form."[218]

In *Le petit bleu de la côte ouest* (1976), Manchette experiments with narrative structure. Where Amila had eschewed the typical *noir* structure in *La lune d'Omaha* of one murder leading to a series of other murders by having his murder in the final chapter,

---

[215] Gilbert Rochu, "Pour saluer Manchette," *Marianne* 1-7 May 2000: 67.

[216] Arnaud Viviant, "Manchette, morgue pleine," *Libération* 05 June 1995: 31.

[217] François Guérif, "Adieu à Manchette," *Le Monde* 16 June 1995: VIII.

[218] Gorrara 60.

Manchette prefers a circular narrative. In *Petit bleu*, the novel ends as it begins: Georges Gerfaut, under the influence of bourbon and barbituates, driving his car on the *périphérique*, destination unknown. Without an emphasis on a particular murder, Manchette is free to use his novel to advance his other agenda of social commentary.

> L'émotion va laisser ici la place à la denunciation d'une société jugée pourrie, mais l'énigme est peu présente car la peinture des moeurs, la description des classes bourgeoises sous leur jour le plus défavorable, des milieux marginaux et violents, prennent le dessus.[219]

By announcing that Georges Gerfaut "a tué au moins deux hommes au cours de l'année"[220] at the end of the first chapter, the reader questions whether Georges is a sympathetic narrator, and wonders if the two murders will lead to more death. As it turns out, they do, and while Georges is sympathetic though flawed, not all of Manchette's narrators can be trusted. After witnessing a car crash, Georges, a young *cadre* with a wife and two *fillettes*, takes the wounded driver to a local hospital, where he realizes that the man had been shot before crashing his car. But rather than tell the hospital, he abandons the body in the emergency room, gets back in his car, and continues driving. He then becomes the target of the driver's murderers, Carlo and Bastien, who follow Georges all over France to try, unsuccessfully, to kill him off. Abandoning his family while on vacation, Georges goes into hiding in the Alps to protect himself, but finds that he does not miss his comfortable, materialistic life as much as he might have thought. With the announcement that Georges has committed two murders, Manchette not only plays with the structure of a *noir*, but also attacks the novel's momentum. In the second chapter, the reader learns that Georges also killed Elizabeth, the bullmastiff of Alonso Emerich y Emerich (Manchette 18), well before reading the actual murder scene in chapter 23. As Georges and his wife Béa prepare for their summer vacation in Saint-Georges-de-Didonne, it is announced "Et le lendemain, on essaya de tuer Georges Gerfaut" (Manchette 40), implying, with the use of the verb "essayer," that the assasination attempt will be unsuccessful. Though the details are lacking, the reader knows what to expect, yet continues to the end

---

[219] Lits 63.
[220] Jean-Patrick Manchette, *Le petit bleu de la côte ouest*, (Paris: Gallimard, 1976) 8.

of the novel to see if the killers get away with their crimes. Georges does get away with the murders of Alonso and Carlo, which turn out to be self-defense, but Bastien dies a horrible death during a gas station fire, where he tries a second time, again unsuccessfully, to kill Georges. The roles of victim and perpetrator are interchangeable, and the justice system, especially the police, has little function in the novel.

Unlike Amila's *noir*, Manchette's novel includes multiple murders which propel the narrative forward, yet unlike Malet's *noir*, there is no detective to solve these crimes. Georges Gerfaut realizes that the two men who attack him on the beach are trying to kill him, as his wife reads her book, his children play in the sand, and crowds of other tourists are oblivious, but he has no idea why this is happening to him. Is it a random act of violence, or has he done something to provoke them? He must become his own detective, piecing together a puzzle of clues, a process which leads him on a Homeric journey of self-discovery away from his job, family, and jazz collection. The novel's title "is both a jazz ballad and an intimation of Georges's own twentieth century 'blues' as an individual alienated by the materialistic dreams of his age. It can also be contrasted to 'le grand bleu', an image of the sea and the expansive freedom that Georges lacks."[221] Though a successful *cadre*, Georges suffers from *ennui*, and is incapable of enjoying his success. When he tells Béa of the car accident he witnessed and the man he abandoned at the hospital, she is outraged.

> -- Tu es parti comme ça sans rien dire à personne? dit-elle. Tu n'as pas donné ton nom, tu ne connais pas celui du type? Tu n'as même pas dit où tu l'as trouvé, est-ce que tu te rends compte?
> -- Je ne sais pas, dit Gerfaut. D'un coup j'en ai eu marre, tout me faisait chier, c'est une impression que j'ai par moments. (Manchette 25-26)

Georges cannot be bothered to notify the authorities of his discovery, but also refuses to involve the police or even Béa after his attack on

---

[221] Gorrara 64. Noreiko adds: "The title is part of a texture of allusion of a kind that makes modern French *polar* – for all by the most primally naïve reader – not simply complex text to be pleasurably unravelled ... but a celebration of, and running commentary on, icons of contemporary culture" (Stephen Noreiko, "'Cigarettes, Whisky et petites pépées': Obscure Allusion and Conspicuous Consumption in a *Polar*," *French Studies Bulletin* 64 (Autumn 1997): 2.)

the beach. She notices the marks of attempted strangulation on his neck but, thinking them sun-related, does not pursue the issue. Georges keeps his attack to himself, and wanders out of the vacation house that evening in the hopes of running into the hitmen again, just to learn more about them.

> Gerfaut ne pouvait plus supporter l'impression qu'il avait. Il dit vers 20 h 25 qu'il allait acheter des cigarettes, il se trimbala à pied dans Saint-Georges, la nuit tombait, Gerfaut avait quasiment envie que les deux hommes réapparaissent et l'attaquent, ne serait-ce que pour mettre fin à son incertitude, il se retrouva sur le bord de mer. Un car passa qui allait à Royan, Gerfaut le prit. (Manchette 55-56)

When he was not attacked immediately outside of his door, Georges returns to his home in Paris, abandoning his family in their vacation rental, temporarily notifying them with telegrams of his whereabouts. Even after he goes on the run, following the explosion at a gas station where Bastien is killed, Georges does not reveal his identity to Raguse, a "dropahoute" (Manchette 114) living in the Alps, who heals Georges's wounds, saying instead that he had left his wife (Manchette 109). Finding an occasional article about his disappearance in a discarded newspaper, he never involves the police, though he knows that they are looking for him. When Gassowitz, who becomes George's accomplice to kill Alonso after Carlo's death, asks Georges why he had not gone to the police earlier, "Gerfaut lui répondit que c'était parce que c'est emmerdant" (Manchette 159). He does not believe that the police can help him, surprising given his affluent, bourgeois status, but not so surprising considering Manchette's disdain for institutions of authority. The only person in whom Georges will confide is his friend Liétard, the owner of a film and camera store in Paris, himself a survivor of police brutality at the Charonne métro station during a demonstration for Algerian independence.[222] After offering him sleeping pills, Liétard gives Georges an abandoned gun with a full clip, but with fifteen-year-old bullets. When Liétard reluctantly encourages him to call the police, Georges replies, "J'ai pas envie" (Manchette 59). Other than his visit with Liétard, he continues to keep his traumatic experience to himself, even after he is

---

[222] Such brutality during the Algerian war of independence will also be chronicled in Daeninckx's *Meutres pour mémoire*.

finally reunited with his family in the final chapter, claiming amnesia rather than answer any questions from Béa or the police about where or why he disappeared.

> La position de Gerfaut est donc inattaquable et il le sait. Comme il était militant de gauche dans sa première jeunesse, il a lu jadis plusieurs manuels et récits vécus bien utiles à qui veut tenir tête à des policiers et juges inquisiteurs. Et il leur a tenu tête, il n'a jamais démordu de son attitude d'ignorance complète, candide, serviable et navrée. Et l'on s'est découragé de lui faire des questions, et les auditions sont devenues plus rares, puis elles ont cessé. (Manchette 179-80)

Had Georges gone to the police after his initial attack on the beach, or after the gas station shootout-explosion which killed Bastien, or after his attack on the train following the explosion in which his identity papers were stolen, he might not have gone into hiding, and would not have had to become self-reliant. He transforms from a man who complains about the vacation rental arranged by his wife (Manchette 46), to a man capable of outsmarting and killing two professional hitmen. Despite this journey, however, he remains unenthusiastic about anything that has happened to him. Manchette's "behaviourist style where all is described from the exterior ... [gives] no access to Georges's thoughts and [denies the reader] any comforting identification with a *roman noir* hero on the run."[223]

Though the "minimalist prose style" and "sardonic and detached narrator"[224] offer little insight into Georges's psyche, Manchette humanizes the criminal elements usually kept mysterious by other *noir* authors. While not necessarily likeable characters, they are neither faceless figures of evil, nor marginalized members of society. Carlo and Bastien are hitmen in the employ of Alonso Emerich y Emerich, a job which they take very seriously. The fact that they fail to kill Georges Gerfaut, despite multiple attempts, affects them personally, as it is a reflection on their job performance. Normally, their contracts for their *patron*

> avaient marché comme sur des roulettes, jusqu'au moment où ils étaient tombés sur ce con de Georges Gerfaut. Un cadre commercial, pourtant, c'est normalement très facile à tuer. Carlo et Bastien pouvaient faire des comparaisons, car ils avaient exercé leur industrie dans les couches les plus

---

[223] Gorrara 66.
[224] Gorrara 66.

variées de la société. Maintenant ils commençaient à être en colère contre Georges Gerfaut. (Manchette 74)

They know that killing *cadres* is usually easy because they had killed many before Georges. Contract killing is its own industry, with such standards as to never shoot at a moving car on the highway, since, according to Bastien, "c'est un vrai piège" (Manchette 80). By breaking their own rules, shooting at the man that Georges takes to the hospital, thus requiring that Georges also be killed, they make their job harder than it needs to be, and they will pay the ultimate price. Throughout the novel, Carlo and Bastien are presented as a bickering couple, contrasting with any prevailing representations of cold-hearted assassins. Since they spend most of their day in the car, either en route to a job, or during surveillance work, they irritate each other with mundane details, such as odors brought into the car:

> L'homme aux mèches livides [Bastien] dilatait nerveusement les narines.
> -- Réellement, Carlo, tu sens la graisse et la friture.
> -- Ce que tu peux être chiant! s'exclama Carlo.
> [Carlo takes his bottle of aftershave out of his *trousse de toilette* and touches up.]
> -- Si on ne presse pas, dit l'homme aux mèches livides, on peut s'arrêter en cours de route au Lude. C'est joli, le Lude. Il y a un joli château.
> -- Si tu veux, d'accord, dit Carlo. Tu démarres, oui ou merde? On ne va pas rester ici cent ans. (Manchette 43)

Until chapter 10, Bastien is known only as "l'homme aux mèches livides," while Carlo, at first described as "le brun d'un ton rancuneux" (Manchette 43) is named almost immediately. His dialogue is the only in Manchette's narrative to include slang, mostly cursing. The day after Georges's attack, though Georges has abandoned his family and returned to his Paris apartment, Carlo and Bastien are staking out his vacation rental in Saint-Georges-de-Didonne, arguing with each other over whether Georges is still in town. They learn of Georges's true location when a telegram is delivered while the family is at the beach, and Bastien ventures out of the car.

> -- C'est de lui, dit-il [Bastien]. C'est de Gerfaut. C'est signé Georges et c'est un télégramme téléphoné, c'est expédié par Georges Gerfaut de chez lui à Paris. Il n'est pas ici, il est rentré chez lui. Alors? Qui est-ce qui avait raison?
> -- Chiotte! s'exclama Carlo.

-- Alors? Qui est-ce qui avait raison? Dis-moi qui est-ce qui avait raison.
-- C'est toi, Ducon.
Bastien remonta en voiture, prenant cette fois place à l'avant, au volant. Il démarra.
-- Holà, dit Carlo. Où est-ce qu'on va?
-- A Paris, Dunoeud. (Manchette 69)

Instead of being relieved to have found a new clue in their pursuit of Georges Gerfaut, the hitmen argue like children over who was right in his assessment. The winner of this latest scuffle momentarily determines the power structure of the relationship, and, more importantly, determines who will drive. Despite their near constant bickering, Carlo is lost after Bastien's death at the gas station. Himself on the run, unable to secure a proper burial for his friend, Carlo buries some of Bastien's personal belongings, including a Spiderman comic book, from which he reads "avec componction le texte de la page de garde qui est toujours le même et précède chaque aventure de Spiderman" (Manchette 99). That Carlo finds solace in this opening passage is representative of the hitman's childlike nature, but is also Manchette's commentary that the most sacred text that Carlo can read at his best friend's funeral is a comic book. Popular culture has become sacred, and is prone to the same misinterpretation as the Bible. Carlo delights in this particular passage before each Spiderman comic because it tells of "un véritable empereur du crime" (Manchette 99) a criminal's Neverland. After selling his Lancia, the car that he worked in with Bastien which now has too many memories, Carlo buys a Peugeot, and vows revenge on Georges: "Amen, dit-il. Ainsi soit-il. Je te vengerai, j'en fais serment. Je crèverai le cul de ce con. *Ite missa est*" (Manchette 99). With the Latin invocation, Carlo dismisses himself, not to go and serve the Lord, but to serve his own agenda.

The hitmen's boss, Alonso Emerich y Emerich, is humanized differently. Where Carlo and Bastien are depicted as childlike, Alonso is depicted as much worse: not only a grownup, but a complacent bourgeois who used to be dangerous. A political exile from the Dominican Republic after the election of Juan Bosch, Alonso had been a successfully corrupt member of the Dominican military, dealing in smuggling and torture, and had smartly set up overseas accounts in anticipation of exile after his partner in crime, Elias

Wessin y Wessin, had been exiled to Miami by the CIA[225]. In his retirement in France, where he refers to himself as Colonel Taylor, Alonso lives alone in a large house in Vilneuil, which he rarely leaves, accepting only the visits of Carlo and Bastien.

> Alonso vieillissait. Lorsqu'il vint s'installer en France à peu de distance de Magny-en-Vexin, il était brisé. Suffisamment en tout cas pour décider de ne plus bouger. Souvenons-nous d'ailleurs qu'il s'agit d'un homme qui, comme la veuve d'un condamné refusait de croire à la mort de son mari, lui avait fait envoyer par colis postal la tête du mort, avec quelque chose entre les dents. Et convenons que si ses craintes n'étaient pas raisonnables, leur racine l'était. (Manchette 14)

Alonso is a shell of the violent man he once was, preferring instead to surround himself in the comforts of a bourgeois lifestyle. His neighbors, oblivious to his violent past, wish only that he would take better care of his abandonded garden.

> Les paysans alentour grognaient de voir cette terre improductive. Ils parlèrent plusieurs fois de manifester à ce sujet. Ils auraient sûrement fini par se décider. La mort d'Alonso a résolu la question. (Manchette 15)

Had the neighbors taken the time to know Alonso the person, they would have realized that his sociopathic behavior, as contracted to his hitmen employees, presents much more of a threat to their standard of living than his lack of gardening. They allow Gerfaut and Gassowitz to escape unquestioned after Alonso's murder (Manchette 174), and are unable to give the police a physical description of either man. The complacent bourgeois order is ineffective, even in their backyard. Alonso's full name, Alonso Eduardo Rhadamès Philip Emerich y Emerich (Manchette 173), suggests nobility with Latin American exoticism. This is a different class of criminal, who gives his guard dog, a bullmastiff, the noble name Elizabeth, as if she were the queen of the house. A victim of his age, Alonso is practically powerless to defend himself without Carlo and Bastien, and this impotence extends to all details of his life, where "De temps à autre chaque soir il se masturbait sans grand success" (Manchette 17). Manchette humanizes the criminal element beyond the reader's expectations. In the absence

---

[225] Gorrara explains how Manchette "himself enacts with his Marxist analysis of capitalism in the pages of a *polar*" (69) by having Emerich y Emerich's activities in the Dominican Republic closely parallel similar atrocities during the Algerian war.

of heroes, everyone in the novel is at times incompetent, pathetic, and self-absorbed. The novel's final resolution, of Georges once again in his Mercedes on the *périphérique*, is less a reflection of some sort of moral order, like in most of Malet's *noirs*, than a representation of coincidence. The novel could have just as easily ended with Carlo driving his Peugeot coupe.

Where Malet took ordinary objects and made them *merveilleux* with the use of surrealist techniques, Manchette takes objects of wealth and privilege and renders them ordinary. Georges's Mercedes (Manchette 8) and apartment are obsessively inventoried, with special attention given to anything with a brand name, from his stereo (Sanyo) to his cigarette (Gitane-filtre), from his whisky (Cutty Sark with ice and Perrier) to his choice of vacation shirt (Lacoste). The reader first meets Georges, and encounters Manchette's detailed style, in the car:

> Georges Gerfaut est un homme de moins de quarante ans. Sa voiture est une Mercedes gris acier. Le cuir des sièges est acajou, et de même l'ensemble des décorations intérieures de l'automobile. L'intérieur de Georges Gerfaut est sombre et confus, on y distingue vaguement des idées de gauche. Au tableau de bord de la voiture, au-dessus des cadrans, se voit une petite plaque métallique mate où sont gravés le nom de Georges, son adresse, son groupe sanguin et une représentation merdeuse de saint Christophe. Par le truchement de deux diffuseurs – un sous le tableau de bord, un sur la plage arrière – un lecteur de cassettes diffuse à bas niveau du jazz de style West-Coast: du Gerry Mulligan, du Jimmy Giuffre, du Bud Shank, du Chico Hamilton. Je sais par exemple qu'à un moment, ce qui est diffusé est Truckin', de Rube Bloom et Ted Koehler, par le quintette de Bob Brookmeyer. (Manchette 8)

With obsessive attention to detail, Manchette sets the scene to the point of distraction. He places the reader inside the car with Georges, but almost forgets that he is telling a mystery. Jazz is a source of intertext in the title and "runs as a leitmotif through the novel, situating Georges as a figure who has assimilated American, and therefore consumerist, values." [226] But given Manchette's own appreciation of jazz, we can see a continuation of the slippage used by Malet to bring some of the author's own personality into his fiction, perhaps explaining the only use of the word "je" in the novel.

---

[226] Gorrara 65.

The contents of Carlo and Bastien's suitcases are given the same detailed attention. In addition to an extensive arsenal containing at least eight different weapons for the two of them, in Carlo's bag is "des vêtements, des affaires de toilette, un roman de science-fiction en langue italienne" (Manchette 41). Their Italian car, a Lancia Beta Berline 1800, contrasts with Georges's Mercedes. After Bastien's death, Carlo buys a sportier Peugeot coupe, which also allows him to better blend in with pre-European Union French material culture. Raguse's cabin in the Alpine woods, however, represents a mishmash of anti-materialism, where a photo of Josef Stalin hangs next to one of Louis Pasteur, and a character-revealing jazz collection is replaced by a personal library including "l'almanach Vermot, la Vie des fourmis de Maeterlinck et l'étonnante autobiographie d'un certain père Bourbaki, missionnaire et aviateur" (Manchette 107). While in Raguse's care, Georges abandons Cutty Sark and Perrier for Four Roses Bourbon, the one change that he keeps after returning to his normal life. Manchette's penchant for detail, however, does not extend to Georges's family – his fillettes are never named, and barely stop watching television long enough to speak. Items "are given the weight and status of a living thing."[227] Where Malet fetishized women's lingerie and high-heeled shoes, Manchette turns to stereo equipment and whisky.

Manchette continues the legacy of both Malet and Amila, adding his own politicized agenda to the tradition of the French *roman noir*. Having revitalized a stagnant genre, the *néo-polar* inspires still another generation of writers to blend popular fiction with current and historical events. The *roman noir engagé*, embodied by Didier Daeninckx, borrows from its predecessors and forges ahead in the 1980s.

Didier Daeninckx, *Meutres pour mémoire*

The *roman noir engagé* develops in the 1980s as writers such as Didier Daeninckx and Thierry Jonquet begin to use the genre not only to express their personal politics, but to generate social change as well. As Gorrara explains, this activism coincided with a "resurgence of interest in the Second World War,"[228] when "historical

---

[227] Gorrara 65.
[228] Gorrara 73.

reinterpretations of the Occupation were complemented by a wave of Holocaust testimonies."[229] Despite the increased popularity of the *roman noir* during this period, with writers including Daniel Pennac and Pierre Magnan[230] continuing to blur the lines between Série Noire and *la série blanche* originally muddied by Malet and Manchette, Daeninckx and Jonquet pushed the envelope even farther by including a socio-economic message with the narrative, producing "texts that are as much a social history of their times as a murder intrigue."[231] While Daeninckx's message is innovative, his narrative style is reminiscent of Malet: an initial murder leading to more murders, solved by a detective figure (though a public servant rather than a private investigator) who makes use of *faits divers* and archival materials, and who is prone to surrealist episodes.[232] His novels "mêlent mémoire individuelle et mémoire collective, histoire personnelle et histoire sociale"[233] with a challenge to right what has been wronged. In his historical *roman noir*, Daeninckx brings the genre full circle, evoking Malet's Paris in the beginning of *Meutres pour mémoire*, and bringing a *banlieue* sensibility to an urbanized form.

Born in 1949 in Aubervilliers, a suburb north of Paris in the Seine Saint-Denis, Daeninckx is the product of a family closely affected by historical events. With one grandfather a World War I deserter who "narrowly avoided the firing squad,"[234] and another one of the youngest Communist mayors elected in France in 1935, who was expelled from the party "after he expressed opposition to the Germano-Soviet pact during the Second World War,"[235] and with his mother a champion for colonial independence, Daeninckx was raised with a radical political sensibility. He was profoundly affected when

---

[229] Gorrara 74.

[230] For more on Pennac and Magnan's contributions to the genre, as well as Christian Jacq, Fred Vargas, Estelle Monbrun, and Anne de Leseleuc, refer to Verdaguer's study.

[231] Gorrara 77.

[232] Though not provoked by a *coup de crâne*, Cadin has a surreal dream sequence in which the police commissioner, wearing a cape and mask, "distribuait à une multitude d'êtres chétifs des petits carrés de carton verts ornés de la photo de Prodis. Je me trouvais sur son passage, nu" (Didier Daeninckx, *Meutres pour mémoire* (Paris: Gallimard, 2003) 180).

[233] Denis Fernández-Recatala, *Didier Daeninckx: Un écrivain en Seine Saint-Denis*, ([Paris?]: n.p., n.d.) 3.

[234] Gorrara 73.

[235] Gorrara 73.

"a close family friend, Suzanne Martorell, was one of eight victims crushed to death when police herded peaceful demonstrators into the closed entrance of the Charonne metro station in February 1962."[236] Following a brief stint as an *animateur culturel*, Daeninckx began working as a journalist in the early 1980s, after receiving unemployment benefits for several years. During those years, he wrote *Mort au premier tour*, his first *roman noir*, though it was not published until 1982 by Le Masque. Reminiscent of Malet's own foray into writing, Daeninckx was inspired by both the surrealism of Aragon, and American hardboiled fiction.

> Je lisais Aragon et les romans noirs américains. Le premier comme les autres traitait de l'actualité. Ils se saisissaient d'évènements contemporains et produisaient des effets immédiats. C'est ce qui m'a séduit et motivé.[237]

Daeninckx's fiction is colored by current and historical events, from the installation of nuclear power plants in *Mort au premier tour*, to World War I deserters in *Le der des ders* (1985), throughout which he is an "outspoken opponent of racism and right wing extremism."[238] It is perhaps for this reason that Daeninckx never mentions Léo Malet as an influence among Amila and Manchette, though *Meutres* has significant parallels to *Les nouveaux mystères de Paris*. In the April 1996 issue of *A Suivre*, where writers and comic book artists including Jacques Tardi, Frédéric Dard, Jean Vautrin and Thierry Jonquet paid tribute to Malet, Daeninckx wrote only, "Je prends un grand plaisir à lire Léo Malet dans les bandes dessinées de Tardi. En parler davantage juste après sa mort me paraît déplacé."[239] Malet's racist diatribes in his fiction and in interviews toward the end of his life made him unpopular with many *néo polar* and *roman noir engagé* writers, though they could not escape the influence of the Nestor Burma series, nor the popularity of Malet's character after the 1980s and 1990s with the television and bande dessinée adaptations.

While researching the Charonne massacre in the early 1980s, Daeninckx noticed a connection between a number of unsettling events in French history and Maurice Papon, secretary-general of the

---

[236] Gorrara 79.

[237] *Avez-vous lu Didier Daeninckx* (Saint Ouen: Bibliothèque Municipale, 1993) 2.

[238] Gorrara 80.

[239] Laurence Harlé, "Léo Malet vu par...," *A Suivre* 219 (April 1996): 9.

Gironde prefecture (1942-1944), inspector-general of North-Eastern Algeria (1956-1958), and chief of police in Paris (1958-1967), among many governmental appointments. [240] Daeninckx responded by refusing to pay his taxes during the years 1979-1981, which were now under Papon's authority as Ministre de budget. In 1982, when *Le Canard enchaîné* revealed Papon's role in the deportation of thousands of Jews from the Bordeaux region during World War II, Daeninckx found inspiration for his second novel: "Un seul homme et trois périodes, vingt ans – une génération – entre chacune d'elle: la structure du roman est là."[241] *Meutres pour mémoire* connects two historical events – the brutal repression of a peaceful protest against a newly imposed curfew for "Français-Musulmans" on October 17, 1961, and the deportation of Jews from Drancy in 1942 – to the murders of a father and son, both historians, twenty years apart. The novel begins in third-person narration, following three characters – Saïd Milache, Kaïra Guelanine, and Roger Thiraud – as they reach the site of the protest, whether on purpose or by accident. All three of them die in the melee. Roger, a professor of history and Latin, finds himself in the wrong place at the wrong time, coming out of an afternooon screening of "Invasion of the Body Snatchers" before going home to his pregnant wife, just as the CRS agents arrive on the scene. He is killed at point blank range. Twenty years later, Bernard Thiraud, the son Roger never knew, leaves Paris for a short research trip to Toulouse before a month in Morocco with his girlfriend. Walking back to his hotel after a day of researching dossiers at the prefecture's archives, Bernard is also shot at point blank range, though it requires several bullets, by a man in his sixties. Robbery is quickly ruled out, since Bernard's wallet and identity papers were still in his pockets. Bernard, it is revealed, had taken up the unfinished research of his late father, a monograph about Roger's hometown of Drancy. During his research, Roger had uncovered the connection of André Veillut, a character based on Papon, and the transport of Jews from the Toulouse region to Drancy. When Veillut first learns of Roger's

---

[240] Steele suggests, "il peut paraître hors sujet qu'un article issu de la chronique quotidienne du process Papon donne à penser literature." (Stephen Steele, "Daeninckx, Quand le roman policier part en guerre," *French Studies Bulletin* 71 (Summer 1999): 9.)
[241] Marion Jacquelin, *Actualité, réalité et fiction dans Meutres pour mémoire de Didier Daeninckx*, (Master's Thesis. U Montpellier III, 2001) 5.

research, he hires a CRS agent, Pierre Cazes, to assassinate the historian during an Algerian demonstration. Twenty years later, when Veillut learns of Roger's son's interest in the project, he must kill Bernard himself to protect his secret, since Cazes is now too ill. But Cazes takes revenge on Veillut for tricking him into believing that Roger had been a subversive, and for other deceptions. Veillut has committed crimes against humanity, much more than the average *noir* villain guilty of blackmail or infidelity. Verdaguer writes:

> L'être vil ... n'agit pas simplement pour son propre compte mais au nom de toute une nation, et même selon les directives de l'État auquel il a juré fidélité. Le mal s'en trouve d'autant plus aggravé, puisqu'il devient affaire de société. Les histoires de Daeninckx ne cessent, de ce fait, de poser la question de la responsabilité de l'homme au sein de sa communauté.[242]

Even more important than Veillut being brought to justice by his death at the hand of Cazes is the public exposé of his past actions. In solving Bernard's murder, Inspector Cadin must also solve Roger's murder, making connections between the two at first seemingly unrelated crimes, while encountering strange people, false leads, and more deaths along the way. With Cadin's arrival, the narration changes to first-person, except for one chapter written from the point of view of Cazes as an old man. With regard to genre, Geldof argues that

> Les récits policiers de Daeninckx ne se conforment donc que très partiellement aux lois actantielles du genre: leur enjeu fondamental est moins la solution d'une quelconque énigme que la volonté de commémorer le passé ou plutôt ... le passé que l'Histoire officielle ignore, efface, refoule ou dégrade au rang de fait divers insignifiant. L'écriture implique pour Daeninckx un acte de *témoignage.*[243]

While it is true that the social message overrides the murder mystery to solve, in *Meutres*, Daeninckx returns to the *noir* formula and narrative momentum of Malet and others, of one murder leading to other murders, but also maintains the legacy of Amila and Manchette's distrust for authority. "L'écrivain," writes Guiou, "veut

---

[242] Verdaguer 251.
[243] Koenraad Geldof, "Une écriture de la résistance: Histoire et fait divers dans l'oeuvre de Didier Daeninckx," *Ecrire l'insignifiant: dix études sur le fait divers dans le roman contemporain*, Eds. Paul Pelckmans and Bruno Tritsmans (Amsterdam: Rodopi, 2000) 138.

témoigner sur son époque et donner la parole à ceux qui ne l'ont pas."[244]

Unlike Malet's *détective de choc*, Nestor Burma, Inspector Cadin is a policeman resisting the orders of his superiors and inviting trouble with his disregard for police protocol and his requests for classified documents. Cadin's request for information from an old friend, Dalbois, working at Renseignements généraux, is met with a response typical in Nestor Burma's world: "Je ne vois pas ce que tu espères trouver de ce côté-là, sinon des emmerdements" (Daeninckx 74). "Créé peut-être en vue d'une série, mais sitôt mis en place, esquissé,"[245] Cadin is a "Colombo sans imperméable, sans femme et sans humour,"[246] a *flic contestataire*. Unmarried, with few friends, he can disappear on assignment for weeks or months at a time. When he first appears in *Meutres*, he is recently returned from six months in Lozère. During the course of the novel, he travels from Toulouse to Paris to Brussels and back, but there is no one to miss him. He is contrasted with his colleague Lardenne, who tries to play with a Rubik's cube (Daeninckx 46) and learn videogames (Daeninckx 149) to better relate to his young son. Cadin is an antihero, in the tradition of Nestor Burma, but lacks the self-confidence to achieve Burma's professional or sexual success. In *Meutres*, he is attracted to Claudine, the girlfriend of Bernard Thiraud, though she is much younger, and has recently suffered the tragic loss of her fiancé. After a failed flirtation (Daeninckx 70), he keeps his attraction to himself until she is lonely enough to call him (Daeninckx 209), but their relationship remains relatively chaste. Cadin, Audusse writes, is "une éponge absorbant la boue du monde, ni chevalier rédempteur ni juge suprême, juste un homme à l'innocence définitivement perdue" ("Adieu"). During the four-novel series in which Cadin appears,[247] he is "un homme ordinaire, vaguement mélancolique et sombrant dans un état

---

[244] Dominique Guiou, "Les verts broient du noir," *Le Figaro* 27 Mar 1997: 40.

[245] Fernáandez-Recatala 9.

[246] Guiou 40.

[247] *Mort au premier tour* (1982), *Meutres pour mémoire* (1984), *Le géant inachevé* (1984), *Le bourreau et son double* (1986). He also appears in the novel *Lumière noire* (1987), the short story collection *Le facteur fatal* (1990), and in the short story "Main courante"(1994). *Meutres pour mémoire* won the Prix Paul Vaillant-Couturier in 1984 and the Grand Prix de la Littérature Policière in 1985, 37 years after Malet won the same award.

de plus en plus dépressif",[248] becoming increasingly vulnerable to failure, eventually leaving the police force, and briefly becoming a private detective before committing suicide in *Le facteur fatal* (1989). The death of Cadin leaves Daeninckx free to continue his politicized writing outside the form of the *roman noir*. Aware of his short-comings, Cadin makes references to other literary detectives, including Sherlock Holmes (Daeninckx 48) and Hercule Poirot, noting, "Si je m'appelais Hercule Poirot, je noterais le numéro de billet et je filerais au Centre National du Cinéma pour relever la date exacte à laquelle ce coupon a été délivré" (Daeninckx 80) recalling a similar line in Malet's *Pas de bavards à la Muette* where Burma speculates that Sherlock Holmes would be able to analyze cigarette butts left on the floor at a crime scene and tell the approximate ages of the smokers who had been in the room (*Enquêtes*, 2: 152). Other scenes in *Meutres* are reminiscent of Malet's series, beyond mere *noir* clichés.

Setting *Meutres* in both 1961 and 1981, Daeninckx evokes the Paris of Malet's *Nouveaux mystères* and gives insight into the result of "progress" toward the end of the century. The novel begins in the second *arrondissement*, the same *arrondissement* as Burma's Fiat Lux detective agency, near Richelieu-Drouot. The first chapter is divided into three sections, for Saïd Milache, Roger Thiraud, and Kaïra Guelanine, detailing the final day of each of their lives up to the violent demonstration on October 17, 1961. Saïd is on his way into the city with his friend Lounès after a long day working at a printing press, and has blue ink all over his hands. His *bidonville* is like many others in Paris.

> Chez Rosa, chez Marius, Café de la Justice, l'Amuse Gueule, le Bar du Gaz. Les cafés, restaurants, hôtels, plus misérables les uns que les autres se succédaient maintenant. Au fil des années les propriétaires avaient revendu leur affaire à des Algériens et ceux-ci conservaient l'enseigne d'origine. Seule exception, le Djurdjura, dernier commerce arabe avant le quartier espagnol. (Daeninckx 12-13)

Though the French have moved out of these neighborhoods, the Algerians retain the original names of the businesses they buy to maintain continuity. Like Malet and Simenon, Daeninckx makes use of local smells and odors: "L'odeur habituelle, mélange de sciure et

---

[248] Geldof 137.

d'humidité, montait du parquet désinfecté à l'eau de Javel" (Daeninckx 13). Saïd and Lounès park their car to take the *métro*. Daeninckx notes the composition of their train car en route to Bonne-Nouvelle, "A chacun de ses arrêts, le métro se remplissait d'Algériens. A «Stalingrad», il était bondé; les rares Européens se lançaient des regards angoissés. Saïd souriait" (Daeninckx 15). He then takes out a piece of paper that he had been printing at work: a poster for Jacques Rivette's film "Paris nous appartient" with a photo of Giani Esposito and Betty Schneider. He says to his friend, "Tu te rends compte Lounès, Paris nous appartient," to which Lounès responds, "Pour un soir … Si cela ne tenait qu'à moi, je leur laisserais bien Paris. Paris et tout le reste, pour un petit village du Hodna" (Daeninckx 15). Unfortunately, Paris would never belong to Saïd, nor to Kaïra, who also sneaks into the city from her *bidonville*, getting a ride from her friend Aounit. She is unlike the other women of her community.

> Elle ne ressemblait pas aux autres jeunes femmes du bidonville. A vingt-cinq ans, toutes ses amies étaient mariées depuis des années et traînait derrière elles une armée de marmots. Cette cour, ou une autre toute semblable, constituait leur seul univers avec le Prisunic de Nanterre. Un horizon de terrains vagues coincé entre les usine de la Seine, à dix minutes d'autobus des Champs-Elysées! Kaïra connaissait des femmes dont le dernier pas en dehors du bidonville remontait à deux, voire trois ans. Sa mère était ainsi. (Daeninckx 21)

Kaïra is also different from her friends as she chooses to wear pants and can be seen in public without a companion. When Aounit asks her how she intends to return home from the rally, she replies, "Je ne sais pas, dix ou onze heures, mais ne t'inquiète pas, Saïd et Lounès me ramèneront à la maison" (Daeninckx 23). The stories of Saïd and Kaïra "highlight the cultural hybridity"[249] of Paris in the early 1960s. The Algerian community evoked in Malet's *Les eaux troubles de Javel* is not humanized, but consists mostly of criminal elements, from illegal arms dealers to murderous FLN rebels. Daeninckx instead uses the vignettes of Saïd and Kaïra, as well as Roger Thiraud, to

> bring everyday life into what is considered scientific historical discourse. At the same time, they establish a social geography of the city which helps to

---

[249] Gorrara 83.

account for the political explosion of October 17, 1961. The text moves quickly, as does the very present implicit narrator.[250]

Daeninckx not only presents immigrants as "desirables," through Cadin he condemns those with racist tendencies, such as a cab driver who "tentait de lancer la conversation sur les tares de conduite comparée des Arabes et des Africains. Désespéré par mon silence il essaya de nouer un contact antisémite sans plus de success" (Daeninckx 88). Rather than tell the driver how he feels, however, Cadin gives the driver an exact fare without tip.

Daeninckx also comments on then contemporary France when the focus of the novel changes to present day. In a 1993 interview, on the subject of physical description, he said

> Pour moi, il y a deux éléments: le décor et les corps. Ça m'intéresse toujours de fixer le décor de manière fouillée. Une ville, un quartier disent de l'histoire sociale, des enjeux économiques. Les lieux disent de la mémoire, des affrontements, des lâchetés. Quand je commence à écrire, c'est ce qui me passionne: montrer que le temps du roman, le présent de l'action est gros de tout ce qui a existé auparavant dans la tête du personnage, dans son corps et dans le décor lui-même.[251]

The portrait of urbanized space is a vital narrative element for Daeninckx, further linking him to the tradition of the *roman noir*, and to Léo Malet in particular. Cadin notes the influx of American retail when he visits Roger's widow: "Peu de choses avaient changé depuis lors, à part l'affiche du Rex qui annonçait un dessin animé de Walt Disney et le self-service de l'Humanité qui s'était mué en «Burger King» " (Daeninckx 111). Obviously, this is only the tip of the iceberg of the Disney onslaught, ten years before EuroDisney. The city is in a constant state of change, but like both Malet and Manchette, Daeninckx preserves a piece of Paris's character in his fiction.

The *roman noir engagé* sets itself apart from its *noir* predecessors in its use of historical and contemporary events to impart

---

[250] Josiane Peltier, "Didier Daeninckx and Michel de Certeau: A Historiography of Affects," *Crime Scenes: Detective Narratives in European Culture Since 1945*, Eds. Anne Mullen and Emer O'Beirne (Amsterdam: Rodopi, 2000) 273.
[251] Mehdi Aïssaoui and Serge Kaganski, "Avenue d'Humaine," *Les Inrockuptibles* 50 (November 1993): 66.

with the reader a missive for social change. While murder is an element in the *noir* formula,

> Didier Daeninckx préfère analyser le passé de ses personnages, reconstituer une époque et en reveler certains faits occultés. L'histoire et la mémoire que nous avons de cette époque sont au centre d'un dispositif qui ne laisse pas le lecteur indemné et le force à s'interroger.[252]

The reader is presented with an alternate interpretation of recent historical events from the point of view of fictional characters. Daeninckx "defamiliarizes history, providing a 'history from below' that focuses on the victims of French state aggression."[253] Cadin approaches his investigation of Roger and Bernard Thiraud's deaths in the same manner that a historian might use: by consulting archives, searching documentation (though some of it had not yet been officially declassified), and interviewing witnesses to the events. Cadin's quest leads him to Brussels, where he interviews a filmmaker who inadvertently shot footage of the riot while following Jacques Brel to Paris (Daeninckx 104). Nestor Burma would also begin each of his investigations with a trip to the archives, though he would often send Hélène. Geldof writes

> Par son intervention originale et critique dans un genre dit populaire, Daeninckx veut désautomatiser une certaine perception du passé et du social et la mise en forme littéraire n'est fonctionnelle que dans la mesure où elle se conforme au souci de communiquer avec le lecteur.[254]

By profiling the lives of two murdered historians, the surviving girlfriend (also a historian), and by using a historian's method in the investigation, Daeninckx reminds the reader of how history can be recorded, that it sometimes comes from the desks of ordinary people, and not always from authorities. Daeninckx also makes use of slippage, harkening back to Malet's series, but where Malet inserted clever details of his own biography into his fiction, Daeninckx bases the character of Veillut on Maurice Papon.

Didier Daeninckx takes the *roman noir* as evolved by Amila and Manchette one step further by incorporating history and activism into his political stance. The *roman noir engagé* champions a cause

---

[252] *Avez-vous lu Didier Daeninckx* 5
[253] Gorrara 83.
[254] Geldof 149.

and makes a difference rather than just complaining. Yet it also brings the genre full circle by incorporating some of the elements used by Malet in the 1940s and 1950s: surrealist dreams, portrait of urbanized space, a detective character on the fringe of authority (even though Inspector Cadin is officially an authority figure), use of slang and slippage. Daeninckx "s'engage (dans un sens presque sartrien) à faire de l'oubli du passé l'objet d'un débat public,"[255] and provokes readers to come to terms with their own, often ugly, history. By reviving the use of a recurring character, only to kill him off, Daeninckx frees himself to explore other characters, themes, and politics, thereby escaping the writer's block which plagued both Malet and Manchette. In recent years, he has turned his attention to critiquing the media in works such as *Zapping* and *En marge*, in which he "sort du cadre policier pour se faire commentateur de société, un peu à la manière de Sinclair Lewis, proposant des series d'historiettes révélatrices des travers du monde postindustrial."[256]

The French *roman noir* continues to develop in the twentieth century well after Léo Malet abruptly ended his series *Les Nouveaux Mystères de Paris*. The detective novel is "entièrement un produit d'époque, fortement ancré dans un temps où font alliance modernisme et esprit fin de siècle."[257] While Malet's contemporary Jean Amila experiments with narrative structure and offers a different version of Americanized detective fiction, Manchette and Daeninckx move the genre into a more political realm with the *néo polar* and the *roman noir engagé*. These writers "a su donner à la noirceur qu'il cultive une profondeur idéologique évidente; quelque peu nihiliste, il dénonce, provoque, revendique."[258] Each author makes the genre his own, yet still show tell-tale signs of what they might have previously read. Malet makes his mark on each of these writers who both embrace and reject his legacy. At the turn of the new millennium, we find Daeninckx moving into politicized media criticism, yet the *roman noir*

---

[255] Steele 10.

[256] Verdaguer 17. Platten writes of the "escalation of a cultural debate in France that has run parallel to the proliferation of interest in crime fiction," and the impact of both Daeninckx and Daniel Pennac's recent writings. (David Platten, "The Impact of the Contemporary Roman Noir: Pennac, Daeninckx, and the Question of a Cultural Evolution," *French Prose in 2000,* Eds. Michael Bishop and Christopher Elson (Amsterdam: Rodopi, 2000) 156)

[257] Dubois 219.

[258] Dubois 220.

lives on in Gallimard's Série Noire, approaching its 60th anniversary. In 2001, the series published Patrick Pécherot's *Les brouillards de la Butte*, "inspired" by the work of Léo Malet, proving that the genre lives on, but has not forgotten its founding fathers.

Conclusion

Léo Malet's use of slang, surrealist imagery, and first-person narration expands the boundaries of the French detective novel, but his series, *Les nouveaux mystères de Paris*, also serves as a political commentary on Parisian life in the face of the renovation that began in the 1950s. What Ross refers to as the unexpected swiftness of the renovation process[259] is played out during Malet's series which ends when the author himself is displaced to an HLM and develops a depressive writer's block. The series depicts the "urbanistes" as a new army of aggressors with the mission to turn all that is beautiful in Paris into a concrete slab. As an alternative tour guide, Burma attempts to focus the reader's attention on districts that are taken for granted in the hope that further demolition can be avoided. He thus ignores the more "obvious" points of interest in each *arrondissement*: the catacombes in the fourteenth, Notre Dame in the fourth, and Les Halles in the first, among others. Suggesting details of everyday Parisian life, Burma looks beyond Paris's touristic mask to present an in-depth portrait of a city that is both "infâme" and "merveilleuse."

Nestor Burma, Malet's postwar icon, is the "détective de choc" on several levels. There is the "choc," as in impact, from the *coups de crâne* which Burma gives as well as receives, and there is the "choc," as in shock, from the outrageous comments that he makes in a hybrid literary form heretofore not present in French detective fiction. Coupez calls Malet a "témoin de son temps," adding, "On découvre en lui l'anarchiste des années 20, le surréaliste des années 30, le père du roman noir,"[260] but, in light of Malet's use of slippage, the same comments could be made about Burma. The detective represents the

---

[259] Ross 4.
[260] Nathalie Coupez, "Léo Malet: Souvenirs épuisés," *Télérama* 9 (1988): 4.

evolution of a generation from the activism of youth to the "esprit canaille"[261] of middle age.[262]

As Burma juggles his anarchistic upbringing with his capitalistic career, he tries to make sense of his new adult priorities while, at the same time, adjusting to new social order in the years following the war. This juggling, however, is complicated by his racist fears of the post-colonial immigrant influx. The bilious outbursts throughout the text against blacks, *magrhébins*, and gypsies, among others, convey the resentment that Burma feels as his French identity is threatened by this invasion of the unknown. To counterbalance the hatefulness of these outbursts, Malet injects a celebration of French artistic culture, including challenging works of literature which might otherwise be ignored by the reader of popular fiction.

Burma's xenophobic personality is tempered by his interactions with his friends and colleagues who serve as his surrogate family. Because of his frequent encounters with Commissioner Faroux, Burma must confront his leftover anarchist feelings toward authority. He ultimately appreciates Faroux as a high-placed friend whom he can call at any time for any reason. Covet is another useful friend, keeping Burma's name in the newspapers and granting him access to restricted areas reserved for the press corps. Hélène keeps the detective's life together, making sure that his business runs smoothly while he is distracted by a new assignment or a new woman, and taking care of his unavoidable wounds. Their symbiotic relationship with Burma balances the narrative as Burma's colorfully candid dialogue with his friends lightens the mood and shows the reader the softer side of Burma. Without Covet, Faroux, and Hélène, the moments of comic relief would be sparse between the scenes of violence and sordid crime. The humanity of these episodes contributes to the popularity of Malet's series, as well as of the television adaptation featuring Guy Marchand, in which all three characters figure alongside Burma.[263]

---

[261] Rivière, *Cadavre* 28.

[262] A representation of what Burma might have been like as an septuagenarian can be found in Malet's posthumously published *Journal secret* (Paris: Fleuve Noir, 1997), in which Malet provides a glimpse into his daily life as well as insight into his depression during the 1980s in the years following the suicide of his wife.

[263] Chatenier explains how Antenne 2 (now France 2) bought the rights to the character of Nestor Burma and not to Malet's novels. Such a deal gives the network

Malet's *roman noir* differs from Simenon's *roman policier* in content, language, and location, even though both the Burma and Maigret series make use of the Parisian topos. Malet juxtaposes the menancing darkness of the crime-ridden city with the calm beauty of the forgotten districts of Paris. His use of slang evokes the urbanized space in which he works, with first-person narration suggesting camaraderie between the reader and the detective. The content of Malet's *roman noir* yields a higher body count than the traditional *policier*, but the reader can be assured that no murder will go unpunished in Burma's personalized justice system.

Malet's series marks a turning point in the progression of the French detective genre, a progression evidenced by both Caillois's and Todorov's studies. Detective fiction evolves from a stagnant genre praised for adhering to a predictable formula and resisting the influence of experimental theater and poetry to a collection of subgenres providing differently flavored mysteries for different sensibilities. By remaining true to detective fiction's constants – violence, sordid crime, and amorality – Malet can expand the boundaries of the genre. He successfully ventures into new artistic directions by bringing a cultivated literary sensibility to the popular milieu. Evocative rather than descriptive, his imagery alludes to his surrealist past as well as to well-known works of the French canon. The constants of detective fiction retain the readers of the classic *policier* while attracting new readers. The surrealist techniques employed by Malet – dream sequences, altered states of consciousness, the appreciation of *faits-divers* and the *merveilleux* – lend a new perspective with which to consider the formulaic items of the detective genre – detective, cadaver, weapon – not present in Malet's contemporaries.

This study of Léo Malet's *Les nouveaux mystères de Paris* has demonstrated multiple literary and cultural influences within the frame of a wildly entertaining series of novels. Presenting vivid avant-garde imagery, well-drawn characters, and detailed insight into the daily life of the generation which survived the war and occupation, Malet

---

"la possibilité d'inventer de nouvelles aventures de Nestor Burma, bien au-delà de la série des quinze romans des *Nouveaux mystères de Paris*." As a result, the bi-weekly television series, which alternates with the "Maigret" series during the fall programming schedule, is set in contemporary France, and not in the 1950s. (Pierre Chatenier, "Les mystères de Paris à la mode Malet," *Murs Murs* 8 (1995): 54.)

expands the boundaries of the French detective novel, paving the way for his detective fiction contemporaries including Jean Amila, the writing team of Pierre Boileau and Thomas Narcejac, Sébastien Japrisot, and, later, new generations of writers such as Jean-Patrick Manchette and Thierry Jonquet with the *néo-noir* of the 1970s, and Didier Daeninckx with the *roman noir engagé* of the 1980s. Though the character of Nestor Burma is better known in contemporary France for the previously mentioned television series and the bande-dessinée adaptation of Jacques Tardi than for a series of novels[264], the legacy of Burma is in his portrait of a transitional era in French culture. Malet's œuvre is notable for the subgenre it creates and the imagery it introduces to popular literature, whereas Burma is notable for the attitudes and concerns that he represents. "Répétons-nous," Lebrun and Schweighaeuser write, "Léo Malet ne doit rien à personne, mais le roman policier lui doit tout."[265]

---

[264] Peter Schulman analyzes "pourquoi et comment Tardi a pu effectuer une telle synergie dans son adaptation en code 'bande dessinée' des codes littéraires des romans de Malet" (Peter Schulman, "Le 'stylo-camera': Léo Malet vu par Jacques Tardi," *De l'écrit à l'écran: literatures populaires: mutations génériques, mutations médiatiques* (Limoges: PULIM, 2000) 523).

[265] Schweighaeuser 81.

Appendix A

Individual titles of Léo Malet's
Les nouveaux mystères de Paris

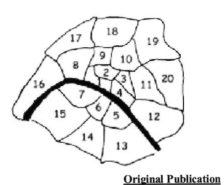

Title	**Original Publication**	***Arr.***
Le soleil naît derrière le Louvre	July 1954	1st
Des kilomètres de linceuls	January 1955	2nd
Fièvre au Marais	February 1955	3rd
La nuit de Saint-Germain-des-Près *	May 1955	6th
Les rats de Montsouris	August 1955	14th
M'as-tu vu en cadavre?	January 1956	10th
Corrida aux Champs-Elysées	February 1956	8th
Pas de bavards à la Muette	June 1956	16th
Brouillard au pont de Tolbiac	October 1956	13th
Les eaux troubles de Javel	February 1957	15th
Boulevard...ossements	May 1957	9th
Casse-pipe à la Nation	September 1957	12th
Micmac moche au Boul'Mich'	December 1957	5th
Du rébecca rue des rosiers	April 1958	4th
L'envahissant cadavre de la Plaine Monceau	February 1959	17th
Les neiges de Montmartre	(one chapter completed)	18th

Titles chosen for:

"300 mètres d'agonie" — 7th
"Méprise de la Bastille" — 11th

No titles chosen for the 19th and 20th *arrondissements*.

* First published as *Le sapin pousse dans les caves*; retitled in 1973

Appendix B

Frequently used slang in Malet's series (as defined by Colin and Mével's *Dictionnaire de l'argot*)

A

abattoir	guillotine
affranchir	voleur
Amerloque	américain
anar	anarchiste
andouille	individu stupide
apéro	apéritif

B

bagnole	véhicule (généralement une voiture, souvent médiocre)
bain (être dans le)	se trouver dans une situation désagréable ou compromettante
balle	monnaie d'une livre, puis d'un franc
bésef	beaucoup (surtout précédé de pas)
bicot	désignation raciste de l'Arabe
blair	nez
blé	argent
bloc	prison ou salle de police
bonniche	bonne, domestique
bouffe/bouffer	nourriture; manger
boul'	boulevard
brique	liasse de 1000 billets de 1000 anciens francs
brouillard	dans un début d'ivresse
buter	tuer
burlingue	bureau

C

calcif	caleçon, slip

canard	journal médiocre et, par extension, tout journal
casse-pipe	action ou situation très dangereuse (surtour en parlant de guerre)
cérbère	gardien intraitable
cibiche	cigarette
ciboulot/cigare	tête
cinoche	cinéma
cinquième	la mort
citron	Citroën
clamser/clapser	mourir
clignotants	yeux
clodo	clochard
clope	mégot
collabo	collaborateur
corniaud	imbécile
corrida	scène plus ou moins violente, en gestes et en paroles

D

dalle (que)	"rien du tout"

F

flic	membre de la police ou de la gendarmerie
flingue	arme à feu
foutaise	propos ou chose sans valeur
fric	argent
fric-frac	vol avec effraction
frusques/fringues	vêtements

G

galure	chapeau
gazer (Ça gaze.)	aller bien
godasses	chaussures
gonzesse	fille ou femme
goumi (coup de)	matraque de caoutchouc
grand-père	surnom donné au directeur du Palais du Justice
grisbi	argent
gueule	bouche; visage
guibolles	jambes

H

herbe	tabac
horizontale	vieilli; prostituée

J

jus de chique	café

K

kif-kif.	pareil

L

larbin	domestique
loge	surveiller de loin le déroulement des opérations pour intervenir au bon moment
loufiat	individu médiocre ou sale

M

macchabée	cadavre
mécano	mécanicien
micmac	intrigue secrète et embrouillée
mollo	doucement
môme	enfant

N

nichon	sein d'une femme
noraf	Nord-Africain
numéro	activité considérée comme représentative d'un individu

P

pétard	arme à feu
pétrin	situation difficile
pige	année
pipe	tête
pissoir	urinoir public
le P.J	Palais de Justice
plumard	lit
pogne	main
pognon	argent
poireauter	attendre longtemps et sur place
pote	ami
pouffiasse	prostituée de bas étage; femme quelconque
poule	vieilli, prostituée; maîtresse; fille ou femme en général
poupée	fille ou femme

pruneau	projectile d'arme à feu
punaise	fille ou femme

R

rébecca	protestation, opposition violente
rince-cochon	boisson légère, composée soit de vin blanc additionné de citron et d'eau de Seltz, soit d'un simple verre d'eau minérale, qu'on absorbe au lendemain de trop copieuses libations
robert	sein d'une femme
robinet	personne excessivement bavarde et prolixe

S

sbire	surveillant de prison, policier
schlass	ivre
schlinguer	puer
sèche	cigarette
sidi	désignation péjoratif de l'Arabe
sous-verge	employé subalterne, adjoint

T

tifs	cheveux
tocbombe	un peu dérangé mentalement
torgnole	coup, gifle
toubib	médecin

V

viande	corps humain, individu
vinasse	vin de qualité médiocre

Y

youpin(e)	désignation raciste du juif

Z

zigue	individu quelconque (variations: mézigue, ce zigue, tézigue, etc.)
zigoto	individu douteux, incapable, ou excentrique
zinc	comptoir d'un marchand de vin, d'un café

Bibliography

Abbas, Akbar. *Hong Kong: Culture and the Politics of Disappearance*. Minneapolis: U of Minnesota P, 1997.

Abescat, Michel. "Léo Malet a quitté pour toujours Nestor Burma." *Le Monde* 09 Mar. 1996: 22.

Aïssaoui, Mehdi and Serge Kaganski. "Avenue d'Humaine." *Les Inrockuptibles* 50 (November 1993): 62-69.

Alexandrian, Sarane. *Le surréalisme et le rêve*. Paris: Gallimard, 1974.

Alfu. *Léo Malet: Parcours un œuvre*. Amiens: Encrage, 1998.

Amila, Jean. *La lune d'Omaha*. Paris: Gallimard, 1964. 2003.

Aragon, Louis. *Le paysan de Paris*. Paris: Gallimard, 1926.

Audusse, Bertrand. "L'adieu à Cadin." *Le Monde* 16 Nov. 1990. N. pag.

---. "Jean Amila: un écrivain réfractaire." *Le Monde* 11 Mar 1995. N. pag.

"Au revoir au pont de Tolbiac." *Le Parisien* 06 May 1996: 4.

Avez-vous lu Didier Daeninckx? Saint Ouen: Bibliothèque Municipale, 1993.

Balakian, Anna. *Surrealism: The Road to the Absolute*. New York: Noonday, 1959.

Baudou, Jacques, ed. *Nestor Burma détective de choc, un monde étrange*. Spec. issue of *Enigmatika* 18 (1981). Paris: Butte-aux-Cailles, 1982.

Benevuti, Stefano, et al. *Le roman policier*. Nantes: L'Atlante, 1982.

Biro, Adam and René Passeron, eds. *Dictionnaire général du surréalisme et de ses environs*. Fribourg, Suisse: Office du Livre, 1982.

Blaha, Franz G. "Detective/Mystery/Spy Fiction." *Handbook of French Popular Culture*. Ed. Pierre L. Horn. Westport: Greenwood, 1991. 39-57.

Bob le Flambeur. Dir. Jean-Pierre Melville. Organisation Générale Cinématographique/La Cyme/Play Art, 1956.

Borie, Jean. *Le célibataire français*. Paris: Livre de Poche, 2002.

Boileau, Pierre and Thomas Narcejac. *Le roman policier*. 3rd ed. Paris: PUF, 1988.

Bott, François. "La guinche des antinomies." *Le Monde* 08 Aug. 1975: 7.

Breton, André. *Manifestes du surréalisme*. Paris: Gallimard, 1963.

---. *Nadja*. Paris: Gallimard, 1963.

Bridgeman, Teresa. "Paris-Polar in the Fog: Power of Place and Generic Space in Malet's *Brouillard au pont de Tolbiac*." *Australian Journal of French Studies* 35.1 (1998): 58-74.

Caillois, Roger. *Le roman policier*. Buenos Aires: Editions des lettres françaises, 1941.

Chandler, Raymond. *Farewell, My Lovely.* New York: Vintage Crime/Random House, 2001.

Chatenier, Pierre. "Les mystères de Paris à la mode Malet." *Murs Murs* 8 (1995): 53-55.

Chenieux-Gendron, Jacqueline. *Le Surréalisme.* Paris: PUF, 1984.

Chlastacz, Michel. "Les Trains de Nestor Burma." *La vie du Rail* 2356 (1992): 10-17.

Cohen, Margaret. *Profane Illumination: Walter Benjamin and the Paris of Surreal Revolution.* Berkeley: U of California P, 1993.

Colin, Jean-Paul and Jean-Pierre Mével, eds. *Dictionnaire de l'argot.* Paris: Larousse, 1994.

Corty, Bruno. "Malet: le journal du malheur." *Le Figaro* 23 Oct. 1997: 7.

Coupez, Nathalie. "Léo Malet: Souvenirs épuisés." *Télérama* 9 (1988): 3-4.

D'Aubarède, Gabriel. "Je suis contre le roman policier fonctionnant comme un mécanisme d'horlogerie,' dit Léo Malet." *Nouvelles Littéraires* 20 Mar. 1958: 1-2.

Daeninckx, Didier. *Meutres pour mémoire.* Paris: Gallimard, 2003.

Delcroix, Olivier. "Léo Malet, entre Fantômas et le roman noir." *Le Figaro* 29 Apr. 1996: 27.

Deleuse, Robert. *Les maîtres du roman policier.* Paris: Bordas, 1991.

Dimanno, Yves. "Roman policier et société." *Europe* 571-72 (1976): 117-25.

Doisneau, Robert and Léo Malet. Interview. "Paris et autres aventures." Ed. France Debray. *Leitmotiv* 1 (1988): 31-39

Driancourt, Christophe. "Le charme discret d'un écrivain non-conformiste." *France-Soir Ouest* 08 Dec. 1989: 14.

---. "Léo Malet casse sa pipe." *France-Soir* 08 Mar. 1996: 5.

Dubois, Jacques. *Le roman policier ou la modernité*. Paris: Nathan, 1992.

Duplessis, Yvonne. *Le surréalisme*. Paris: PUF, 1995.

Durozoi, Gérard. "Esquisse pour un portrait anthume de Léo Malet en auteur de romans policiers." *Revue des sciences humaines* 64.193 (1984): 169-78.

Eisenzweig, Uri. "Madness and the Colonies: French and Anglo-Saxon Versions of the Mysterious Origins of Crime." *L'Esprit créateur* 26.2 (1986): 3-14.

Evans, Christophe. "Pourquoi lit-on des romans policiers? Une enquête sur les lecteurs," *Bulletin BPI*, 12 (2005): 6.

Evrard, Franck. *Lire le roman policier*. Paris: Dunod, 1996.

Fernández-Recatalá, Denis. *Didier Daeninckx: Un écrivain en Seine Saint-Denis*. [Paris?]: n.p., n.d.

Forest, Philippe. *Le mouvement surréaliste*. Paris: Vuibert, 1994.

France, Peter, ed. *The New Oxford Companion to Literature in French*. Oxford: Oxford UP: 1995.

Fric-frac, Johnny. "Léo Mallet [sic]: le mal de Paris." *Le Bien-Public* 12 Mar. 1985. N. pag.

Freud, Sigmund. *On Dreams*. Trans. James Strachey. New York: Norton, 1952.

Gaillard, Noé. *Du surréalisme au roman policier de Léo Malet.* Master's Thesis. U Toulouse le Mirail, 1978-79.

---. "Nestor Burma et Cie . . ." Baudou 35-38.

Gauteur, Claude. "Léo Malet et le cinéma: un rendez-vous manqué." *La revue du cinéma image et son* Apr. 1979: 50-66.

Geldof, Koenraad. "Une écriture de la résistance: Histoire et fait divers dans l'oeuvre de Didier Daeninckx." *Ecrire l'insignifiant: dix études sur le fait divers dans le roman contemporain.* Eds. Paul Pelckmans and Bruno Tritsmans. Amsterdam: Rodopi, 2000. 135-153.

Goebel, Rolf. "Paris, Capital of Modernity: Kafka and Benjamin." *Monatshefte* 90.4 (1998): 445-64.

Gorrara, Claire. *The Roman Noir in Post-war French Culture: Dark Fictions.* Oxford: Oxford UP, 2003.

Grève, Claude de. "Des *Mystères de Paris* d'Eugène Sue aux *Nouveaux Mystères de Paris* de Léo Malet." *Cahiers de l'association internationale des études françaises* 40 (1988): 151-66.

Guérif, François. "Adieu à Manchette." *Le Monde* 16 June 1995: VIII.

Guiou, Dominique. "Les verts broient du noir." *Le Figaro* 27 Mar 1997: 40.

Hamilton, Deborah E. "The French Detective Fiction Novel 1920s to 1990s: Gendering a Genre." *DAI* 55 (1994): 1576A. Pennsylvania State U.

Harlé, Laurence. "Léo Malet vu par…" *A Suivre* 219 (April 1996): 7-12.

Hoog, Armand. "Mythologie du Pistolet: Romans policiers de Léo Malet." *Carrefour* 07 Sept 1949. Rpt. in Baudou 118-22.

Hoveyda, Fereydoun. *Histoire du roman policier*. Paris: Editions de Pavillon, 1965.

Jacquelin, Marion. *Actualité, réalité et fiction dans Meutres pour mémoire de Didier Daeninckx*. Master's Thesis. U Montpellier III, 2001.

Jonzac, Gérard. "Sur les pas de Nestor Burma." *Le journal du dimanche* 2172, 31 Jul. 1988. 2.

Klein, Richard. *Cigarettes are Sublime*. Durham: Duke UP, 1993.

Kost, Rudi. "Mit Nestor Burma durch Paris: Annaherung an den Scriftsteller Léo Malet oder Das Leben, wie's brullt und lacht." *Die Horen* 32.4 (1987): 23-30.

Lacassin, Francis. *Mythologie du roman policier*. 2 vols. Paris: Union générale d'éditions, 1974.

---. *Sous le masque de Léo Malet: Nestor Burma*. Amiens: Encrage, 1991.

Lamy, Jean-Claude. "Léo Malet, chroniqueur du pavé parisien." *Le Figaro* 08 Mar. 1996: 16.

Le Bris, Michel. "Les malheurs de Malet." *Le Nouvel Observateur* 18 June 1979: 80.

Lebrun, Michel. *Almanach du crime, 1982*. Paris: Veyrier?, 1981.

Lebrun, Michel and Jean-Paul Schweighaeuser, eds. *Le guide du polar: Histoire du roman policier français*. Paris: Syros, 1987.

"Léo Malet: mon 'paletot sans manches' m'a valu une veste, ou polémique autour d'une paire de godasses." *France-

Dimanche 04 Dec. 1949. Rpt. in *Cahiers du Silence: Léo Malet.* Ed. Daniel Mallerin. Paris: Kesselring, 1974. 14-15.

Léonardini, Jean-Pierre. "Léo Malet: Nestor Burma est orphelin." *L'Humanité* 08 Mar. 1996: 21.

"Le père du roman noir français meurt . . . dans son lit!" 14 Mar. 1996. <http://www.gallimard-mtl.com/eseriesn.html>.

Lits, Marc. *Le roman policier: introduction à la théorie et à l'histoire.* Liège: Editions du Céfal, 1999.

Malet, Léo. *Dernières enquêtes de Nestor Burma.* Paris: Laffont, 1987.

---. "Entretien avec Léo Malet." Eds. François Guérif and Richard Bocci. *Polar* 8 (1980): 11-18.

---. Interviews with Hubert Juin. *À voix nue.* France Culture. 9-11 Oct. 1995.

---. "Interview de Léo Malet en 1986." Ed. Noël Simsolo. Rpt. in *Léo Malet: sous pli discret.* Mons (Belgium): Séries B, 1988.

---. *Journal Secret.* Paris: Fleuve Noir, 1997.

---. *La vâche enragée.* Paris: Hoëbeke, 1988.

---. "Le faucon Malet." Ed. Phil Casoar. *Libération* 11 June 1985: 30-31.

---. "Léo Malet." Ed. Jean-Louis Ezine. *Lire* 105 (1984): 86-92.

---. "Léo Malet: Fétichiste moyen et obsédé sexuel total." Ed. Noël Simsolo. *L'Organe* 2 (1985): 4-6.

---. "Léo Malet, Piéton de Paris: Fragment d'une lettre adressée à Monsieur Geslin." *Les Cahiers du Silence: Léo Malet.* Ed. Daniel Mallerin. Paris: Kesselring, 1974. 101.

---. *Les Confrères de Nestor Burma*. Paris: Laffont, 1988.

---. *Les Enquêtes de Nestor Burma et les nouveaux mystères de Paris*. 2 vols. Paris: Laffont, 1985.

---. *Romans, nouvelles, et poèmes*. Paris: Laffont, 1989.

---. "Titres." Baudou 51.

---. "Treize questions à Léo Malet." Baudou 15-22.

---. "Trotsky, Breton, Burma et les autres." Ed. Renaud Monfourny. *Les Inrockuptibles* 13 (1988): 45-48.

Malet, Léo and Jacques Tardi. *120, rue de la gare*. Paris: Casterman, 1996.

Manchette, Jean-Patrick. *Le petit bleu de la côte ouest*. Paris: Gallimard, 1976.

Marin La Meslée, Valérie. "Léo Malet ne reconnaît plus le Paris de Nestor Burma." *France-Soir* 11 Dec. 1989: 29.

Melly, George. *Paris and the Surrealists*. London: Thames & Hudson, 1991.

Moran, John. "How to Ask: Question Formation in Written Representations of Spoken French." *Georgetown University Roundtable on Languages and Linguistics* (1992): 135-46.

Morand, Paul. "Réflexions sur le roman détective." *Revue de Paris* (1934): 481-92

Morel, Jean-Paul. "Amila l'anar de la Série Noire." *Le Matin* 26-27 Oct. 1985: 24-25.

---. "Le retour de Nestor Burma." *Le Matin* 14-15 July 1979: 21.

Narcejac, Thomas. *Esthétique du roman policier*. Paris: Le Portulan, 1947.

---. "Le roman policier." *Histoire des littératures: littératures françaises connexes et marginales*. Vol. 3. Paris: Gallimard, 1978.

Nogueira, Rui. *Le cinéma selon Jean-Pierre Melville*. Paris: Éditions de l'Étoile/Cahiers du cinéma, 1996.

Noreiko, Stephen. 'Cigarettes, Whisky et petites pépées': Obscure Allusion and Conspicuous Consumption in a *Polar*. *French Studies Bulletin* 64 (Autumn 1997): 1-3.

Palmer, Jerry. *Potboilers: Methods, Concepts, and Case Studies in Popular Fiction*. London; New York: Routledge, 1991.

Peltier, Josiane. "Didier Daeninckx and Michel de Certeau: A Historiography of Affects." *Crime Scenes: Detective Narratives in European Culture Since 1945*. Eds. Anne Mullen and Emer O'Beirne. Amsterdam: Rodopi, 2000.

Perec, Georges. *Perec/rinations*. Paris: Zulma, 1997.

Pinçonnat, Crystel. "Maigret contre Metal: Georges Simenon et Léo Malet face à la tradition américaine du roman noir." *Études Littéraires* 29.2 (1996): 111-22.

Platten, David. "The Impact of the Contemporary Roman Noir: Pennac, Daeninckx, and the Question of a Cultural Evolution." *French Prose in 2000*. Eds. Michael Bishop and Christopher Elson. Amsterdam: Rodopi, 2000.

Prendergast, Christopher. "Framing the City: Two Parisian Windows." *City Images: Perspectives from Literature, Philosophy, and Film*. Ed. Mary Ann Caws. New York: Gordon and Breach, 1991. 179-95.

Renault, Maurice. "En bavardant avec Léo Malet." *Magazine Littéraire* 21 (1949). 109-11.

Richard, Jacques. "Malet en verve." *Le Figaro* 01 Mar. 1989: 38.

Rispail, Jean-Luc. *Les surréalistes: Une génération entre le rêve et l'action*. Paris: Gallimard, 1994.

Rivière, François. "Daeninckx fait coup double." *Libération* 28 Oct. 1986: 40.

---. "Léo Malet: l'envahissant cadavre." *Libération* 08 Mar. 1996: 28-29.

---. "Léo Malet: un noir jeu de l'oie." *Magazine Littéraire* 332 (1995): 61-63.

Rochu, Gilbert. "Pour saluer Manchette." *Marianne* 1-7 May 2000: 66-67.

Ross, Kristin. *Fast Cars, Clean Bodies: Decolonization and the Reordering of French Culture*. 3rd ed. Cambridge: MIT P, 1988.

Sartre, Jean-Paul. *Les mots*. Paris: Gallimard, 2003.

Schlor, Joachim. *Nights in the City: Paris, Berlin, London*. London: Reaktion, 1998.

Schulman, Peter. "Paris en jeu de l'oie: Les fantômes de Nestor Burma." *The French Review* 73.6 (May 2000): 1155-64.

---. "Le 'stylo-camera': Léo Malet vu par Jacques Tardi." *De l'écrit à l'écran: literatures populaires: mutations génériques, mutations médiatiques*. Limoges: PULIM, 2000.

Schweighaeuser, Jean-Paul. *Le roman noir français*. Paris: PUF, 1984.

Sheringham, Michael. "City Space, Mental Space, Poetic Space: Paris in Breton, Benjamin, and Réda." *Parisian Fields*. Ed. Michael Sheringham. London: Reaktion, 1999.

Shutoff, Carl. "Simenon's Maigret Novels." *DAI* 41A no. 1 (1980), 277. Indiana U.

Simonin, Albert. "Conseils aux futurs historiens de moeurs." *Les Cahiers du Silence: Léo Malet*. Ed. Daniel Mallerin. Paris: Kesselring, 1974. 105.

Smith, Steve. "Between Detachment and Desire: Léo Malet's French roman noir." *Crime Scenes: Detective Narratives in European Culture Since 1945*. Eds. Anne Mullen and Emer O'Beirne. Amsterdam: Rodopi, 2000. 125-36.

Steele, Stephen. "Daeninckx, Quand le roman policier part en guerre." *French Studies Bulletin* 71 (Summer 1999): 9-10.

Stragliati, Roland. "Léo Malet, cet autre 'Paysan de Paris'." *Le Monde* 09 May 1975: 10.

Todorov, Tzvetan. "Typologie du roman policier." *Poétique de la Prose*. Paris: Seuil, 1971.

Vanoncini, André. *Le roman policier*. Paris: PUF, 1993.

Verdaguer, Pierre. *La séduction policière: Signes de croissance d'un genre réputé mineur: Pierre Magnan, Daniel Pennac et quelques autres*. Birmingham: Summa, 1999.

Vilar, Jean-François. "Les pas perdus de Nestor Burma." *Le Monde* 01 Aug 1986: 9.

Viviant, Arnaud. "Manchette, morgue pleine." *Libération* 05 June 1995: 31.

Walz, Robin R. *Pulp Surrealism*. Berkeley: U of California P, 2000.

Wichir, Ralph. "Roman noir comme anar." *Le combat syndicaliste* (November 1995): 12-13.

Williams, Raymond. "The Politics of the Avant-garde." Introduction. *Visions and Blueprints: Avant-Garde Culture and Radical Politics in Early Twentieth-Century Europe.* Eds. Edward Timms and Peter Collier. Manchester: Manchester UP, 1988. 1-15.